The Question of Sacrifice

The Question of Sacrifice

Dennis King Keenan

INDIANA UNIVERSITY PRESS
Bloomington and Indianapolis

This book is a publication of

Indiana University Press
601 North Morton Street
Bloomington, IN 47404-3797 USA

http://iupress.indiana.edu

Telephone orders   800-842-6796
Fax orders   812-855-7931
Orders by e-mail   iuporder@indiana.edu

Library of Congress Cataloging-in-Publication Data

Keenan, Dennis King, date
   The question of sacrifice / Dennis King Keenan.
      p. cm.—(Studies in Continental thought)
   Includes bibliographical references and index.
   ISBN 0-253-34582-0 (alk. paper)—ISBN 0-253-21769-5 (pbk. : alk. paper)
   1. Sacrifice.   2. Philosophy, European.   3. Sacrifice—Christianity.   4. Philosophical
theology.   I. Title.   II. Series.
   BJ1533.S4K44 2005
   177'.7—dc22   2004022313

1 2 3 4 5 10 09 08 07 06 05

To my family:

James Thomas Keenan (1925–1993)

Alice Marie (Peterson) Keenan (1933–)

John Thomas Keenan (1962–)

Patrick Edwin Keenan (1963–)

Teresa Marie (Keenan) Rouse (1969–)

Contents

ACKNOWLEDGMENTS

This work was made possible, in part, by a sabbatical leave (academic year 1999–2000) and summer research stipends (1996 and 1998) from Fairfield University. Portions of this work have appeared earlier in altered form in journals: a version of chapter 2 appeared as "Kristeva, Mimesis, and Sacrifice," in *Philosophy Today*, David Pellauer, editor; a version of chapter 4 appeared as "Nietzsche and the Eternal Return of Sacrifice," in *Research in Phenomenology*, John Sallis, editor; a version of chapter 6 appeared as "Irigaray and the Sacrifice of the Sacrifice of Woman," in *Hypatia: A Journal of Feminist Philosophy*, Hilde Lindemann, editor; and a version of chapter 10 appeared as "The Sacrifice *of* the Eucharist," in *The Heythrop Journal: A Quarterly Review of Philosophy and Theology*, M. J. Walsh, editor. I am grateful to the editors for permission to use these materials here. I am also grateful to John Cayer of the DiMenna-Nyselius Library at Fairfield University for locating a number of references through interlibrary loan.

Thank you . . .

to my community of friends spread throughout the world: Jason Aldrin, Travis Anderson, Ellen Armour, Robert Bernasconi, Cynthia Brincat, Josh Cohen, Janet Donohoe, Paul French, John Llewelyn, Maria LaMonaca, David Livingston, Rene McGraw, John Sallis, Tom Sheehan, and David Wood.

to my community at Fairfield University in Fairfield, Connecticut: Sharon Abbott, Mark Andrejevic, Beth Boquet, Matt Coleman, Nancy Dallavalle, Elizabeth Dreyer, Dina Franceschi, April Hill, Malcolm Hill, Nalini Jones, Paul Lakeland, Jim Long, Harriet Luckman, Kathy Nantz, Marcie Patton, John Thiel, and Kathi Weeks.

to my community at Smith College in Northampton, Massachusetts: Kirsten Blumhardt, Stephanie Bryson, Sue Dana, Bill Etnyre, Sherri Ettinger, Ann Marie Garran, Jeana Hayes-Carrier, Mary Krieger, Kim McNamara, Susan Patania, Lisa Werkmeister Rozas, and to Gail Adametz, Klara Dienes, and Patricia Nadeau, of the Young Science Library in Bass Hall for providing me with a carrel ("straight back and to the right") and one of the most ideal work environments one could imagine.

Special thanks to my beautiful wife Liz.

Finally, this book is dedicated to my family: my dad Jim, my mom Alice, my brothers John and Pat, and my sister Teresa.

ABBREVIATIONS

AE/OB   Emmanuel Levinas, *Autrement qu'être ou au-delà de l'essence.* Dordrecht: Kluwer Academic Publishers, 1991 / *Otherwise than Being or Beyond Essence.* Translated by Alphonso Lingis. The Hague: Martinus Nijhoff Publishers, 1981.

AEC   Georges Bataille, "L'art, exercice de cruauté." In *Œuvres complètes,* vol. XI, 480–486. Paris: Éditions Gallimard, 1988.

AM   Marc Shell, *Art and Money.* Chicago: University of Chicago Press, 1995.

AM/AD   Jacques Derrida, *Apories: Mourir—s'attendre aux «limites de la vérité.»* In *Le passage des frontières: Autour du travail de Jacques Derrida,* 309–338. Paris: Éditions Galilée, 1994 / *Aporias: Dying—Awaiting (One Another at) the "Limits of Truth."* Translated by Thomas Dutoit. Stanford, Calif.: Stanford University Press, 1993.

ASZ/TSZ   Friedrich Nietzsche, *Also sprach Zarathustra: Ein Buch für Alle und Keinen.* In *Werke: Kritische Gesamtausgabe,* bd. 1, abt. 6. Edited by Giorgio Colli and Mazzino Montinari. Berlin: Walter de Gruyter & Co., 1968 / *Thus Spoke Zarathustra: A Book for All and None.* Translated by Walter Kaufmann. Harmondsworth, Middlesex, England: Penguin Books, 1978.

CCS   Mark C. Taylor, "Christianity and the Capitalism of Spirit." In *About Religion: Economies of Faith in Virtual Culture,* 140–167. Chicago: University of Chicago Press, 1999.

CD/CG   Augustine, *De civitate dei.* In *Œuvres de Saint Augustin,* vols. 33–37. Paris: Desclée de Brouwer, 1959 / *The City of God.* Translated by Marcus Dods. New York: Random House, 1950.

CDH/WGBM   Anselm, *Cur deus homo.* In *S. Anselmi, Cantuariensis Archiepiscopi: Opera Omnia,* vol. 2, 37–133. Edited by Franciscus Salesius Schmitt. Edinburgh: Thomas Nelson and Sons, 1946 / *Why God Became a Man.* In *Anselm of Canterbury,* vol. 3, 39–137. Edited and translated by Jasper Hopkins and Herbert Richardson. Toronto: Edwin Mellen Press, 1976.

CI/UC   Maurice Blanchot, *La communauté inavouable.* Paris: Les Éditions de Minuit, 1983 / *The Unavowable Community.* Translated by Pierre Joris. Barrytown, N.Y.: Station Hill Press, 1988.

CM/BI   Luce Irigaray, "La croyance même." In *Sexes et parentés,* 35–65. Paris: Les Éditions de Minuit, 1987 / "Belief Itself." In *Sexes and*

CP/PC
Genealogies, 23–53. Translated by Gillian C. Gill. New York: Columbia University Press, 1993.

CP/PC
Jacques Derrida, *La carte postale: de Socrate à Freud et au-delà*. Paris: Flammarion, 1980 / *The Post Card: From Socrates to Freud and beyond*. Translated by Alan Bass. Chicago: University of Chicago Press, 1987.

DA/DE
Max Horkheimer and Theodor W. Adorno, *Dialektik der Aufklärung: Philosophische Fragmente*. In *Theodor W. Adorno: Gesammelte Schriften*, vol. 3. Frankfurt am Main: Suhrkamp, 1981 / *Dialectic of Enlightenment*. Translated by John Cumming. New York: Continuum, 1972.

DA/TA
Friedrich Nietzsche, *Der Antichrist: Fluch auf das Christenthum*. In *Werke: Kritische Gesamtausgabe*, bd. 3, abt. 6, 163–251. Edited by Giorgio Colli and Mazzino Montinari. Berlin: Walter de Gruyter & Co., 1969 / *The Anti-Christ*. In *Twilight of the Idols and The Anti-Christ*, 113–187. Translated by R. J. Hollingdale. Harmondsworth, Middlesex, England: Penguin Books, 1968.

DEE/EE
Emmanuel Levinas, *De l'existence à l'existant*. Paris: Librairie Philosophique J. Vrin, 1990 / *Existence and Existents*. Translated by Alphonso Lingis. Dordrecht: Kluwer Academic Publishers, 1988.

DJ
Robert M. Price, *Deconstructing Jesus*. Amherst, New York: Prometheus Books, 2000.

DM/GD
Jacques Derrida, *Donner la mort*. In *L'éthique du don: Jacques Derrida et la pensée du don*, 11–108. Paris: Métailié-Transition, 1992 / *The Gift of Death*. Translated by David Wills. Chicago: University of Chicago Press, 1995.

DP/GP
Emmanuel Levinas, "Dieu et la philosophie." In *De Dieu qui vient à l'idée*, 2nd ed., 93–127. Paris: Librairie Philosophique J. Vrin, 1992 / "God and Philosophy." In *Of God Who Comes to Mind*, 55–78. Translated by Bettina Bergo. Stanford, Calif.: Stanford University Press, 1998.

E/ES
Jacques Lacan, *Écrits*. Paris: Éditions du Seuil, 1966 / *Écrits: A Selection*. Translated by Alan Sheridan. New York: W. W. Norton & Company, 1977.

ED/WD
Maurice Blanchot, *L'écriture du désastre*. Paris: Éditions Gallimard, 1980 / *The Writing of the Disaster*. Translated by Ann Smock. Lincoln: University of Nebraska Press, 1986.

EdP/EoP
Jacques Lacan, *Le séminaire de Jacques Lacan: Livre VII: L'éthique de la psychanalyse: 1959–1960*. Edited by Jacques-Alain Miller. Paris: Éditions du Seuil, 1986 / *The Seminar of Jacques Lacan, Book VII: The Ethics of Psychoanalysis, 1959–1960*. Edited by Jacques-Alain Miller. Translated by Dennis Porter. New York: W. W. Norton & Company, 1992.

EH/HE   Maurice Merleau-Ponty, "L'existentialisme chez Hegel." In *Sens et non-sens*, 125–139. Paris: Les Éditions Nagel, 1948 / "Hegel's Existentialism." In *Sense and Non-Sense*, 63–70. Translated by Hubert L. Dreyfus and Patricia Allen Dreyfus. Evanston, Ill.: Northwestern University Press, 1964.

EI/IC   Maurice Blanchot, *L'entretien infini*. Paris: Éditions Gallimard, 1969 / *The Infinite Conversation*. Translated by Susan Hanson. Minneapolis: University of Minnesota Press, 1993.

EI/IE   Georges Bataille, *L'expérience intérieure*. In *Œuvres complètes*, vol. V, 7–189. Paris: Éditions Gallimard, 1973 / *Inner Experience*. Translated by Leslie Anne Boldt. Albany: State University of New York Press, 1988.

EL/SL   Maurice Blanchot, *L'espace littéraire*. Paris: Éditions Gallimard, 1955 / *The Space of Literature*. Translated by Ann Smock. Lincoln: University of Nebraska Press, 1982.

EREG/RGE   Jacques Derrida, "De l'économie restreinte à l'économie générale: Un hegelianisme sans réserve." In *L'écriture et la différence*, 369–407. Paris: Éditions du Seuil, 1967 / "From Restricted to General Economy: A Hegelianism without Reserve." In *Writing and Difference*, 251–277. Translated by Alan Bass. Chicago: University of Chicago Press, 1978.

EYS   Slavoj Žižek, *Enjoy Your Symptom! Jacques Lacan in Hollywood and out*. London: Routledge, 1992.

FA   Slavoj Žižek, *The Fragile Absolute—or, Why Is the Christian Legacy Worth Fighting For?* London: Verso, 2000.

FB/FT   Søren Kierkegaard, *Frygt og Bæven: Dialektisk Lyrik*. In *Søren Kierkegaards Samlede Værker*, vol. III, 53–168. Edited by A. B. Drachmann. Copenhagen: Gyldendalske Boghandels Forlag, 1901 / *Fear and Trembling: Dialectical Lyric*. In *Fear and Trembling and Repetition*, 1–123. Edited and Translated by Howard V. Hong and Edna H. Hong. Princeton, N.J.: Princeton University Press, 1983.

FEVR/EFRL   Émile Durkheim, *Les formes élémentaires de la vie religieuse: Le système totémique en Australie*, 3rd ed. Paris: Librairie Félix Alcan, 1937 / *The Elementary Forms of Religious Life*. Translated by Karen E. Fields. New York: The Free Press, 1995.

FS/FK   Jacques Derrida, "Foi et savoir: Les deux sources de la «religion» aux limites de la simple raison." In *La Religion: Séminaire de Capri*, 9–86. Paris: Éditions du Seuil / Éditions Laterza, 1996 / "Faith and Knowledge: The Two Sources of 'Religion' at the Limits of Reason Alone." In *Religion*, 1–78. Edited by Jacques Derrida and Gianni Vattimo. Stanford, Calif.: Stanford University Press, 1998.

FSA/WSM   Luce Irigaray, "Les femmes, le sacré, l'argent." In *Sexes et parentés*, 87–102. Paris: Les Éditions de Minuit, 1987 / "Women, the Sacred,

Abbreviations

	Money." In *Sexes and Genealogies*, 73–88. Translated by Gillian C. Gill. New York: Columbia University Press, 1993.
FTK	Slavoj Žižek, *For They Know Not What They Do: Enjoyment as a Political Factor*. London: Verso, 1991.
GB	James George Frazer, *The Golden Bough: A Study in Magic and Religion*, 3rd ed. New York: St. Martin's Press, 1990.
GD/TI	Friedrich Nietzsche, *Götzen-Dämmerung, oder Wie man mit dem Hammer philosophirt*. In *Werke: Kritische Gesamtausgabe*, bd. 3, abt. 6, 49–157. Edited by Giorgio Colli and Mazzino Montinari. Berlin: Walter de Gruyter & Co., 1969 / *Twilight of the Idols, or How to Philosophize with a Hammer*. In *Twilight of the Idols and The Anti-Christ*, 19–112. Translated by R. J. Hollingdale. Harmondsworth, Middlesex, England: Penguin Books, 1968.
GdM/GoM	Friedrich Nietzsche, *Zur Genealogie der Moral: Eine Streitschrift*. In *Werke: Kritische Gesamtausgabe*, bd. 2, abt. 6, 257–430. Edited by Giorgio Colli and Mazzino Montinari. Berlin: Walter de Gruyter & Co., 1968 / *On the Genealogy of Morals: A Polemic*. Translated by Walter Kaufmann and R. J. Hollingdale. In *On the Genealogy of Morals and Ecce Homo*, 13–163. New York: Random House, 1967.
Gf/Ge	Jacques Derrida, *Glas*. Paris: Éditions Galilée, 1974 / *Glas*. Translated by John P. Leavey, Jr., and Richard Rand. Lincoln: University of Nebraska Press, 1986.
GSP/GSH	Jean Hyppolite, *Genèse et structure de la* Phénoménologie de l'esprit de Hegel. Paris: Aubier, Éditions Montaigne, 1946 / *Genesis and Structure of Hegel's* Phenomenology of Spirit. Translated by Samuel Cherniak and John Heckman. Evanston, Ill.: Northwestern University Press, 1974.
HHdI/HHtI	Martin Heidegger, *Hölderlins Hymne «Der Ister»*. In *Gesamtausgabe*, vol. 53. Frankfurt am Main: Vittorio Klostermann, 1984 / *Hölderlin's Hymn "The Ister."* Translated by William McNeill and Julia Davis. Bloomington: Indiana University Press, 1996.
HMS/HDS	Georges Bataille, "Hegel, la mort et le sacrifice." In *Œuvres complètes*, vol. XII, 326–345. Paris: Éditions Gallimard, 1988 / "Hegel, Death and Sacrifice." Translated by Jonathan Strauss. In *Yale French Studies* 78 (1990): 9–28.
HNg/HNe	Walter Burkert, *Homo Necans: Interpretationen altgriechischer Opferriten und Mythen*. Berlin: Walter de Gruyter & Co., 1972 / *Homo Necans: The Anthropology of Ancient Greek Sacrificial Ritual and Myth*. Translated by Peter Bing. Berkeley: University of California Press, 1983.
I/U	Jean-Luc Nancy, "L'insacrifiable." In *Une pensée finie*, 65–106. Éditions Galilée, 1990 / "The Unsacrificeable." Translated by Richard Livingston. In *Yale French Studies* 79 (1991): 20–38.

IR   Slavoj Žižek, *The Indivisible Remainder: An Essay on Schelling and Related Matters*. London: Verso, 1996.

JGB/BGE   Friedrich Nietzsche, *Jenseits von Gut und Böse: Vorspiel einer Philosophie der Zukunft*. In *Werke: Kritische Gesamtausgabe*, bd. 2, abt. 6, 1–255. Edited by Giorgio Colli and Mazzino Montinari. Berlin: Walter de Gruyter & Co., 1968 / *Beyond Good and Evil: Prelude to a Philosophy of the Future*. Translated by R. J. Hollingdale. Harmondsworth, Middlesex, England: Penguin Books, 1973.

JL/BPP   Sigmund Freud, *Jenseits des Lustprinzips*. In *Gesammelte Werke*, vol. 13, 1–69. Frankfurt am Main: S. Fischer Verlag, 1940 / *Beyond the Pleasure Principle*. In *The Standard Edition of the Complete Psychological Works of Sigmund Freud*, vol. XVIII, 1–64. Translated and edited by James Strachey, in collaboration with Anna Freud, and assisted by Alix Strachey and Alan Tyson. London: Hogarth Press and The Institute of Psycho-analysis, 1955.

KPV/CPR   Immanuel Kant, *Kritik der praktischen Vernunft*. In *Gesammelte Schriften*, vol. V, 1–163. Edited by Königlich Preussischen Academie der Wissenschaften. Berlin: Georg Reimer, 1908 / *Critique of Practical Reason*. Translated by Lewis White Beck. Indianapolis, Ind.: Bobbs-Merrill Company, 1956.

KS   Valerio Valeri, *Kingship and Sacrifice: Ritual and Society in Ancient Hawaii*. Translated from the author's unpublished French manuscript by Paula Wissing. Chicago: University of Chicago Press, 1985.

KU/CJ   Immanuel Kant, *Kritik der Urteilskraft*. In *Gesammelte Schriften*, vol. V, 165–485. Edited by Königlich Preussischen Academie der Wissenschaften. Berlin: Georg Reimer, 1908 / *Critique of Judgement*. Translated by J. H. Bernard. New York: Hafner Press, 1951.

LDM/LRD   Maurice Blanchot, "La littérature et le droit à la mort." In *La part du feu*, 291–331. Paris: Éditions Gallimard, 1949 / "Literature and the Right to Death." Translated by Lydia Davis. In *The Work of Fire*, 300–344. Translated by Charlotte Mandell. Stanford, Calif.: Stanford University Press, 1995.

LeP/LaP   Emmanuel Levinas, "Langage et proximité." In *En découvrant l'existence avec Husserl et Heidegger*, 2nd ed., 217–236. Paris: Librairie philosophique J. Vrin, 1967 / "Language and Proximity." In *Collected Philosophical Papers*, 109–126. Translated by Alphonso Lingis. Dordrecht: Martinus Nijhoff Publishers, 1987.

ME   Slavoj Žižek, *The Metastases of Enjoyment: Six Essays on Women and Causality*. London: Verso, 1994.

Mf/Me   Jacques Derrida, "Mnemosyne." In *Mémoires pour Paul de Man*, 23–57. Paris: Éditions Galilée, 1988 / "Mnemosyne." Translated by

Abbreviations

	Cecile Lindsay. In *Memoires for Paul de Man*, 1–43, rev. ed. New York: Columbia University Press, 1989.
MGD	John Burbidge, "Man, God, and Death in Hegel's *Phenomenology.*" In *Philosophy and Phenomenological Research* 42.2 (1981): 183–196.
MMM	William H. Desmonde, *Magic, Myth, and Money: The Origin of Money in Religious Ritual*. New York: The Free Press of Glenco.
MP/DF	Emmanuel Levinas, "«Mourir pour . . . »." In *Entre Nous: Essais sur le penser-à-l'autre*, 219–230. Paris: Éditions Grasset & Fasquelle, 1991 / "Dying for . . ." In *Entre Nous: On Thinking-of-the-Other*, 207–217. Translated by Michael B. Smith and Barbara Harshav. New York: Columbia University Press, 1998.
NF/WP	Friedrich Nietzsche, *Nachgelassene Fragmente*. In *Werke: Kritische Gesamtausgabe*, bd. 1, abt. 8. Edited by Giorgio Colli and Mazzino Montinari. Berlin: Walter de Gruyter & Co., 1974 / *The Will to Power*. Translated by Walter Kaufmann and R. J. Hollingdale. New York: Random House, 1967.
NFS/SNF	Henri Hubert and Marcel Mauss, *Essai sur la nature et la fonction du sacrifice*. In *L'Année sociologique* 2 (1899): 29–138 / *Sacrifice: Its Nature and Function*. Translated by W. D. Halls. Chicago: University of Chicago Press, 1964.
NR	E. E. Evans-Pritchard, *Nuer Religion*. Oxford: Oxford University Press, 1956.
NWM/PWM	Martin Heidegger, "Nachwort zu: «Was ist Metaphysik?»." In *Wegmarken*. In *Gesamtausgabe*, vol. 9, 303–312. Frankfurt am Main: Vittorio Klostermann, 1976 / "Postscript to 'What Is Metaphysics?'" Translated by William McNeill. In *Pathmarks*, 231–238. Edited by William McNeill. Cambridge: Cambridge University Press, 1998.
OeG/OaG	Jacques Derrida, "*Ousia et grammè*: Note sur une note de *Sein und Zeit*." In *Marges de la philosophie*, 31–78. Paris: Les Éditions de Minuit, 1972 / "*Ousia and Grammē*: Note on a Note from *Being and Time*." In *Margins of Philosophy*, 29–67. Translated by Alan Bass. Chicago: University of Chicago Press, 1982.
OS	Raymond Firth, "Offering and Sacrifice: Problems of Organization." In *Journal of the Royal Anthropological Institute* 93 (1963): 12–24.
OVM/OCM	Martin Heidegger, "Die onto-theo-logische Verfassung der Metaphysik." In *Identität und Differenz*, 35–73. Pfullingen: Günther Neske, 1957 / "The Onto-theo-logical Constitution of Metaphysics." In *Identity and Difference*, 42–74. Translated by Joan Stambaugh. New York: Harper & Row, 1969.
P	Jacques Derrida, *Points . . . : Interviews, 1974–1994*. Translated by Peggy Kamuf & others. Edited by Elisabeth Weber. Stanford, Calif.: Stanford University Press, 1995.
PCES/CPSS	Marcel Detienne, "Pratiques culinaires et esprit de sacrifice." In *La cuisine du sacrifice en pays grec*, 7–35. Marcel Detienne and Jean-

Pierre Vernant. Paris: Éditions Gallimard, 1979 / "Culinary Practices and the Spirit of Sacrifice." In *The Cuisine of Sacrifice among the Greeks*, 1–20. Marcel Detienne and Jean-Pierre Vernant. Translated by Paula Wissing. Chicago: University of Chicago Press, 1989.

PdSF/PoSF   Ernst Cassirer, *Philosophie der Symbolischen Formen*. Berlin: Bruno Cassirer Verlag, 1925 / *The Philosophy of Symbolic Forms*. Translated by Ralph Manheim. New Haven, Conn.: Yale University Press, 1955.

PeI/PaI   Emmanuel Levinas, "La philosophie et l'idée de l'infini." In *En découvrant l'existence avec Husserl et Heidegger*, 2nd ed., 165–178. Paris: Librairie philosophique J. Vrin, 1967 / "Philosophy and the Idea of Infinity." In *Collected Philosophical Papers*, 47–59. Translated by Alphonso Lingis. Dordrecht: Martinus Nijhoff, 1987.

Pf/Pe   Blaise Pascal, *Pensées*. In *Œuvres complètes*, 1079–1345. Paris: Librairie Gallimard, 1954 / *Pensées*. Translated by A. J. Krailsheimer. Harmondsworth, Middlesex, England: Penguin Books, 1966.

Pg/Pe   Plato, *ΦΑΙΔΩΝ*. In *Platonis Opera*, vol. I, 79–172. Edited by Ioannes Burnet. Oxford: Oxford University Press, 1900 / *Phaedo*. In *The Dialogues of Plato*, vol. 1, 101–175. Translated by Benjamin Jowett. Edited by R. M. Hare and D. A. Russell. London: Sphere Books, 1970.

PG/PM   Georg Simmel, *Philosophie des Geldes*, 4th ed. München and Leipzig: Duncker & Humblot, 1922 / *The Philosophy of Money*. Translated by Tom Bottomore and David Frisby. London: Routledge & Kegan Paul, 1978.

PG/PS   G. W. F. Hegel, *Phänomenologie des Geistes*. Edited by Wolfgang Bonsiepen and Reinhard Heede. In *Gesammelte Werke*, vol. 9. Hamburg: Felix Meiner Verlag, 1980 / *Phenomenology of Spirit*. Translated by A. V. Miller. Oxford: Oxford University Press, 1977.

PIH   Maurice Bloch, *Prey into Hunter: The Politics of Religious Experience*. Cambridge: Cambridge University Press, 1992.

POf/POe   Jacques Derrida, *Positions*. Paris: Les Éditions de Minuit, 1972 / *Positions*. Translated by Alan Bass. Chicago: University of Chicago Press, 1981.

PR/REM   Gerardus van der Leeuw, *Phänomenologie der Religion*. Tübingen: J.C.B. Mohr (Paul Siebeck), 1970 / *Religion in Essence and Manifestation*. Translated by J. E. Turner. Princeton, N.J.: Princeton University Press, 1986.

PS/SM   Claude Lévi-Strauss, *La pensée sauvage*. Paris: Librairie Plon, 1962 / *The Savage Mind*. Chicago: University of Chicago Press, 1966.

RLP/RPL   Julia Kristeva, *La révolution du langage poétique: L'avant-garde à la fin du XIXe siècle: Lautréamont et Mallarmé*. Paris: Éditions du Seuil, 1974 / *Revolution in Poetic Language*. Translated by Margaret Waller. New York: Columbia University Press, 1984.

Abbreviations

RTJ/RJT   Emmanuel Levinas, "La révélation dans la tradition juive." In *L'au-delà du verset: Lectures et discours talmudiques*, 158–181. Paris: Les Éditions de Minuit, 1982 / "Revelation in the Jewish Tradition." In *Beyond the Verse: Talmudic Readings and Lectures*, 129–150. Translated by Gary D. Mole. Bloomington: Indiana University Press, 1994.

SA   Luc de Heusch, *Sacrifice in Africa: A Structuralist Approach*. Translated from the author's unpublished French manuscript by Linda O'Brien and Alice Morton. Bloomington: Indiana University Press, 1985.

SG   Bernhard Lang, *Sacred Games: A History of Christian Worship*. New Haven, Conn.: Yale University Press, 1997.

Sl/Se   Augustine, "Sermo CCLXXII." In *Patrologiæ cursus completes*, [. . .] *series Latina*, vol. XXXVIII, 1246–1248. Edited by J. P. Migne. Paris, 1844–1864 / "Sermon 272." In *The Works of Saint Augustine*, part III, vol. 7, 300–301. Translated by Edmund Hill. Edited by John E. Rotelle. New Rochelle, N.Y.: New City Press, 1993.

SNT/TNT   Martin Luther, "Eyn Sermon von dem newen Testament, das ist von der heyligen Messe." In *Werke: Kritische Gesamtausgabe*, vol. 6, 353–378. Weimar: Hermann Böhlau, 1888 / *A Treatise on the New Testament, that is, the Holy Mass*. Translated by Jeremiah J. Schindel. Revised by E. Theodore Bachmann. In *Luther's Works*, vol. 35, 79–111. Edited by E. Theodore Bachmann. General Editor: Helmut T. Lehmann. Philadelphia: Fortress Press, 1960.

SOI   Slavoj Žižek, *The Sublime Object of Ideology*. London: Verso, 1989.

SS   John Milbank, "Stories of Sacrifice: From Wellhausen to Girard." In *Theory, Culture & Society* 12 (1995): 15–46.

SS/MS   Emmanuel Levinas, "La signification et le sens." In *Humanisme de l'autre homme*, 15–70. Montpellier: Fata Morgana, 1972 / "Meaning and Sense." In *Collected Philosophical Papers*, 75–107. Translated by Alphonso Lingis. Dordrecht: Martinus Nijhoff Publishers, 1987.

SZ/BT   Martin Heidegger, *Sein und Zeit*, 9th ed. Tübingen: Max Niemeyer, 1960 / *Being and Time*. Translated by John Macquarrie and Edward Robinson. New York: Harper & Row, Publishers, 1962.

T   John Sallis, "Tremorings—Withdrawals of the Sublime." In *Spacings—Of Reason and Imagination in Texts of Kant, Fichte, Hegel*, 82–131. Chicago: University of Chicago Press, 1987.

TA/T   Claude Lévi-Strauss, *Le totémisme aujourd'hui*. Paris: Presses Universitaires de France, 1962 / *Totemism*. Translated by Rodney Needham. Boston: Beacon Press, 1963.

TCU/TCD   Jan Patočka, "Je technická civilizace úpadková, a proč?" In *Kacířské eseje o filosofii dějin*, 105–126. Praha: Academia, 1990 / "Is Technological Civilization Decadent, and Why?" In *Heretical Essays*

	in the Philosophy of History, 95–118. Translated by Erazim Kohák. Edited by James Dodd. Chicago: Open Court Publishing, 1996.
TdR/ToR	Georges Bataille, *Théorie de la religion*. In *Œuvres complètes*, vol. VII, 281–361. Paris: Éditions Gallimard, 1976 / *Theory of Religion*. Translated by Robert Hurley. New York: Zone Books, 1989.
TeI/TaI	Emmanuel Levinas, *Totalité et infini: Essai sur l'extériorité*, 4th ed. The Hague: Martinus Nijhoff, 1984 / *Totality and Infinity: An Essay on Exteriority*. Translated by Alphonso Lingis. Pittsburgh, Pa.: Duquesne University Press, 1969.
TM/MT	Emmanuel Levinas, "Textes messianiques." In *Difficile liberté: Essais sur le judaïsme*, 2nd ed., 83–129. Paris: Editions Albin Michel, 1963 and 1976 / "Messianic Texts." In *Difficult Freedom: Essays on Judaism*, 59–96. Translated by Seán Hand. Baltimore, Md.: Johns Hopkins University Press, 1990.
TPR	E. E. Evans-Pritchard, *Theories of Primitive Religion*. Oxford: Oxford University Press, 1965.
TS	Slavoj Žižek, *The Ticklish Subject: The Absent Centre of Political Ontology*. London: Verso, 1999.
TTg/TTe	Sigmund Freud, *Totem und Tabu: Einige Übereinstimmungen im Seelenleben der Wilden und der Neurotiker*. In *Gesammelte Werke*, vol. 9. Frankfurt am Main: S. Fischer Verlag, 1940 / *Totem and Taboo: Some Points of Agreement between the Mental Lives of Savages and Neurotics*. In *The Standard Edition of the Complete Psychological Works of Sigmund Freud*, vol. XIII, vii–162. Translated and edited by James Strachey, in collaboration with Anna Freud, and assisted by Alix Strachey and Alan Tyson. London: Hogarth Press and The Institute of Psycho-analysis, 1955.
TWN	Slavoj Žižek, *Tarrying with the Negative: Kant, Hegel, and the Critique of Ideology*. Durham, N.C.: Duke University Press, 1993.
TYGF	Nancy Jay, *Throughout Your Generations Forever: Sacrifice, Religion, and Paternity*. Chicago: University of Chicago Press, 1992.
UK/OWA	Martin Heidegger, "Der Ursprung des Kunstwerkes." In *Holzwege*. In *Gesamtausgabe*, vol. 5, 1–74. Frankfurt am Main: Vittorio Klostermann, 1977 / "The Origin of the Work of Art." In *Poetry, Language, Thought*, 15–87. Translated by Albert Hofstadter. New York: Harper & Row, 1971.
VC II	*Sacrosanctum Oecumenicum Concilium Vaticanum II: Constitutiones, Decreta, Declarationes*. Typis Polyglottis Vaticanis, 1974 / *Vatican Council II: The Conciliar and Post Conciliar Documents*, 1988, rev. ed. Edited by Austin Flannery. Northport, N.Y.: Costello Publishing Company, 1975.
VeM/VaM	Jacques Derrida, "Violence et métaphysique: Essai sur la pensée d'Emmanuel Levinas." In *L'écriture et la différence*, 117–228. Paris:

Abbreviations

| | Éditions du Seuil, 1967 / "Violence and Metaphysics: An Essay on the Thought of Emmanuel Levinas." In *Writing and Difference*, 79–153. Translated by Alan Bass. Chicago: University of Chicago Press, 1978. |

VeS/VaS   René Girard, *La violence et le sacré*. Paris: Éditions Bernard Grasset, 1972 / *Violence and the Sacred*. Translated by Patrick Gregory. Baltimore, Md.: Johns Hopkins University Press, 1977.

WL/SL   G. W. F. Hegel, *Wissenschaft der Logik*. Edited by Friedrich Hogemann and Walter Jaeschke. In *Gesammelte Werke*, vols. 11–12. Hamburg: Felix Meiner Verlag, 1978–1981 / *Science of Logic*. Translated by A. V. Miller. New York: Humanities Press, 1969.

WM/TSM   C. G. Jung, "Das Wandlungssymbol in der Messe." In *Von den Wurzeln des Bewusstseins: Studien über den Archetypus*, 217–350. Zürich: Rascher & Cie. AG., Verlag, 1954 / "Transformation Symbolism in the Mass." In *The Collected Works of C. G. Jung*, vol. 11, *Psychology and Religion: West and East*, 2nd ed., 201–296. Translated by R.F.C. Hull. Princeton, N.J.: Princeton University Press, 1969.

The Question of Sacrifice

The Sacrifice of Sacrifice

Waiting without Hope

Sacrifice sacrifice. Ours is the moment in history that calls for this strange imperative. This moment in the genealogy of sacrifice is (in the words of Derrida) a dissident and inventive rupture with respect to tradition. It is a moment in history that calls for the sacrifice of sacrifice. It is a strange moment and a strange imperative. But this "work" — of sacrificing sacrifice, on sacrificing sacrifice — will accomplish very little, almost nothing. And that will make all the difference.

In the genealogy of Western sacrifice, one can trace an increasing interiorization, spiritualization, and dialecticization of sacrifice. Throughout this genealogy, sacrifice has predominately been understood as a necessary passage through suffering and/or death (of either oneself or someone else) on the way to a supreme moment of transcendent truth. Sacrifice effects the revelation of truth that overcomes the negative aspect of the sacrifice. In a word, sacrifice pays. One gets a return on one's investment. But this economical understanding of sacrifice only makes "sense" if it is pushed to its "logical" extreme. Ironically, it is as if the economical understanding of sacrifice inevitably unworks itself. The work of sacrifice unworks itself. To be what it "is" sacrifice must sacrifice itself.

Sacrifice is essentially a holocaust. In sacrifice, all (*holos*) is burned (*caustos*). There is no remainder. As such, it is essentially essenceless. It involves selflessness, giving without reserve. Sacrifice has to be beyond calculation and hope of a reward, so as not to be construed as self-serving (and, therefore, not a genuine sacrifice). Sacrifice must necessarily be a sacrifice *for nothing*, a sacrifice for no reason, no goal. It must necessarily be a nonsensical aneconomical sacrifice. According to the Gospel of Matthew, Jesus exhorts his disciples to sacrifice, specifically to give alms, pray, and fast. The sacrifice must be performed without calculation. This extends even to the simple *intention* of sacrificing. It extends to whatever takes recognition into account. As such, the exhortation to sacrifice comes with the *supplemental* instruction that it must be done *in secret:* "do not let your left hand know what your right hand is doing." But this exhortation to sacrifice without reserve is only half of the story.

The *an*economical understanding of sacrifice inevitably gets sublated by an economical understanding of sacrifice. Even though sacrifice must be aneconomical to genuinely be what it "is," sacrifice inevitably has been interpreted in economic terms. The sublation of the aneconomical understanding of sacrifice by the economical understanding of sacrifice is likewise evident in the Gospel of Matthew. Though Jesus exhorts his disciples to give alms, pray, and fast in secret, he adds that God the Father sees in secret.

- But when you give alms, do not let your left hand know what your right hand is doing, so that your alms may be done in secret; and your Father who sees in secret will reward you. (Matt. 6:3, NRSV)
- But whenever you pray, go into your room and shut the door and pray to your Father who is in secret; and your Father who sees in secret will reward you. (Matt. 6:6, NRSV)
- But when you fast, put oil on your head and wash your face, so that your fasting may be seen not by others but by your Father who is in secret; and your Father who sees in secret will reward you. (Matt. 6:17, NRSV)

Though the sacrifice must be performed without expectation of a *terrestrial* reward, it comes with a *celestial* reward. Sacrifice is sacrificed. The aneconomy is sublated by a transcendent economy. If one sacrifices without reserve here on earth, then one's reward will be great in heaven. The *supplemental* instruction that the sacrifice must be done *in secret* ("do not let your left hand know what your right hand is doing") is the condition of the possibility and (at the same time) the condition of the *im*possibility of sacrifice. The *supplemental* instruction is necessary, yet impossible.

If the essence of a sacrificial action precludes receiving a return on one's investment of suffering and/or death, and if a sacrificial action only has meaning insofar as it is essentially an all-burning holocaust, and if this all-burning holocaust is essentially an essenceless *an*economical sacrifice that is inevitably sacrificed to an economy, then what is (if it "is" anything at all) sacrifice *as such?* How does it transform the transcendental intention of sacrifice? How does it transform the very intentionality of sacrifice (i.e., can one perform such a sacrifice)? How does sacrifice *as such* transform our understanding of sacrificial action and responsibility?

Sacrifice is sacrifice only as the sacrifice of sacrifice. Sacrifice is (genuinely) sacrifice only as the sacrifice of (an economical understanding of) sacrifice. It is necessary for sacrifice to consume *itself* in an all-burning holocaust in order to be what it "is."

Sacrifice sacrifice. This is an imperative that "works" in a variety of ways (and should be read as such). The first "sacrifice" in this strange imperative is an ethical action that one is obliged to do (for sacrifice to genuinely be sacrifice), but that interrupts itself *in the very "doing" of the action*. Rather than merely a work to be accomplished, or an action to be performed, sacrifice is experienced as a call to action that calls itself into question. It becomes a work that unworks itself *in the very performance of the work*. But the imperative to sacrifice sacrifice is, at the same time, an imperative that calls into question (sacrifices) the sacrifice without reserve (as well the imperative itself). It is inevitably impossible, for the very intention to sacrifice (even sacrifice) is the sublation of the aneconomical understanding of sacrifice by the economical understanding of sacrifice. Said otherwise, the all-burning holocaust of the sacrifice of sacrifice burns *itself* (as sacrifice without reserve) up; that is, it burns itself into the existence of the phenomenal economy of sacrifice. Therefore, the imperative to sacrifice sacrifice is at one and the same time the imperative to sacrifice (economical) sacrifice and the imperative of not being able to sustain this pure sacrifice without reserve (as well as the imperative itself). The *necessary* **sacrifice of** (economical) **sacrifice** (= aneconomical sacrifice) is inevitably *impossible*; it is inevitably the **sacrifice of** (aneconomical) **sacrifice** (= economical sacrifice). **Ours is the moment in history, if only for a moment, that calls for dwelling with this aporia of sacrifice** rather than stilling this strange oscillation between the aneconomical and the economical (by sublating the aneconomical into the economical). At this moment, if only for a moment, the possibility of sacrifice *is* its impossibility. At this moment, if only for a moment, the meaning of sacrifice undergoes slippage. Said otherwise, ours is the moment in history when sacrifice is experienced at a certain distance from itself. It is experienced as approach, as "not yet." The necessary step beyond economical sacrifice is inevitably not beyond. One is called to necessarily, yet impossibly, dwell in (borrowing a phrase from Blanchot) the step/not beyond (*le pas au-delà*) sacrifice. Sacrifice can only sacrifice itself over and over (in an eternal return of the same) because what it seeks to overcome (the nihilistic revelation of truth that sublates the negative aspect of sacrifice) makes this sacrifice of itself both *necessary* and *useless*. The truth is eternally postponed in a *necessary* sacrificial gesture that can only sacrifice itself, thereby rendering itself *useless*.

Sacrifice begins—echoing Blanchot in "Literature and the Right to Death"—at the moment when sacrifice becomes a question. This question—the "question" that seeks to pose itself in sacrifice, the "question" that is its essence—is posed *to* sacrifice *by* sacrifice that has become *an*economical. This question *is* the irreducible *double meaning* of sacrifice as economical and sacrifice as *an*economical. **The question of sacrifice**, sacrifice's question, is the essence of sacrifice. Sacrifice is what it is only in the necessary, yet impossible (and useless), turning of sacrifice as economical into sacrifice as aneconomical. "The question awaits an answer, but the answer does not appease the question, and even if it puts an end to the question, it does not put an end to the waiting that is the question of the question" (EI 16/IC 14). This question that seeks to pose itself in sacrifice, the question that is its essence, is the necessary, yet (paradoxically)

3

impossible (and useless), sacrifice of the sacrifice. This question is the waiting (without hope) that is the sacrifice of the sacrifice.

The necessary, yet impossible (and useless), sacrificing of sacrifice does *not*, however, absolve one of the responsibility of sacrificing sacrifice. Dwelling with this aporia or question alerts one to the self-serving aspect of sacrificial responsibility without thereby absolving one of the necessity of sacrificial responsibility. Dwelling with this aporia or question means undertaking the necessary yet humbling task of incessant vigilance and questioning that is philosophy itself. Emphasizing either the "necessity" or the "impossibility" (and "uselessness") of sacrificing sacrifice (at the expense of the other) misses what the strange "logic" of sacrificing sacrifice *forces* one to think, and leaves one vulnerable to naively justifying a self-serving sacrifice that is obviously nothing but irresponsible. One is called to dwell with the aporia or question characteristic of the strange "logic" of sacrificing sacrifice. Dwelling with the aporia or question of sacrifice will disturb sacrifice on one level while at the same time reinforcing its most extreme ramifications.

This "work" — *of* sacrificing sacrifice, *on* sacrificing sacrifice — begins with a genealogy of theories of sacrifice. One is called — in the spirit of Nietzschean genealogy — to use the resources of the tradition to interrupt the tradition, to interrupt the economics, sexism, and Christo-centric evolutionism of past theories of sacrifice and momentarily open them to other possibilities. This genealogy of theories of sacrifice requires, paraphrasing a passage from the Preface of Nietzsche's *On the Genealogy of Morals*, a knowledge of the conditions and circumstances in which sacrifice grew, under which sacrifice evolved and changed. What is called for is "going through" the tradition to retrieve what the tradition could only have overlooked, and which even now only reveals itself in the form of a question. The necessary, though brief, genealogy of theories of sacrifice traced in the opening chapter sets the stage for the remaining chapters of the book, which interrupt not only these theories (and their underlying presuppositions of economics, sexism, and Christo-centric evolutionism), but sacrifice itself. It sets the stage for a consideration of the condition of the possibility and the condition of the impossibility of each of these theories and their presuppositions.

The remaining chapters of the book (with the exception of the final chapter) are each organized around the work of either a single thinker or a constellation of thinkers. Through a close reading of the work of Hegel, Kierkegaard, Nietzsche, Heidegger, Bataille, Lacan, Levinas, Blanchot, Irigaray, Derrida, Kristeva, Nancy, and Žižek, I argue that an attentiveness to the question of sacrifice (i.e., the sacrifice of sacrifice, and the multiplicity of ways it calls for being read) corrects a too-easy reading of their work and opens it to new horizons of thought. Though each chapter can (for the most part) be read independently of the others, they are all gathered together around this question. And though each chapter considers the question of sacrifice, this is not done out of ignorance of the essential differences between the thinkers. It is not done out of ignorance of the different horizons of thought from which their works emerge. It is not done with an eye toward synthesizing these thinkers. It is done with an attentiveness to those decisive moments in their work when work is discovered to be at a certain distance from itself. At this moment, if only for a moment, one can think the question of the proximity of these thinkers to one another. This work proceeds from chapter to chapter (quoting Derrida's reading of Levinas's *Totality and Infinity*) "with the infinite insistence of waves on a beach: return and repetition, always, of the same wave against the same shore, in which, however, as each return recapitulates itself, it also infinitely renews and enriches itself" (VeM 124n1/VaM 312n7). In this particular work, the thematic development of the question of sacrifice proceeds in this way.

The first thinker considered is Kristeva. Sacrifice haunts her work. For Kristeva, the genesis of the subject is a scene of (what may be called) sacrifice. The rhythm of drives and their stases characteristic of the unconscious or semiotic is confined (through sacrifice) to generate the signification of the symbolic order. This confinement of semiotic violence through sacrifice (which tends toward ideological truth, which in turn represses the semiotic) is to be interrupted by the mimesis of the poet. Kristeva thinks that the "truest" truth is not the unicity of ideological truth effected by sacrifice, but the moment of the institution of symbolism, which is situated *between* the semiotic and the symbolic. However, through a close reading of *Revolution in Poetic Language*, I argue that insofar as mimesis is the "reversed reactivation" of the contradictory sacrificial process (understood as simultaneously violent and confining), the poet *mimics sacrifice*. Therefore, the radicality of Kristeva's work is at risk (despite her intentions) of being reinscribed back into the economical understanding of sacrifice as the revelation of (the unicity of ideological) truth. By way of a reading of Nancy's reading of Bataille in "The Unsacrificeable," I argue that despite Kristeva's intentions, mimesis is still governed by an economical understanding of sacrifice as the revelation of truth. I argue that sacrifice must not be mimicked by the poet. Sacrifice is obliged, rather, to mimic *itself* in a gesture that infinitely postpones the revelation of truth (whether this truth is the unicity of traditional doxy *or* the plurality characteristic of Kristeva's "new dialectic").

Nancy's reading of Bataille sets the stage for a more detailed reading of Bataille, whose reading of sacrifice is incessantly at risk of being misread. I argue that a reading of Bataille's reading of sacrifice must be attentive to the sacrifice of sacrifice characteristic of the question of death (the moment when death as possibility turns into death as impossibility) that is the interruption of the Hegelian dialectic. Reading Bataille's "Hegel, Death and Sacrifice" alongside Derrida's "From Restricted to General Economy: A Hegelianism without Reserve," I argue for a way to (1) reread Nancy's reading of Bataille in "The Unsacrificeable," (2) establish a proximity between Blanchot's "literature" in "Literature and the Right to Death" and Bataille's "fiction," (3) correct a too-quick association of sacrifice in Bataille with either a crude reading of Freud's reflections on the origin of society or Girard's reading of sacrifice as integral to the origin of community, and (4) correct Žižek's reading of Bataille in *The Indivisible Remainder*.

The next chapter begins with the reading of a passage from *Beyond Good and Evil* — quoted by Bataille in *Inner Experience* — in which Nietzsche traces a genealogy of sacrifice. Though it may seem obvious to a reader of the work of Nietzsche that sacrifice is to be overcome, I argue that a careful reading of it will reveal that in the attempt to step beyond sacrifice, one becomes inextricably implicated in the move of nihilistic sacrifice. Through a close reading of (1) the stroke of genius on the part of Christianity from *On the Genealogy of Morals*, (2) the step/not beyond (*le pas au-delà*) nihilism described by Blanchot in *The Infinite Conversation*, and (3) the action characteristic of Jesus' evangelic practice described in *The Anti-Christ*, I argue that sacrifice can only sacrifice itself over and over (in an eternal return of the same) because what it seeks to overcome (the nihilistic revelation of truth) makes this sacrifice of itself both necessary and useless.

The fact that sacrifice can only sacrifice itself over and over in an eternal return of the same, making it both necessary and impossible (and useless), helps to correct a too-easy reading of Levinas. I first explore why Levinas's work necessarily resorts to ethical language. Levinas's resorting to an ethical language arises, I argue, insofar as his work describes a *moment* when philosophy encounters what can only be described as paradoxical. The ethical language Levinas resorts to does *not* proceed from a special moral experience that is independent of the description developed until then. This "description" refers to those moments in the work of Levinas that describe the irreducibly paradoxical "not yet" of approach. Two instances of this moment are (1) Levinas's reading of Descartes's *Meditations*, and (2) his concretization of that reading in the phenomenological description of the irreducibly paradoxical body. The ethical language resorted to comes from the very meaning of approach, from those paradoxical or aporetical moments in the work of Levinas. The meaning of the ethical language of sacrifice is aporetic. For Levinas, sacrifice (like responsibility) requires, paradoxically, both singularity and being nothing but "for the other." But Levinas is careful to point out that this sacrifice is *not* an *action* performed *by* the same *for* the other. There is no intentionality of sacrifice in the work of Levinas. Though necessary, it is *useless*; it is *for nothing*.

Like the chapters that precede it, the chapter on Irigaray considers the necessity, yet impossibility (and uselessness), of the sacrifice of sacrifice, but specifically within the context of her concern with how sacrifice is relevant to women. Irigaray states that most of our societies have been built on sacrifice, and though numerous instances of social space existing only through immolation are offered by the work of Girard, she points out that he writes very little about how his work is relevant to women. In "Belief Itself" and "Women, the Sacred, Money" — both from *Sexes and Genealogies* — Irigaray sets out to correct this omission. She inquires whether, under the sacrificed victim, another victim is hidden. According to Irigaray, this other victim is woman, and the revelation of the hidden sacrifice ultimately involves a *new* sacrifice. I argue that this new sacrifice is the sacrifice of sacrifice. This new sacrifice is the sacrifice *of* the revealed sacrifice of man that conceals the sacrifice of woman. I argue that

Irigaray addresses what this sacrifice of sacrifice gives one to think about the all too easily understood words *revelation, sacrifice,* and *woman.* A radical reading of the words *revelation, sacrifice,* and *woman* is opened up, I argue, when one reads the work of Irigaray alongside the work of Lacan and Žižek (and Levinas). This reading proceeds by way of a consideration of (1) Žižek and safe belief, (2) Derrida, Freud, and Lacan, on the work of mourning, and (3) woman('s body) as the hidden victim of sacrifice and the elemental substrate of life. I conclude the chapter by considering the risks associated with this new sacrifice, specifically, the risks of *belief* in the sacrifice of sacrifice.

The work of Irigaray, as well as the work of Kristeva, is situated in the wake of Lacan. For all three thinkers, the status of the human being as a "being of language" is defined by a primordial sacrifice. Žižek argues that this sacrifice is a sacrifice of sacrifice. With this sacrifice of sacrifice (which Lacan calls the "empty gesture" of the "forced choice"), the subject emerges as alienated in/by the symbolic order. Exculpating oneself from this constitutive alienation requires a *repetition* of the "forced choice," a *repetition* of the sacrifice of sacrifice. This repetition involves not *alienation* in/by, but rather *separation* from, the symbolic order. This is (in a Lacanian sense) an authentic ethical act. Žižek argues that dialectical analysis is a *repetition* of the sacrifice of sacrifice. I argue, drawing upon Levinas's vocabulary, that this analysis *produces* (i.e., is the effectuation of being of and the revelation of) the "true meaning" (or essence) of the symbolic order. Four paradigmatic moments of the repetition of this sacrifice of sacrifice are: (1) Antigone's suicidal "No!" to Creon's command to leave the body of her brother Polynices unburied, (2) Abraham's binding (and intention to sacrifice) his son Isaac in unconditional obedience to the command of God, (3) the sacrifice of Jesus Christ, and (4) St. Paul's reading of *agape* (love) as the spontaneous enjoyment of doing one's duty without expectation of a reward.

Though Žižek often situates his work in opposition to the work of Derrida, I argue that the work of Derrida and Lacan/Žižek forms an equivocal chiasm. But before doing that it will be necessary to consider the work of Derrida on sacrifice. I argue that everything on sacrifice in the work of Derrida hinges on the aporetic moment of the double bind of sacrifice: the moment when the sacrifice of (economical) sacrifice turns into the sacrifice of (aneconomical) sacrifice, and vice versa. Following his reading of the work of Bataille in "From Restricted to General Economy: A Hegelianism without Reserve," Derrida's next sustained consideration of sacrifice—*Glas*—again occurs within the context of the work of Hegel. The remarks on *Glas* in this chapter are limited to a reading of Derrida's reading of the first shape of natural religion in Hegel's *Phenomenology of Spirit.* I then go on to do a close reading of Derrida's *The Gift of Death,* which is one of his most sustained considerations of the question of sacrifice. The reading begins with a consideration of Patočka's genealogy of responsibility, which includes four sections: (1) Plato and "practicing (for) death," (2) Christianity and the terrifying mystery, (3) Heidegger and Being-towards-death (which traces sacrifice through the work of Heidegger), and (4) a heretical and hyperbolic form of Christianity. I then go on to consider Kierkegaard and the binding of Isaac, the Gospel of Matthew and the God who sees in secret, and Nietzsche and Irigaray on the risk of belief. The chapter concludes with a close reading of "Faith and Knowledge: The Two Sources of 'Religion' at the Limits of Reason Alone," where Derrida again refers to a sacrifice of sacrifice.

Despite protestations to the contrary (on the part of Žižek), I argue that the work of Derrida and Lacan/Žižek forms an equivocal chiasm: an atemporal non-spatial momentary point of intersection that is the sacrifice of sacrifice. The work of Hegel plays a pivotal role at this sacrificial intersection. The starting point of this consideration of the chiasm of the work of Derrida and Lacan/Žižek is "The Revealed Religion" from the *Phenomenology of Spirit*, specifically the appropriation of the sacrifice of Jesus Christ (the mediator between the divine and the human) by the religious community. I argue that everything turns on the reading of the *identity* of finite human beings and God. This point of intersection is the sacrifice of sacrifice, radical negativity, death.

I argue that "The Revealed Religion" from Hegel's *Phenomenology of Spirit* is a work on the incessant dying of God. A responsible attentiveness to this phenomenon is, I argue, a responsible attentiveness to the sublime commandment of the Hebrew Scriptures against idolatry. I, in turn, argue that this is ritualized in (among other events) the sacrifice *of* the Eucharist.

Eucharistic theology has traditionally been divided between understanding eucharistic sacrifice as a *repetition* of the sacrifice of Jesus Christ and understanding it as a memorial of the *singular* sacrifice of Jesus Christ. I argue that what is called for is (paradoxically) an incessant *repetition* of the *singular* sacrifice of Jesus Christ (whether it be in a good work or in liturgy). I show this by way of a consideration of (1) Augustine on the Church as the mystical body of Christ, (2) Derrida on God as nothing but *agape* (love), and (3) Žižek on God as nothing but *agape* (love). I conclude by arguing not for a change in the liturgy of the sacrifice of the Eucharist, but rather for a radical change in perspective on the sacrifice *of* the Eucharist as it is currently performed. I argue that the ritual appropriation of the sacrifice of Jesus Christ (whose death is the death of God himself) is the ritual appropriation of the sacrifice of the sacrifice that is a mourning of the incessant dying of God and an unconditional call to responsibility. This final chapter, which draws upon the work of the preceding chapters, will disturb the sacrifice *of* the Eucharist on one level while at the same time reinforcing its most extreme ramifications.

This "work"—*of* sacrificing sacrifice, *on* sacrificing sacrifice—will accomplish very little, almost nothing. And that will make all the difference. Sacrifice is sacrifice only as the sacrifice of sacrifice, and the sacrifice of sacrifice is necessary, yet impossible and useless. But that is precisely what makes sacrifice sacrifice. This is the question of sacrifice. This moment in the genealogy of sacrifice is the moment in history when the work of sacrifice unworks itself. Ours is the moment in history, if only for a moment, that calls for dwelling with this question

8

of sacrifice. *In* the (im)possible moment of the unworking of the work of sacrifice, *in* the moment of this (im)possible sacrifice, one is called (in the words of T. S. Eliot) to "wait without hope / For hope would be hope for the wrong thing" (in "East Coker" from *Four Quartets*).

1

A Genealogy of Theories of Sacrifice

A History of Economics, Sexism, and Christo-centric Evolutionism

The history of the theories of sacrifice has been subtly (and not so subtly) influenced by economics, sexism, and Christo-centric evolutionism. Most theories of sacrifice are predicated on an economy of debts and credits in which one gets a return on one's sacrificial investment. One particular economy of sacrifice — the Christian doctrine of sacrifice — has subtly worked its way into the very heart of (particularly as the *telos* of) numerous late nineteenth-century and early twentieth-century theories of sacrifice. But even when social anthropologists and historians of religion concentrated less on Christo-centric evolutionary sequences and more on investigations of sacrifice within particular cultures, the construction of worldwide typologies was still prevalent. And even in those theories that attentively attempted to avoid the construction of worldwide typologies, two things remained constant: an economic understanding of sacrifice and a persistently pervasive sexism.

Sacrifice has come to be understood as a necessary passage through suffering and/or death (of *either* oneself *or* someone else) on the way to a supreme moment of transcendent truth. Sacrifice effects the revelation of truth. Sacrifice is the price to be paid for this gain. This economic understanding of sacrifice plays an important role in sociological theory at the turn of the twentieth century. In *The Protestant Ethic and the Spirit of Capitalism* (1904–1905), Max Weber explores the role that one form of sacrifice — asceticism — plays in the relationship between religion and the economic and social life of modern culture. The Calvinistic doctrines of predestination and of a calling to act in a disciplined, ascetic manner encouraged the view that worldly success was a confirmation that one was acting as an instrument of God's will and a sign that one had been predestined to an elite salvational status. This Protestant ethic was instrumental, Weber argues, to the rise of the spirit of modern capitalism, which is a form of economic life involving rational conduct in the form of disciplined work, careful calculation, and a willingness to sacrifice short-term gains for long-term gains. Sacrifice also plays an important role in Georg Simmel's central theory of economic exchange. In *The Philosophy of Money* (1900; 2nd ed. 1907), Simmel writes that "economic exchange [. . .] always signifies the sacrifice [*Opfer*] of an otherwise useful good, however much eudaemonistic gain is involved" (PG 35/PM 83). Simmel interprets economic life as an exchange of sacrifices. Simmel writes:

> The sacrifice [*Opfer*] does not in the least belong in the category of what ought not to be, as superficiality and avarice would have us believe. Sacrifice is not only the condition of specific values, but the condition of value as such; with reference to economic behavior, which concerns us here, it is not only the price to be paid for particular established values, but the price through which alone values can be established. (PG 38/PM 85)

It is interesting to note that *money* itself has a sacrificial origin. According to Gerardus van der Leeuw, the oldest Greek measure of value was the sacred sacrificial ox, the tribute that was to be paid to the deity. "Thus the sacrificial meal, in the course of which the meat was equally divided, was the 'germ of public financial administration'. Later, coin appeared instead of the sacrifice; but that the coin was money, that is valid, was also due to its originating in the sphere of sacrifice and bringing with it its powerfulness, or as we should say, its credit" (PR 398/REM 353). The Greek work *drachma* (the name of a common coin) once was used to designate a handful of sacrificial meat (*oblos*). The Latin word *pecunia*, which is the root of the English word *pecuniary*, derives from *pecus* (cattle) (CCS 150). The English word *money* derives from Juno Moneta, the sister and wife of the Roman god Jupiter. "The oldest altar to Moneta was located at Mons Albanus, where a bull sacrifice, the central ritual of the Latin confederacy, was annually held" (MMM 124). Roman coins were first minted in the Temple of Juno Moneta (the association of money with cattle extends to Wall Street, where the bull is a familiar symbol of rising stock prices). It has been common practice since the early years of Christianity to produce communion wafers that resemble coins. The communion wafer

> was expressly manufactured like coin: it was pressed between wafer irons and impressed with insignia like those of coins. [. . .] That the manufacturing process of making the Eucharistic wafer from flour paste was often technically similar to making coins from metal ingots allowed thinkers like Nicholas of Cusa in fifteenth-century Germany to observe how the Eucharistic wafer's symbolic representation of the body of Jesus—or its actually being the body— has a numismatically iconic character. (AM 15)

The Question of Sacrifice

This association of the sacrifice of the Eucharist with money serves as a reminder that an economy of sacrifice is at the heart of the predominant doctrine of sacrifice. Economic models for the process of salvation exist throughout the Christian tradition. One of the most influential economic models of Christology is developed in *Why God Became a Man* (1094–1098) by Anselm of Canterbury. Summarizing his argument for the necessity for the incarnation of God, Anselm writes:

> The crux of the problem was why God became a man [*cur deus homo*] in order to save mankind through His death, although he was apparently able to accomplish man's salvation in some other way. Responding to this problem, you showed by many compelling reasons that the restoration of human nature ought not to be left undone, and yet could not be done unless man paid what he owed to God for his sin. *This debt was so great that only God was able to pay it,* although only a man ought to pay it; and, thus, the same [individual] who was divine was also human. Hence, it was necessary for God to assume a human nature into a unity of person, so that the one who with respect to his nature ought to make payment, but was unable to, would be the one who with respect to this person was able to. Next, you showed that the man who was God had to be taken from a virgin by the person of the Son of God; and you showed how he could be taken sinless from the sinful mass. You proved very clearly that the life of this man was so sublime and so precious that it could suffice to make payment for what is owed for the sins of the whole world—and even for infinitely more [sins than these]. (CDH 126–127/WGBM 129–130, emphasis added)

This understanding of Christ as a token of exchange that restores the balance of payments between the divine and the human is echoed in Nietzsche's *On the Genealogy of Morals*. Nietzsche writes: "[S]uddenly we stand before the paradoxical and horrifying expedient that afforded temporary relief for tormented humanity, that stroke of genius on the part of Christianity: God himself sacrifices himself for the guilt of mankind, *God himself makes payment to himself, God as the only being who can redeem man from what has become unredeemable for man himself*—the creditor sacrifices himself for his debtor, out of *love* (can one credit that?), out of love for his debtor!—(GdM 347/GoM 92, emphasis added, except to "love"). This "stroke of genius" on the part of Christianity is that God (in the person of Jesus Christ) sacrifices himself for the forgiveness of our sins. Though a necessary condition for salvation, the incarnation and sacrifice of God is not the sufficient condition for salvation. A common interpretation of Christian sacrifice is that it is a work done to overcome alienation or expiate sins. The redemptive power of Christ becomes effective in the lives of believers through the incorporation of the body and blood of Christ in the sacrifice of the Eucharist.

From the perspective of this particular economy of sacrifice—Christianity—sacrifice had long been perceived as the cultic act central to *all* religions of the world. This is repeatedly verified, Marcel Detienne points out, in numerous voyage narratives. For example, in 1724, Lafitau writes that sacrifice "is as ancient

12

as Religion itself, and as widespread as the Nations subject to Religion, since there is not one of them in which Sacrifice is not the custom, and among which it is not at the same time a proof of Religion" (*Les Mœurs des sauvages américains comparées aux mœurs des premiers temps*, I: 163; see PCES 26/CPSS 15). With the emergence in the nineteenth century of the science of religion and the consciousness of historical development (fostered by the work of Hegel, Marx, and Darwin), sacrifice (in particular, Christian sacrifice) was accorded a theoretical status that was dominated by the perspective of evolutionism. This evolutionary perspective, Detienne writes in "Culinary Practices and the Spirit of Sacrifice" from *The Cuisine of Sacrifice among the Greeks*, enabled these early theories of sacrifice to argue that what is latent in embryonic form in *all* cultures is the necessity of a self-sacrifice that was remarkably Christo-centric. Detienne concludes the essay: "Today [...] it seems important to say that the notion of sacrifice is indeed a category of the thought of yesterday [...] both because it gathers into one artificial type elements taken from here and there in the symbolic fabrics of societies and because it reveals the surprising power of annexation that Christianity still subtly exercises on the thought of these historians and sociologists who were convinced they were inventing a new science" (PCES 34–35/CPSS 20).

Another reason to perhaps relegate the category of "sacrifice" to the status of a contemporary anachronism is the persistently pervasive sexism in theories of sacrifice. In *Throughout Your Generations Forever: Sacrifice, Religion, and Paternity*, Nancy Jay writes, "Theories of sacrifice commonly exhibit notions of gender ranging from taken-for-granted male domination to explicit misogyny" (TYGF 128). Jay's work reveals an affinity between sacrifice and patriliny unacknowledged in most theories of sacrifice. Along similar lines of thought, Luce Irigaray argues in "Women, the Sacred, Money" from *Sexes and Genealogies* that under the sacrificed victim of those societies built on sacrifice, another victim is often hidden: woman (FSA 89–90/WSM 75–76). In *The Gift of Death*, Jacques Derrida writes, "Does the system of this sacrificial responsibility and of the double 'gift of death' [i.e., wherein the gift of death consists in *both* putting to death by killing someone *and* putting death forward by giving it as an offering (DM 71/ GD 72)] imply at its very basis an exclusion or sacrifice of woman? A woman's sacrifice or a sacrifice of woman, according to one sense of the genitive or the other?" (DM 75/GD 76).

Given that many theories of sacrifice are subtly influenced by Christo-centric evolutionism, and that they tend to perpetuate sexist attitudes, is sacrifice merely a category of the thought of yesterday, as Detienne argues? I would argue that one cannot merely step beyond the tradition. Such a step would unwittingly repeat the very dynamic that it tries to contain and distance itself from; that is, such a step would be a sacrifice of sacrifice, which, if performed naively (i.e., without dwelling with the question of sacrifice), would unwittingly preserve some form of sacrifice. One would be duped into believing that one could be done with sacrifice, which could then return (relatively unchanged) in far more subtle and pernicious forms. One is called to use the resources of the tradition to interrupt the tradition (rather than unwittingly repeat it). One is called to remain attentive to the irreducible ambiguity of the sacrifice of sacrifice.

One is called, I would argue, not to relegate the category of "sacrifice" to the status of a contemporary anachronism. What is called for is not retrieving what the tradition merely overlooked, for example an idyllic presacrificial time. For it is impossible to merely turn back the hands of time. We are creatures of time. We are creatures of our particular context in history. What is called for is "going through" the tradition. What follows is a necessary, though brief, beginning of a genealogy of the theories of sacrifice. It will be concerned primarily with identifying the underlying presuppositions of the theories: economics, sexism, and Christo-centric evolutionism.

In *Primitive Culture* (1871), Edward Burnett Tylor proposes that sacrifice was originally a gift to the gods to secure their favor or minimize their hostility, then as homage (with no expectation of a return on one's sacrificial investment), and finally renunciation (in which the sacrificer more fully offered him or herself). This theory presupposes that religion was originally animism; the spirits residing in nature, indifferent to moral considerations and having a limited sphere of power, could be enriched, and therefore influenced, by gifts. Though sacrifice evolved into an activity with moral significance, it was originally an activity without moral significance.

In *Prolegomena to the History of Israel* (1883), Julius Wellhausen advances the theory that sacrifice is a universal spontaneous feeling and asserts the naturalness among "primitive" people of a notion of (private) giving to the gods or even a (communal) sharing of a meal with them. He associates both of these aspects of sacrifice (which, for him, represent the primitive character of sacrifice) with a time of closeness to nature, spontaneous joy, freedom from the political rule of the centralized state, and a diversity of freely chosen sacred sites. The loss of the primitive idyll was inevitable, he theorizes, given that the communion aspect of primitive sacrifice contains an innate centralizing tendency that ruptures its own private spontaneity. The centralizing divinely ordained (political) state ruptured the primitive idyll by regulating the *oral* anarchy of primitive sacrificial practices with *written* laws. This centralization ruptured the cyclical view of nature characteristic of the primitive idyll and replaced it with a historical linearity characterized by progress (with Deuteronomic centralization, the cultic irregularity and idolatry associated with the primitive character of sacrifice were prevented by restricting all sacrificial practice to the temple in Jerusalem). The historically contingent circumstances of the Babylonian captivity fostered the complexity and artificiality of the (non-political) "wilderness legislation," especially with respect to sacrificial practices, which was set in place entirely in the interests of the power of Israel's priestly caste. This (non-political) sociality in exile was not (according to Wellhausen) divinely ordained. The "church" as an institution independent of the state is (according to Wellhausen) a distortion of the divinely ordained (political) state. As a distortion, it perversely directs sacrificial efforts of individuals toward the (supposed) appeasement of God rather than toward ethical self-giving. In "Stories of Sacrifice: From Wellhausen to Girard," John Milbank argues that Wellhausen constructed his theory of the original sacrifice not from evidence, but from his own liberal Lutheran preferences for private religion and a centralizing divinely ordained (political) state (SS 20). Echoing Detienne's thesis that the vocation of sacrifice is to fulfill the major social function of mobilizing mental and moral energies (PCES 33/CPSS 19), Milbank writes, "Before the sociologists, Wellhausen 'retrieved' sacrifice as the 'highest' religious truth of surrender of the individual to the (political) community" (SS 20).

In *Lectures on the Religion of the Semites* (1889; 2nd ed. 1894), William Robertson Smith proposes that the original motive for sacrifice was communion among members of a group and between the members of the group and their god. Whereas Wellhausen proposes a natural sacrifice that was a spontaneous private gift with an associated aspect of communal sharing, Smith denies the centrality of the gift aspect of sacrifice. This denial is a development of Comte's theory of primitive fetishism (which proposed that the "primitive" person experienced his or her surroundings as imbued with the same sacred forces that course through his or her own body), mediated by J. F. McLennan's pioneering work on totemism (which proposed that a matrilinear, exogamous clan-grouping experienced itself to be of the same species as, and of the lineage of, a totemic plant or animal). This proposal gives a Darwinian twist to Comtean positivism (insofar as the worship of animals recognized as kin exhibits the first intuition of evolutionary descent) as well as a Comtean twist to Darwinian evolutionary theory (insofar as one can construe biological inheritance optimistically) (SS 21). Though under ordinary circumstances it was taboo to kill this totem, Smith argues that a material emergency may have required the consumption of a nomadic tribe's totem. This horror was interpreted as an extreme instance of divine sustaining: the sacrifice and communal resurrection of the deity. This argument, which was based solely upon Nilus's story of the sacrifice and consumption of a camel by North African nomads (the Bedouin of the Sinai), led Smith to propose that sacrifice involved not a gift, but total consumption. Later material emergencies demanded a repetition of the ritual, which was taken as a reconfirmation of tribal strength and unity. Sacrifice was thus originally a meal in which one entered into communion with the totem. An animal sacrifice was essentially a communion through a theriomorphic tribal divinity (an intermediary between the sacred and profane realms). The transition to a sedentary way of life (according to Smith) gave rise to the conception of sacrifice as a gift comparable to a tribute paid to a sovereign (taken as a model for the relation to the divinity). As with Wellhausen, the centralizing power of the state effected the rupture of primitive sacrifice. With Smith, however, it is the perverse notion of sacrifice as *gift* that derives from tribute to a centralized power and the emergence of private property. The rise of this priestly thematic was (according to Smith) the result of a confusion between the religious and the political (between sacrifice and taxation), compounded by the experience of God's absence during exile and persecution, which called for a more stringent safeguarding of the pure and the holy. According to Milbank, Smith's interest in claiming the incoherence of Leviticus and the resulting necessity of an evolutionary decipherment of it was "in order to show that the most characteristic features of Christ's death and the Eucharist—namely the voluntary death of a divine victim, and the total consumption, rather than sending up, of a sacred offering—were fulfillments of primitive sacred communion, rather than primitive substitutionary expiation" (SS 23). Smith wishes to demonstrate the natural evolutionary progress to Christianity, which is the latent truth of the literality of the "one blood" model associated with totemism as the mystical truth of a universal, totemic faith. The emergent essence of religion is a this-worldly community. The latent truth of sacrifice is revealed as the altruistic behavior necessary for this community. Though this community was supported by a transcendent God, the essence of this God is the sacrifice of transcendence to immanent progress.

In *The Golden Bough: A Study in Magic and Religion* (1890), James George Frazer proposes the theory that sacrifice originated from magical practices in which the ritual slaying of a god was performed as a means of rejuvenating the god. The key contrast between Smith and Frazer, according to Milbank, lies in the following: whereas Smith emphasized the discovery of a primitive fetishistic religion, Frazer emphasized Comte's discovery of a primitive science in fetishism (SS 24). Given that Frazer thinks that magical thinking sought (like science) universal laws, he thinks that fetishism (or totemism) was magic (rather than religion), and individualistic and pragmatic (rather than organicist and mystical). In the wake of the work of A. A. Goldenweiser, Frazer concludes that totemism (in the precise sense) was probably either rare or never existed. For Frazer, the totemic plant or animal is not kin, but a depository of the life principle. The separation of the life principle from a person's body, combined with a principle of "pruning," led Frazer to argue that sacrifice was a pruning of one manifestation of the forces of sacred *mana* in order to allow it to flourish more abundantly (GB pt. II, 1–2; pt. III, 198; pt. VI, 226–227). As such, all sacrifice was calculative and proto-scientific. Given this fact, Frazer (more than either Wellhausen or Smith) allows for expiation in primitive sacrifice. For Frazer, all the themes of primitive fetishism are personified in the God-King. Since magic only (apparently) works in the hands of a self-consciously manipulative despot, it was the centralization of magical practices in the person of the God-King that became the source of progress. According to a Comtean thematic, religion mediates between magic and religion. With the wane of magic, human beings attempt to manipulate (i.e., appease) personal controlling forces (gods) operative behind things (GB pt. I, vol. I, 222–223). Like the magical God-King, sacrifice lies at the boundary of magic and science, insofar as it endeavors to manipulate personal forces; these forces are concentrated in the God-King, who must be sacrificed (or pruned) in order that he may (in another incarnation) flourish more abundantly. To this end, the personal force or life principle of the God-King was deposited in a totem (paradigmatically, the totemic plant mistletoe, i.e., Virgil's

"Golden Bough"). This sacrifice may secondarily involve the expiatory transfer of evil or contamination (GB pt. VI, 1). Frazer's implied critique of Christianity took the form of interpreting Christianity *itself* as a perverse deviation from primitive sacrificial practice, "just as Wellhausen so interpreted the Jewish temple system and the Catholic Church—both taken as examples of non-natural, *non-political politics*, misdirecting political energies towards transcendent ends" (SS 26). The God-King is, for Frazer, a progressive figure who dies in an illusory fashion for the ultimately non-illusory security of the (political) state and the strength of character of the culture. The God-King reveals the truth of sacrifice to be "sacrificing the present to the future" (GB pt. I, vol. II, 119). According to Milbank, Frazer completes a process begun by Wellhausen and Smith. For Wellhausen and Smith, the meaning of Christ's sacrifice (which is not held within the tradition of the Church) is latent in the original type of sacrifice (gift for Wellhausen; communion for Smith), which Christ's sacrifice fulfills. Science and state inherit the typological space of the Church (which perverted primitive sacrifice) and claim that their new typology (of an *un*perverted sacrifice) can be demonstrated in fact and as an evolutionary process. The Church and expiation (as well as gift, in Smith's case) are evolutionary redundancies, a vestige of the original meaning of sacrifice. For Frazer, Christianity *itself* is a redundancy, and the primal sacrifice that permits science and the state occurs *not* in a perversely contingent circumstance in the middle of history (i.e., as a tribute to a centralized power), but at its inception (SS 28).

In *Sacrifice: Its Nature and Function* (1899), Henri Hubert and Marcel Mauss propose that "[s]*acrifice is a religious act which, through the consecration of a victim, modifies the condition of the moral person who accomplishes it or that of certain objects with which he is concerned*" (NFS 41/SNF 13). The victim is not holy by nature (as is the case in Smith's theory), the consecration of a victim is effected by destruction, and the connection with the sacred world is completed by a sacred meal (implied here is the view of the French sociological school, going back to Durkheim, that the sacral world is nothing more than a projection of society). Though they abandon the search for the origin of sacrifice, they did not similarly abandon the search for the unity of sacrifice. Like Smith, they think that a sacrifice establishes a relationship between the sacred and profane realms. Sacrifices "are all the same in essence. [. . .] They are the outer coverings of one single mechanism" (NFS 47/SNF 18). Hubert and Mauss propose that sacrifice's "single mechanism" is a double process of communication between the sacred and the profane by means of a victim who plays a mediating role between the sacrificer and the divinity. The relationship between the two realms is effected by two complementary processes: sacralization and desacralization. Sacrifice establishes a relationship between the two separate realms that the sacrificial action simultaneously brings together and keeps apart. Despite their refusal to derive sacrifice from totemism, Hubert and Mauss continue to regard totemic religion as an advance toward the *telos* of a self-sacrificing god; whereas every "normal" sacrifice adheres to the gift-logic of the Latin formula *do ut des* ("I give that you may give") in which every renunciation is performed with an eye toward self-interest, in the divine sacrifice "the god who sacrifices himself gives himself irrevocably" (NFS 136/SNF 101). According to Hubert and Mauss, the totemic hypothesis fails to grasp that sacrifice *of* the god had to come after sacrifice *to* the god. The *self*-sacrificing god points (for them) to the ultimate form of the sacrificial process (if sacrifice *to* the god came first, and if the renunciation found at the heart of this sacrifice is the operative principle of the social system of a society, then sacrifice *of* the god defines the ideal of renunciation). "[T]ransformed and, so to speak, purified, sacrifice has been preserved by Christian theology" (NFS 131/SNF 93). However, Detienne points out that this ultimate form of sacrifice is not governed by the complementary processes of sacralization and desacralization that effect a relationship between the sacred and profane, but rather by the extreme self-renunciation of the god. This is the vanishing point of the mediating term (which *defines* the very sacrificial process for Hubert and Mauss [NFS 136/SNF 100]) insofar as the self-sacrificing god is confused with the (mediating) victim and with the sacrificer. "The triumph reserved for 'abnegation' — so total that it brings with it the end of the contractual and the communional — would not be so striking were not the final term in Mauss' theory also a point of departure: i.e., the only possible locus for a unitary image of sacrifice in a society in which any question pertaining to religion must necessarily be posed in the field circumscribed by dominant Christian mentality" (PCES 27–28/CPSS 16). In an endnote here, Detienne responds to a sentence by Hubert and Mauss — "The Christian imagination has built according to ancient blueprints" — with the following rejoinder: "This is true, but it is no less true that the imagination of the sociologists, and others, has built according to Christian blueprints" (PCES 28n1/CPSS 223n53). Though E. E. Evans-Pritchard (in *Theories of Primitive Religions*) considers *Sacrifice: Its Nature and Function* "an unconvincing piece of sociologistic metaphysics" (TPR 70), he admires the attempt to construct what he calls a "grammar" of sacrifice. "In fact," Luc de Heusch counters, "the essay provides neither a 'grammar' nor a correct vocabulary, but merely conveys the authors' own ideology of the sacred" (SA 7). It is Latin that opposes *sacer* to *profanus*. Hubert and Mauss's analysis is relevant for Roman religion, but it is a misleading starting point for the analysis of ritual (SA 4–6; see TYGF 136–137). It is further pointed out by de Heusch that Evans-Pritchard's study of Nuer sacrifice (which largely follows Hubert and Mauss) is compromised by his translation of Nuer concepts into Christian theology and vocabulary (SA 6–14). Even though he agrees with Detienne's argument regarding the Christo-centric evolutionism of Hubert and Mauss's work, and Detienne's argument that most anthropologists have failed to see the importance of cooking and eating in sacrifice, Maurice Bloch (in *Prey into Hunter*) cannot entirely follow Detienne when he uses the point about cooking and eating as though it negated the significance of *both* the identification of victim and sacrificer *and* the self-sacrifice and substitution elements that interested Hubert and Mauss (PIH 29–30). Though Detienne thinks that the significance of these two points can be attributed to nothing more than Hubert and Mauss's Christo-centric evolutionism, Bloch writes that "[t]he evidence of some form of self identification [. . .] seems inescapable though perhaps the general idea needs reformulating" (PIH 30). In addition to the retention of Christo-centric evolutionism, Hubert and Mauss preserve an economy of sacrifice. Despite their rejection of gift-logic of *do ut des* and valorization of disinterested renunciation, they (like Durkheim) conceive of modern social sacrifice as a fulfillment of gift-logic: individual renunciation sustains social forces, but the individual gains back social legitimation for his or her needs (material, erotic, spiritual) (NFS 137/SNF 102; see SS 30).

In *The Elementary Forms of Religious Life* (1912), Émile Durkheim (according to Detienne) best expresses the presuppositions motivating theoretical reflection on the phenomenon of sacrifice between 1880 and 1930 (PCES 28/ CPSS 16). He proposes that people represent society to themselves in ritual, making aspects of society available to consciousness in conceptual form for the first time. In these "collective representations" originated the categories of understanding. These categories are, for Durkheim, products of religion, but the sacred/profane dichotomy is a precondition for religion, based on the eternal and universal dichotomy between social and individual. The soul/body dichotomy represents the opposition between what is social in us (and consequently transcendent and sacred) and what is individual in us (and consequently amoral, unenduring, and profane, e.g., our bodies). The opposition of social and individual is a soul/body dichotomy in which moral rules and stable conceptual thought are opposed to sensual appetites and shifting sense perceptions. Like Hubert and Mauss, he understands sacrifice in terms of this opposition, but he (unlike them) again turns to totemism and the search for origins (he places totemism at the origin of conceptual thought itself). Though he pays homage to Smith for recognizing an act of alimentary communion in the original sacrifice (a meal in which human beings effect communion with a divinity through the incorporation of the clan's vital principle), he insists that there is no communion without a gift, without an act of renunciation (FEVR 490/EFRL 347). He shows that even the most primitive sacrifices are inspired by a moral force. The fact that many historians of religion put the sacrament of the Eucharist on a parallel with the ancient practice of the worshipers of Dionysus (who tear an animal apart and eat it, believing it is the flesh of their god) forced apologists for the singularity of the Christian faith (such as M.-J. Lagrange) to make a distinction between abject tendencies of a carnal relationship that devour flesh and noble tendencies of a purely spiritual relationship where the alimentary aspects of the sacrifice are negligible. This sacrifice appears, according to the apologists, only with the emergence of moral needs at the level of human civilization (PCES 30–31/CPSS 18). For Durkheim, however, there is no break between the original sacrifice and the Christian Eucharist, but only a difference of degree. At both extremes is the *same* moral force, which minimizes the alimentary aspects of the sacrifice, the details of the killing, and the status of the victim. Given that the sacred principle is, according to Durkheim, nothing other than society hypostasized and transfigured (FEVR 495/EFRL 351), he argues that the effect of the rites of sacrifice is periodically to recreate a moral being on which we depend as much as it depends upon us: society (FEVR 497/EFRL 352). Like Tylor's science of civilization, Durkheim's social analysis is animated by a reforming spirit (PCES 32/CPSS 19). Like Hubert and Mauss, Durkheim conceives of modern social sacrifice as a fulfillment of gift-logic: individual renunciation sustains social forces, but the individual gains back social legitimation for his or her needs (material, erotic, spiritual) (NFS 137/SNF 102; see SS 30).

In *Der Ursprung der Gottesidee* (1912–1955) and in "Ethnologische Bemerkungen zu theologischen Opfertheorien" (1922), Wilhelm Schmidt proposes that the original meaning of sacrifice can be seen in the firstlings sacrifices of early hunters and food gatherers. These firstlings sacrifices were sacrifices of homage and thanksgiving to the supreme being. This being could not be enriched (and, therefore, bribed) by these sacrifices insofar as it was understood that everything already belonged to it. In *Das Opfer auf den uns heute noch erreichbaren ältesten Stufen der Menschheitsgeschichte: Eine Begriffsstudie* (1956), Anton Vorbichler proposes that what was offered in firstlings sacrifices was not food, but life itself. In *La grande festa: Vita rituale e sistemi di produzione nelle società tradizionali* (1959), Vittorio Lanternari proposes, like Schmidt, that the original meaning of sacrifice can be seen in the firstlings sacrifices. However, unlike Schmidt, who sees these sacrifices as sacrifices of homage and thanksgiving to the supreme being, Lanternari sees these sacrifices as the result of anxiety. Lanternari draws upon a certain form of neurosis that is expressed in the undoing (or sacrifice) of earlier achieved successes.

In *Totem and Taboo: Some Points of Agreement between the Mental Lives of Savages and Neurotics* (1913), Sigmund Freud, influenced by the work of Smith, proposes that the ritual slaughter of an animal, which was instituted to re-enact the primeval act of parricide in the primal horde (hypothesized by Charles Darwin), reflected an ambivalent attitude: insofar as some remorse was symptomatic of the slaying of the father, the sacrificial ritual expresses the desire both for the death of the father and for reconciliation and communion with the father through the substitute victim. "The importance which is everywhere, without exception, ascribed to sacrifice [*Opfer*] lies in the fact that it offers satisfaction to the father for the outrage inflicted on him in the same act in which that deed is commemorated" (TTg 180–181/TTe 150).

In "Die *do-ut-des*-Formel in der Opfertheorie" (1920–1921) and in *Religion in Essence and Manifestation* (1933), Gerardus van der Leeuw develops Mauss's idea of the gift in the context of sacrifice. The Latin formula *do ut des* ("I give that you may give") is likewise expressed in the Vedic religion: "Here is the butter; where are your gifts?" He proposes that sacrifice as gift is "no longer a mere matter of bartering with gods corresponding to that carried on with men, and no longer homage to the god such as is offered to princes: it is an opening of a blessed source of gifts" (PR 399/REM 353). Sacrifice as gift does not describe a commercial transaction, but rather a release of a current of force. Instead of the rationalistic *do ut des,* he suggests *do ut possis dare* ("I give power in order that you may be able to give"). This theory combines the gift and communion theories insofar as the two participants (the deity and human beings) are simultaneously givers and receivers (who are strengthened by the gift), but the central role belongs to the gift itself and the current of force it sets in motion.

In *The Philosophy of Symbolic Forms* (1925), Ernst Cassirer proposes that the sacrificial act was the kernel around which intellectual activity developed and the practice of worship was first organized. The intuition that any expansion of the ego is tied to a corresponding limitation or renunciation that the ego imposes on itself grounds the sacrifice that usually comprises an important part of religious faith and activity (PdSF 274/PoSF 222). Drawing on a particular reading of the work of G. W. F. Hegel, Cassirer proposes an ultimately Christocentric dialectical progression (or evolution) of forms of sacrifice. Unlike Hubert and Mauss (and Smith before them), Cassirer proposes that the essential factor in the progressive development of sacrifice is not a process of communication between pre-existing sacred and profane realms by means of a victim who plays a mediating role between the human sacrificer and the divinity, but rather is the very process that establishes the meaning of these two realms. Each new form of sacrifice opens up a new meaning of the human and the divine and a new relation between them. It is the tension of this relation that gives to each form of sacrifice its actual character and meaning. Thus, sacrifice does "not merely bridge a gulf that existed for the religious consciousness from the beginning; rather, the religious consciousness *creates* this gulf in order to close it; it progressively intensifies the opposition between God and man in order to find in this opposition the means by which to surpass it" (PdSF 284/PoSF 230). This surpassing, or *Aufhebung,* of each particular form of sacrifice is a progression (or evolution) toward a Christo-centric form of sacrifice. "The meaning of sacrifice is not exhausted by the sacrifice *to* the god: rather, it seems to stand out fully and reveal itself in its true religious and speculative depth where *the god himself* is sacrificed or sacrifices himself" (PdSF 284/PoSF 230).

In *Dialectic of Enlightenment* (1944), Max Horkheimer and Theodor W. Adorno (following a line of interpretation opened up by Karl Kerényi and C. G. Jung; see Wiggershaus's *The Frankfurt School: Its History, Theories, and Political Significance,* 330) use an equivocal economical theory of sacrifice to show that myth was already enlightenment (the first excursus of *Dialectic of Enlightenment*—"Odysseus, or Myth and Enlightenment"—is, according to the Introduction, intended to provide evidence for the thesis that myth was already enlightenment). Odysseus succeeded in establishing himself against the mythic powers through self-inflicted renunciation. "Odysseus acts as sacrifice and priest at one and the same time. By calculating his own sacrifice, he effectively negates the power to whom the sacrifice is made. In this way he redeems the life he had forfeited" (DA 68–69/DE 50). The mythical powers are outwitted, but it comes at the cost of the internalization of renunciation. Horkheimer and Adorno thus deny that either the victim or the myth had any genuine transcendence. Rather than condemning a world full of sacrifices and striving for a world free of sacrifices, rituals confirmed to the victim that finite existence was fraught with sacrifices.

In *Myth and Cult among Primitive Peoples* (1951), Adolf E. Jensen works within the context of the theory of *Kulturkreislehre* originated by Leo Frobenius. According to this theory, the original significance of a new insight, which assumes a specific form in the expressive phase of a culture, degenerates in the phase of application. Jensen proposes that the origin of blood sacrifice was in the ritual killing of the archaic cultivator cultures (blood sacrifice was not associated with hunter-gatherers), which is grounded in the myth of the primordial slaying of a Dema-deity. From the body of the slain deity crops originated, so that eating these plants is an eating of the deity. Jensen proposes that ritual killing is a cultic re-enactment of this primordial mythological event. These ceremonial repetitions affirm and guarantee the continuous destruction and re-creation of the present world that would otherwise not function. Once the original significance of the myth had been forgotten, or was no longer connected to the ritual, ritual killings were reinterpreted as a sacrificial giving of a gift to divinities (who originally played no role in the rites, because the primordial divine being had been slain). Blood sacrifices are "meaningless survivals" of the "meaningful rituals of killing" of the earlier cultivator cultures.

In the mid-twentieth century, social anthropologists and historians of religion concentrate less on worldwide typologies or Christo-centric evolutionary sequences, and more on investigations of sacrifice within particular cultures. A good example of this trend is the work of Evans-Pritchard. In *Nuer Religion* (1956), Edward Evan Evans-Pritchard proposes that for the Nuer "[m]ost sacrifices are made to prevent some danger hanging over people, for example on account of some sin, to appease an angry spirit, or at the birth of twins; or to curtail or to get rid of a misfortune which has already fallen, as in times of plague or in acute sickness" (NR 198). He proposes that the Nuer established communication with the god in order to keep him away, not to create a fellowship with him. Evans-Pritchard acknowledges that no single typology adequately explained the variety of types of sacrifice of the Nuer, and he maintains that his interpretations of the Nuer did not have universal applicability. Other examples of this trend to concentrate more on investigations of sacrifice within particular African cultures include John Middleton's *Lugbara Religion: Ritual and Authority among an East African People* (1960), Godfrey R. Lienhardt's *Divinity and Experience: The Religion of the Dinka* (1961), and Luc de Heusch's *Sacrifice in Africa: A Structuralist Approach* (1985). While accepting Detienne's genealogy of the anthropological category of "sacrifice," Luc de Heusch is not convinced that all comparative research is definitively compromised (SA 23). Acknowledging not only differences of emphasis, but also different ways of thinking about sacrifice (i.e., different ways of organizing symbolic systems), de Heusch insists that sacrifice "is always a matter of establishing a locus, near or distant—in space or time—where a debt of life is to be paid" (SA 215). Therefore, though he distances his work from the Christo-centrism of earlier interpretations, de Heusch continues to argue that all sacrifices are circumscribed by an economy of sacrifice. Ritual acts of sacrifice, he writes, "are part of a metaphysical calculation of profit and loss" (SA 215). Other examples of this trend to concentrate more on investigations of sacrifice within a variety of different particular cultures include Thomas Gibson's *Sacrifice and Sharing in the Philippine Highlands: Religion and Society among the Buid of Mindoro* (1986), M. E. Combs-Schilling's *Sacred Performances: Islam, Sexuality, and Sacrifice* (1989), J. C. Heesterman's *The Broken World of Sacrifice: An Essay in Ancient Indian Ritual* (1993), and Angela Zito's *Of Body and Brush: Grand Sacrifice as Text/Performance in Eighteenth-Century China* (1997).

In *The Savage Mind* (1962), Claude Lévi-Strauss abandons (unlike Durkheim) the search for the origin of sacrifice, but he does not abandon Durkheim's social/individual dichotomy, which appears in his theory of sacrifice as filtered through the work of Saussure. Influenced by Durkheim, Saussure's *Course in General Linguistics* (1916) describes language as social (a feature of the transcendent collective conscious) in contrast to speech as individual (idiosyncratic and unpredictable). Like Durkheim's social/individual dichotomy, Saussure's language/speech dichotomy is a soul/body dichotomy. Rather than opposing the sacred and the profane (as religious systems), Lévi-Strauss opposes totemism and sacrifice (as modes of classification).

social	individual
language	speech
(spiritual, ordered, intelligible)	(embodied, chaotic, unintelligible)
totemism	sacrifice
	("a private discourse wanting in good sense")

People who have been (mistakenly) described as practicing "totemism" (an institution that, according to Lévi-Strauss, does not exist) have really been making systems of classification. Totemic classification *correlates* differences between natural species and differences between social groups. By adopting the discontinuous differences between natural species, social groups eliminate their own resemblances, for discontinuity is necessary for order and intelligibility (Lévi-Strauss relies on a structural model of language as a system of discontinuous operations within which continuity means unintelligibility). In totemic classification, just as "one beast can never be taken for another," the member of one clan can never be taken for the member of another clan (PS 296/SM 223). Rather than representing the series of natural species as discontinuous, sacrifice represents them as continuous. In sacrifice (echoing the work of Hubert and Mauss), the series of natural species "plays the part of an intermediary between two polar terms, the sacrificer and the deity, between which there is initially no homology nor even any sort of relation," except the one established through the victim "by means of a series of successive identifications" (PS 297/SM 225). Citing the Nuer substitution of a cucumber for an ox as a sacrificial victim from the work of Evans-Pritchard, Lévi-Strauss writes:

> [Totemism] is a quantified system while [sacrifice] permits a continuous passage between its terms: a cucumber is worth an egg as a sacrificial victim, an egg a fish, a fish a hen, a hen a goat, a goat an ox. And this gradation is oriented: a cucumber is sacrificed if there is no ox but the sacrifice of an ox for want of a cucumber would be an absurdity. In totemism, or so-called totemism, on the other hand, relations are always reversible. In a system of clan appellations in which both figured, the oxen would be genuinely equivalent to the cucumbers, in the sense that it would be impossible to confound them and that they would be equally suitable for manifesting the differentiation between the groups they respectively connote. (PS 296–297/SM 224)

Insofar as it *correlates* two systems of difference (natural species and social groups), totemic classification is a metaphorical system. Insofar as neither natural species nor social groups are (according to Lévi-Strauss) really continuous, sacrifice establishes relations of continuity (not resemblance) and is therefore a metonymic system. Sacrifice establishes relations of continuity where there are none, which introduces unintelligibility. Despite what Lévi-Strauss argues, biological evolution describes natural species *as continuous*. Underlying both sacrifice and biological evolution is a common concern with time and continuity, which is entirely lacking in totemic classification (which orders a timeless conceptual "space"). For Lévi-Strauss, time and continuity introduce unintelligibility. Lévi-Strauss's totemic classification, like Saussure's language, is a timeless structure of discontinuities. Totemic classification, like language, is disembodied. Totemic classification, according to *Totemism* (1962), chooses natural species "not because they are 'good to eat' but because they are 'good to think' " (TA 128/T 89). In contrast, sacrifice is fundamentally an alimentary ritual. Totemic classificatory systems "are not, or are not primarily, means of communication. They are means of thinking" (PS 90/SM 67). In contrast, sacrifice is a means of communication (and of severing communication). Sacrifice is an active embodied *doing*, not a disembodied completed system. For Saussure, acts of speech are imperfect because they are individual, but not completely private, and therefore not completely wanting in sense. However, for Lévi-Strauss, sacrifice "represents a private discourse wanting in good sense" (PS 302/SM 228).

In "Offering and Sacrifice: Problems of Organization" (1963), Raymond Firth proposes that sacrifice is a symbolic act that is often conditioned by economic rationality. Firth stresses that his argument is not that concepts of sacrifice can simply be reduced to rational, economic terms. Though sacrifice is a symbolic act that is highly significant to human personality and that has important social components, his basic point of view is that "to understand the operations of a religious system even in such a highly symbolic rite as sacrifice, we must consider the implications of organization in men, material and timing of procedures" (OS 22). These economic considerations primarily affect the magnitude and style of the sacrificial rites, but can also have an effect on their quality, content, and ideology.

In *Violence and the Sacred* (1972), *Things Hidden since the Foundation of the World* (1978), and *The Scapegoat* (1982), René Girard proposes that the sacrifice of a scapegoat was a means of focusing and diverting violence. "[I]f left unappeased, violence will accumulate until it overflows its confines and floods the surrounding area. The role of sacrifice is to stem this rising tide [...] and redirect violence into 'proper' channels" (VeS 24/VaS 10). According to Girard, one learns everything through the imitation (*mimesis*) of others, including to desire what the imitated model desires. At some point, the object of desire becomes an obstacle between the imitator and the imitated (since they both cannot have the object), and they become rivals. "[T]he effects of mimetic rivalry [...] invariably end in reciprocal violence" (VeS 242/VaS 174). Soon the desired object becomes irrelevant, insofar as it is the imitated person that the imitator covets. The imitator seeks to be no longer *like* the imitated person, but to *become* the imitated person. At some point in the escalation of mimetic violence, the mimetic rivals become indistinguishable from one another. They become mimetic twins. At some point, the blame for the escalation of mimetic violence is placed upon a marginalized or otherwise insignificant third party. This scapegoat becomes the "monstrous double" of all involved in the conflict; that is, everyone sees their own rage and culpability in the scapegoat. A united front is formed against the perceived culprit. "Where only shortly before a thousand individual conflicts had raged unchecked between a thousand enemy brothers, there now reappears a true community, united in its hatred for one alone of its number. All the rancors scattered at random among the divergent individuals, all the differing antagonisms, now converge on an isolated and unique figure, the *surrogate victim*" (VeS 118/VaS 79). With this primordial event, which signifies the passage from non-human to human, "reciprocal violence" becomes the "violent unanimity" that creates community. The sacrifice of the scapegoat (temporarily) restores equilibrium. This almost miraculous restoration of equilibrium causes a retroactive exoneration of the scapegoat, who is subsequently perceived as a beneficent savior and is venerated forever after by repeated sacrificial anamnesis. All sacrifice repeats this primordial event, and functions (like it) to focus and redirect violence into "proper" channels. Girard claims (according to Robert M. Price in *Deconstructing Jesus*) that the canonical gospels of the New Testament have exposed the scapegoat mechanism "on which all previous religion rested, which all previous mythology had *embodied*" (DJ 177, emphasis added). This was accomplished by depicting Jesus as an innocent victim. Rather than being a persecution text (typical of mythology), the gospels were written from the standpoint of the victim. Jesus critiqued the scapegoating mechanism by calling into question the Jewish sacrificial system and calling for the end of violence and counterviolence in favor of turning the other cheek and loving the enemy. Therefore, Jesus (according to Girard) called for the end of the mystification of violence as the sacred. But in *Deconstructing Jesus*, Price shows how "Girard himself [. . .] will not see how the gospels *embody* the scapegoating mechanism instead of exposing and exploding it" (DJ 208, emphasis added). Here again, according to Price's reading of Girard, is the resurrection of Christo-centrism. (Several other critiques have been leveled against Girard's theory; see SS 32–44, TYGF 131–132, Kearney's "Myths and Scapegoats: The Case of René Girard," Derrida's "Désistance," and Lacoue-Labarthe's "Typography.")

In *Homo Necans: The Anthropology of Ancient Greek Sacrificial Ritual and Myth* (1972), Walter Burkert proposes a genetic, rather than a psychological, explanation of the origin of sacrifice. He builds his theory on "the fundamental role played in biology by intraspecific aggression" (HNg 8/HNe 1). In the hunt, intraspecific aggression (aggression directed against humans) was directed toward the hunted animal, saving the human beings from self-destruction. The hunted animal was experienced as human, even becoming a father substitute, which partially confirmed (according to Burkert) "Freud's intuition that a patricide stands at the start of human development" (HNg 89/HNe 75). This hunting behavior was genetically fixed, and the behavior was retained in the form of sacrifice of domestic animals.

In *Cannibals and Kings: The Origins of Cultures* (1977) and "The Enigma of Aztec Sacrifice" (1977), Marvin Harris and Michael Harner (respectively) propose that Aztec human sacrifice had nothing to do with astronomy or religion, but was actually a method for the production and distribution of animal protein in an environment where animal protein was in short supply. (For a critique of this interpretation of sacrifice, see Sahlins's "Culture as Protein and Profit.")

In *Kingship and Sacrifice: Ritual and Society in Ancient Hawaii* (1985), Valerio Valeri proposes that sacrifice (like all ritual) is to be understood as a dialectical process. He puts Durkheim's account of ritual in Hegelian terms. For Durkheim, the concept of the collective subject (society) that is produced in ritual is transcendent and sacred. According to Valeri, in the public work of ritual sacrifice, Hawaiians produce the concept of the collective subject (i.e., ritual represents society in conceptual form), but this concept is produced not as transcendent and sacred, but (in Hegelian terms) as objectified and alienated. For Valeri, the sacred and profane, which represents the social and the individual, is not an eternal and universal dichotomy (as it is according to Durkheim), but a historically contingent alienation to be dialectically overcome. Hegel's pupil Feuerbach was also important to Valeri's theory of sacrifice. For both Durkheim and Feuerbach, the content of religious representation (or ritual representation) is the collective subject (society for Durkheim, species-being for Feuerbach). But there is a difference. For Durkheim, religious representation is the way society becomes conscious of itself in conceptual form (therefore, religious representation enriches society). For Feuerbach, religious representation is what is alienated from human beings. In Valeri's synthesis of Durkheim and Feuerbach, ritual representation both reveals and conceals: "[T]he ordering virtue of ritual is not due simply to enlightening, but also to blinding" (KS xi–xii).

In *Prey into Hunter: The Politics of Religious Experience* (1992), Maurice Bloch proposes to situate what has been called "sacrifice" within a three-stage dialectical process that involves an element of violence or conquest. In the initial move of the ritual, the value of the immanent world of the here and now is negated. It is left behind in the move toward the transcendental. But this move into the beyond is ultimately politically unsatisfactory insofar as the enduring entity in the transcendent world (of which one becomes a part) has no political significance. If the initial move represents the transcendental as desirable and the immanent world as of no value, the return is different. In the return, the transcendental neither is left behind nor is its value negated. The return is a conquest of the immanent world by the transcendental. The dialectical process thus leads to what Bloch refers to as "rebounding violence" (PIH 4–5): the violence of the initial move and the violence of the return. Vitality is regained through this ritual, but it is not the homegrown native vitality that was negated in the initial move of the ritual that is regained, but rather a conquered vitality obtained from an external being (usually an animal, but sometimes plants or other human beings).

> In ritual representations, native vitality is replaced by a conquered, external, consumed vitality. It is through this substitution that an image is created in which humans can leave this life and join the transcendental, yet still not be alienated from the here and now. They become part of permanent institutions, and as superior beings they can reincorporate the present life through the idiom of conquest or consumption. (PIH 5)

For Bloch, this conquering and consuming is important because it helps to explain the political outcomes of religious action, insofar as the consumption of the external being "can be represented as merely a preliminary to expansionist violence against neighbors" (PIH 6). Though Bloch acknowledges that this thesis may seem close to that of Girard and Burkert, who likewise see a link between religion and violence, it sees a link for totally different reasons.

> These writers assume an innate aggressiveness in humans which is expressed, and to a certain extent purged, by ritual. In contrast I do not base myself on some innate propensity to violence but argue that violence is itself a result of the attempt to create the transcendental in religion and politics. (PIH 7)

Though this thesis helps to explain the political outcomes of religious action, Bloch points out that that potential of the symbolism to take the form of expansionist violence against neighbors depends on real economic, political, and military circumstances in which people find themselves (PIH 44–45).

In *Throughout Your Generations Forever: Sacrifice, Religion, and Paternity* (1992), Nancy Jay proposes an affinity between sacrifice and patriliny. Rejecting universalizing modes of theorizing, Jay argues that her own general concepts of sacrifice constitute lenses to look through (TYGF 23). Sacrifice joins people together in community and separates them from defilement, disease, and other dangers. Jay proposes to use the logical abstractions of communion and expiation—the traditional terms for joining and separating, or collective and piacular (Evans-Pritchard), or conjunctive and disjunctive (de Heusch)—as the contextually situated lens through which to observe various sacrificial systems (TYGF 17–29). They are abstractions rather than descriptions of any particular actual sacrificial practice. "They are lenses that will bring into focus analogous aspects of differing traditions" (TYGF 23), while attempting to preserve their diverse individuality. Hubert and Mauss recognize the intermingling of the communion and expiation, but consider them to be two distinct and logically separate processes. Unlike Hubert and Mauss, Jay argues that communion and expiation are two reciprocal aspects of a single unified process. This "logic of sacrifice" is revealed in the original etymology of an English word: "atonement is also always at-one-ment" (TYGF 18–19).

Descent "systems"—which are associated with specific types of economic production found predominantly in preindustrial agrarian and pastoral societies— are ideal ways of ordering the social relations of production. The varieties of intergenerational continuity—"lineage" organization—are efficient means of controlling and transmitting (by means of inheritance) productive property (such as farmland and livestock herds) and monopolized skills (such as priestly skills and political office). Such descent "systems" (as well as blood sacrificial religions) are concentrated among preindustrial agrarian and pastoral societies in which rights to productive property are highly valued, as opposed to hunter-gatherer societies (which lack significant durable productive property to pass from generation to generation), and modern economic societies (which are characterized by occupational differentiation and monetary exchange) (TYGF 34–35).

Both the patrilineal and the matrilineal descent "systems" are ways in which men regulate rights over women's reproductive powers. In patrilineages, the descent of authority, and of property, is from father to son. In matrilineages, the descent is from uncle to nephew (from mother's brother to sister's son). In the matrilineal system (as opposed to the patrilineal system), the man with rights over sexual access and the man (and group) with rights over the offspring are different (TYGF 35). Although both descent "systems" are dependent on women's powers of reproduction, this dependence is structurally recognized in matrilineages but transcended in patrilineages. Biological paternity does not have the same natural certainty as birth, which provides certainty of maternity and determines the rights of membership in a matrilineage. No enduring social structure can be structured on the uncertainty of biological paternity. Sacrifice, Jay argues, solves this problem.

> When the crucial intergenerational link is between father and son, for which birth by itself cannot provide sure evidence, sacrificing may be considered essential for the continuity of the social order. What is needed to provide clear

evidence of social and religious paternity is an act as definite and available to the senses as is birth. When membership in patrilineal descent groups is identified by rights of participation in blood sacrifice, evidence of "paternity" is created which is as certain as evidence of maternity, but far more flexible. (TYGF 36)

Sacrifice is (as Jay puts it) "at home" in societies where intergenerational continuity between males (patriliny) is a central concern (TYGF xxiv–xxv). Sacrifice solves a problem that is inherent in patriliny: intergenerational continuity between males is not naturally given, but culturally constructed. Sacrifice is a culturally constructed way to transcend dependence on (and the finitude associated with being born of) childbearing women and be integrated into an "eternal" social order that transcends mortality.

> The twofold movement of sacrifice, integration and differentiation, communion and expiation, is beautifully suited for identifying and maintaining patrilineal descent. Sacrifice can expiate, get rid of, the consequences of having been born of woman (along with countless other dangers) and at the same time integrate the pure and eternal patrilineage. Sacrificially constituted descent, incorporating women's mortal children into an "eternal" (enduring through generations) kin group, in which membership is recognized by participation in sacrificial ritual, not merely by birth, enables a patrilineal group to transcend mortality in the same process in which it transcends birth. In this sense, sacrifice is doubly a remedy for having been born of woman. (TYGF 40)

Sacrifice, according to Jay, works in a performative way. It is what Thomas Aquinas called an "effective sign," one that causes what it signifies. Jay qualifies this by adding that sacrifice does not "cause" patrilineal membership where there are not patrilineages. As with Aquinas, the effective work of symbolic action is reflexively dependent on the existence of other structures (social, religious, etc.) (TYGF 37). Sacrifice is a concrete action situated in a particular social and religious context. As such, one cannot possess *the* meaning of sacrifice. This is not a failure, according to Jay, but a mistaken idea of understanding. Understanding is not an act of acquisition, but an incessant and interminable work. "Like women's work, it is never done but not consequently invalid" (TYGF 13).

Jay's work on the affinity between sacrifice and patriliny calls for a rereading of some of the early theorists of sacrifice. With regard to Wellhausen, Jay accounts for the post-exilic increase in the importance of expiatory sacrifice sociologically. It had to do, she argues, with the rise of a theocratic priesthood organized patrilineally and increasingly differentiated from the rest of the Israelite population (TYGF 95–97). Smith notices the affinity between sacrifice and patriliny, but given that he considers patriliny as a natural blood tie (and not as a cultural construction), he does not consider that sacrifice might identify and maintain patrilineal descent (TYGF 32–33). Jay writes of theories of sacrifice in general: "Theories of sacrifice commonly exhibit notions of gender ranging from taken-for-granted male domination to explicit misogyny" (TYGF 128).

A particular example of the way sacrifice can identify, and maintain through time, other forms of male-to-male succession that transcend dependence on childbearing women is the apostolic succession of the sacrificing priesthood of the Roman Catholic Church. This transcendence of the natural (birth and death) is concomitant with the *super*natural basis of the priestly hierarchical authority. The fundamental hierarchical distinction in Roman Catholic Church social organization is between God (supernatural) and nature (natural). The hierarchy presides, according to Vatican II, "in God's stead over the flock" (VC II: *Lumen Gentium* 20). And the supernatural basis of this hierarchy is absolutely dependent on sacrifice: the priest, in performing eucharistic sacrifice, acts supernaturally as the person of Christ (TYGF 113).

Nowhere in the New Testament is the Eucharist referred to as a sacrifice, nor does it describe a special priestly office for celebrating it. There is no mention of an institutionalized apostolic succession of the sacrificing priesthood. In fact, there is no mention of Christian priests, except the universal priesthood of all believers. Jay points out that the only part of the New Testament about priesthood and sacrifice (the letter to the Hebrews) "is about the end of all sacrificing, whose ultimate goal of transcending 'bodily descent' (having-been-born-of-woman) has been finally attained" (TYGF 115). As opposed to the Levitical sacrificing priesthood, Christ is "one who has become a priest, not through a legal requirement concerning physical descent, but through the power of an indestructible life" (Heb. 7:16, NRSV). This eternal continuity with the God the Father attained by Christ effects the end of the need for, as well as possibility of, all future sacrificing (Heb. 7:27; 9:25–26; 10:5–10, 12, 14, 18, 26).

Threatened by persecution, heresy, and schism, the Church (according to Jay) dealt with the problems of continuity and succession by developing a sacrificially maintained social structure to control and transmit its valued spiritual property. "The Eucharist became *the* Christian sacrifice, increasingly identical with that on Calvary; the bishops who celebrated it became unilineal successors to the apostles; and clerical office became sacrificing priesthood, not charismatic ministry" (TYGF 116). As early as the second century, the Eucharist was called *thusia* (sacrifice) and was celebrated by the bishop for the congregation (see *The Didache*, 14: 1–3), but it was as yet an offering of praise and thanksgiving and not yet of the body and blood of Christ (see Daly's *Christian Sacrifice: The Judaeo-Christian Background before Origen*). By the middle of the third century, Cyprian, Bishop of Carthage, had become the first (in response to the contemporary use of water alone in the Eucharist, and his insistence on a mixture of water and wine) to refer to the body and blood of Christ as the object of sacrifice by priests (see Cyprian's "Letter 63"). Cyprian was the first to call the bishop "priest" (*sacerdos*) and the first (in response to the Novatian schism) to make explicit the transition from a universal apostolic hierarchy to a single line of apostolic descent tied to the episcopate (TYGF 116, 166n10). Jay argues that "[r]itual purity, as distinct from moral purity, became crucial for priests, and the reproductive powers of women were specifically polluting. Celibacy became an ideal for the priesthood, much later a requirement" (TYGF 117). By the ninth and tenth centuries, the priesthood was formally identified by its exclusive sacrificing power, and private masses with no congregation became common (these commonly non-alimentary sacrifices were entirely expiatory) (TYGF 117–118). The sacrificial tradition reached its full development in the thirteenth century, simultaneously with the height of centralized political power of the hierarchy of the episcopate. In 1215, the Fourth Lateran Council accepted the doctrine of transubstantiation, and later Aquinas gave the sacrificial understanding of the Eucharist its classical doctrinal expression: the sacrifice of the cross is repeated in the mass (see Aquinas's *Summa Theologiæ* III Q 83: 1) (TYGF 118).

Jay argues that there is a correspondence between developments of Roman Catholic Church social organization and sacrificial practice and theology. One of the most striking correspondences is that as the line of priestly descent became *more* differentiated from the laity, so did the Eucharist become more expiatory (and an increasingly non-alimentary separating sacrifice), and (after Vatican II) as the line of priestly descent became *less* differentiated from the laity, so did the Eucharist become less expiatory (and an increasingly alimentary communion) (TYGF 112). Vatican II affirms a traditional understanding of the sacrificial priesthood—"[I]n the person of Christ he effects the eucharistic sacrifice" (VC II: *Lumen Gentium* 10)—and the apostolic succession of the priesthood—"[T]he apostles were careful to appoint successors in this hierarchically constituted society. [. . .] Amongst those [. . .] the chief place [. . .] is held by the function of those who, through their appointment to the dignity and responsibility of bishop, and in virtue consequently of the unbroken succession, going back to the beginning, are regarded as transmitters of the apostolic line [*apostolici seminis*]" (VC II: *Lumen Gentium* 20). Though Vatican II affirms these traditional understandings, it blurs the distinction between the line of priestly descent and the laity by desiring "that all the faithful should be led to that full, conscious, and active participation in liturgical celebrations which is demanded by the very nature of the liturgy, and to which the Christian people, 'a chosen race, a royal priesthood, a holy nation, a redeemed people' (1 Pet. 2:9, 4–5) have a right and obligation by reason of their baptism" (VC II: *Sacrosanctum Concilium* 14). This blurring of the distinction between the line of priestly descent and the laity was accompanied by an increasingly alimentary (and less expiatory) understanding of the Eucharist.

Despite the relative merits of the viability of sacrifice as a category for contemporary sociology, anthropology, and religious studies, and even though particular aspects of each of these theories have been criticized (quite legitimately) from the perspective of sociology, anthropology, and religious studies, this chapter

The Question of Sacrifice

has been primarily concerned with beginning what will of necessity be an incessant genealogy of sacrifice. This beginning of a genealogy of sacrifice sets the stage for the necessarily incessant interruption not only of these theories (and their subtle, and not so subtle, presuppositions of economics, sexism, and Christocentric evolutionism), but of sacrifice itself.

2

Kristeva

Mimesis and Sacrifice

Sacrifice haunts the work of Kristeva. Drawing upon the work of Lacan and social anthropologists such as Robertson Smith, Hubert and Mauss, Evans-Pritchard, and Lévi-Strauss, she outlines a contemporary criticism of ideology. For her, the genesis of the subject occurs in the two phases of the thetic, which is a rupture and/or boundary with the unconscious or semiotic *chora*. The genesis of the subject in the two phases of the thetic (the mirror stage and castration) is a scene of (what may be called) sacrifice. Western sacrifice comes to be understood as a violent action that effects the revelation of truth that overcomes the negative aspect of the sacrifice. In the thetic, the rhythm of drives and their stases characteristic of the unconscious or semiotic *chora* is confined (through sacrifice) to generate the signification of the symbolic order. This necessary confinement of semiotic violence through sacrifice (which tends toward the unicity of theological or ideological truth, which in turn represses the semiotic) is subsequently interrupted by mimesis and poetic language, which deploy the expenditure of semiotic violence and question the very principle of the ideological.

I would argue that perhaps the boundary between sacrifice and mimesis (or poetic language) is not distinct. Mimesis or poetic language is the "reversed reactivation" of the contradiction that institutes the thetic characteristic of the symbolic. The "reversed reactivation" of the contradiction that institutes the thetic is a "reversed reactivation" of the contradictory sacrificial process insofar as it is understood as simultaneously violent and confining or regulatory. The poet mimics sacrifice, for the poet, according to Kristeva, is comparable to the scapegoat. But the poet is not merely a scapegoat insofar as the poet's practice, setting itself up as a substitute for the thetic moment (rupture and/or boundary) instituting symbolism, does not allow his or her function to become harnessed (as is the case with sacrifice, which tends toward the unicity of theological or ideological truth). The poet dwells with this rupture, at this boundary. The poet "is" the subject in process/on trial (*en procès*). And the "truth" of this moment is articulated by a "new dialectic." But, I will argue, this scapegoat (who is not merely a scapegoat) remains governed (despite Kristeva's intentions) by the logic of sacrifice, insofar as this moment remains the revelation of truth (whether this truth is the unicity of traditional doxy or the plurality of the "new dialectic" that is likewise vulnerable to theologization). Kristeva wants to prevent such theologization (which she correctly attributes to sacrifice), but the way she describes mimesis (as a "reversed reactivation" of sacrifice) only sets the stage for another form of theologization. Her work must, therefore, be relentlessly corrected. It must be withdrawn from the tendency to sacrifice that haunts mimesis.

Mimesis and Sacrifice

In *Revolution in Poetic Language* (1974), Kristeva posits the ontological status of the unconscious or semiotic *chora*. Kristeva borrows the term *chora* from Plato's *Timaeus* to denote a non-expressive totality formed by the rhythm of drives and their stases in a motility that is as full of ruptures as it is ephemeral regulating stases (a regulation that is, however, different from the symbolic law). Although drives have been described as contradictory structures, insofar as they are simultaneously "negative" and "positive," this doubling generates a dominant "destructive wave" that is these drives' most characteristic trait, and the most instinctual drive, according to Freud, is the death drive.

> In this way, the term "drive" denotes waves of attack against stases, which are themselves constituted by the repetition of these charges; together, charges and stases lead to no identity (not even that of the "body proper") that could be seen as a result of their functioning. This is to say that the semiotic *chora* is no more than the place where the subject is both generated and negated, the place where his unity succumbs before the process of charges and stases that produce him. (RLP 27/RPL 28)

Kristeva next points out that it may be hypothesized that certain semiotic articulations or ephemeral regulating stases are genetically transmitted, and as such form the innate preconditions of the symbolic. But she is quick to add that the symbolic is a social effect of the relation to the other that is established through the constraints of biological differences and historical family structures. The important thing to keep in mind is that it is "possible to specify the *semiotic* as a psychosomatic *modality* of the signifying process; in other words, not a symbolic modality but one articulating (in the largest sense of the word) a *continuum*" (RLP 28/RPL 28, emphasis added, except to "semiotic"). Later in the same work, she writes, "As a precondition of the symbolic, semiotic functioning is a fairly rudimentary *combinatorial system*, which will become more complex only after the break in the symbolic" (RLP 67/RPL 68, emphasis added). She posits, therefore, a kind of continuum between the semiotic and the symbolic even while asserting their difference.

The irruption of the symbolic that is the break with the semiotic is called the thetic (rupture and/or boundary). If one accepts, as Kristeva does, that "the symbolic" and "the social" are synonymous, then they both depend on what she calls the thetic.

> From Mauss to Lévi-Strauss, social anthropology continually reconfirms this equivalence between the symbolic and the social when it considers society's various means of self-regulation—the exchange of women, different kinds of magic, myths, etc.—as languages. In reading the parallels or equivalencies that anthropology establishes between social symbolism and language, it becomes clear that the latter converge in a single place, which we have called the thetic, where positions and their syntheses (i.e., their relations) are set up. (RLP 70/ RPL 72)

Given this convergence of the emergence of the social and the symbolic in the thetic, and given that sacrifice is an "event" in the social order that "may be viewed as the *counterpart* of the thetic moment instituting symbolism" (RLP 72/ RPL 74, emphasis added), then it becomes possible to describe the thetic moment instituting symbolism as a scene of sacrifice.

Kristeva, drawing upon the work of Lacan, identifies two phases of the thetic: (1) the mirror stage, (2) and castration (alienation). These phases of the thetic, around which signification is organized, constitute phases of a scene of (what can be called) sacrifice. The break of the imaginary bond of union with the mother at the end of the mirror phase is the first phase in the process of separation. In order to capture its image unified in a mirror, the child must remain separate from it (RLP 44/RPL 46). The child, therefore, comes to be in a "place" where "it" is not. Castration completes the process of separation that posits the subject as signifiable, that is, as separate. The separation from the mother and the perception of lack (*manque*) is at once the constitution of the subject as want(ing)-to-be (*manque à être*) and the irruption of desire (of the incestuous Thing embodied initially in the mother). Castration involves a primordial sacrifice of the incestuous Thing of enjoyment (*jouissance*). As Lacan, drawing upon Hegel, writes, "[T]he symbol manifests itself first of all as the murder of the thing" (E 319/ES 104).

> This is a decisive moment fraught with consequences: the subject, finding his identity in the symbolic, *separates* from his fusion with the mother, *confines* his jouissance to the genital, and transfers semiotic motility onto the symbolic order. Thus ends the formation of the thetic phase, which posits the gap between the signifier and the signified as an opening up toward every desire but also every act, including the very jouissance that exceeds them. (RLP 45/ RPL 47)

The subject finds its identity in a place where "it" is not, that is, *in* the symbolic Other. As subjects of the symbolic, subjects are characterized by a constitutive and irreducible lack (*manque*). The subject, as a want(ing)-to-be (*manque à être*), supports the functioning of signification. Signification, in turn, exists because there is no subject *in* signification. The subject "is" a lack (*in* the signifier, *in* the symbolic Other). "The subject is hidden 'by an ever purer signifier' [E 800/ ES 299], this want-to-be confers on an *other* the role of containing the possibility of signification; and this other, which is no longer the mother (from which the child ultimately separates through the mirror stage and castration), presents itself as the place of the signifier that Lacan will call 'the Other' " (RLP 45–46/RPL 48). This confining or regulating of *jouissance*, along with simultaneous separation from the mother and transfer of semiotic motility onto the symbolic order, points to what Kristeva calls sacrifice.

Sacrifice is an "event" *in* the social order that may be viewed as the counterpart of the thetic moment instituting symbolism (RLP 72/RPL 74). In all known archaic societies, the regulation of the semiotic in the symbolic through the thetic break is represented by murder (RLP 69/RPL 70). Freud locates this break in the myth of the primal horde, where according to this myth the confinement of the death drive and origin of the law is incarnated in the murder of the father. Kristeva indicates how language, as well as the social order, confines the death drive:

> [L]anguage, already as a semiotic *chora* but above all as a symbolic system, is at the service of the death drive, diverts it, and *confines* it as if within an isolated pocket of narcissism. The social order, for its part, reveals this *confinement* of the death drive, whose endless course conditions and moves through every stasis and thus every structure, in an act of murder. (RLP 69/ RPL 70, emphasis added)

It is important to note that this passage reinforces the fact that there is a certain continuity ("in the largest sense of the word") between the semiotic *chora* — that is, the rhythm of drives and their stases in a motility that is as full of ruptures as it is made up of ephemeral confining or regulating stases — and the symbolic (which is instituted by sacrifice). The difference between the two seems to be a matter of emphasis. The semiotic is characterized by a violence that is momentarily regulated. It is important to recall that this confinement or regulation is different from the symbolic law. As such, a "destructive wave" (the death drive) predominates as the drive's most characteristic trait. The symbolic, however, which is instituted by sacrifice, confines semiotic violence by means of the symbolic law. It is as if the violent sacrificial process, which is a represented or focused violence that confines or regulates the death drive characteristic of semiotic violence, "tips the scales" in favor of the regulating process of stases (as opposed to the continuous rupturing movement of the drives) that is now (as opposed to what was the case in the semiotic *chora*) identical to the symbolic law. And, the instituting of the symbolic effected by the violent sacrificial process tends to be on the way to a unified signified, a monotheism that is the theologized truth of the semiotic *chora*.

Sacrifice, therefore, is a violent process that is not merely an unleashing of animal violence. Drawing upon social anthropology, Kristeva thinks that a more accurate view of sacrifice is that it is simultaneously violent and confining or regulatory. The violent sacrificial process puts an end to previous (semiotic, pre-symbolic) violence. The violence of sacrifice is a focusing of violence. By focusing semiotic violence—that is, by violently sacrificing semiotic violence—the violent sacrificial process displaces or transfers (see RLP 45/RPL 47) semiotic violence onto the symbolic order at the very moment the symbolic order is being established, insofar as violently focusing semiotic violence is (at the same time) the establishment of the symbolic order (RLP 72/RPL 75). The violence of sacrifice, which is a focusing of violence, sets up the symbolic order and the "first" symbol at the same time. The violence of sacrifice is a focusing "that *confines* violence to a single place, making it a signifier" (RLP 73/RPL 75, emphasis added). This "first" symbol is the victim of the murder (sacrifice). This victim (i.e., semiotic violence as focused/confined, semiotic violence "after the fact" of the irruption of language; Lacan writes, "[T]he symbol manifests itself first of all as the murder of the thing") represents the fact that language irrupts as the murder (sacrifice) of something (specifically, semiotic violence). As such, the sacrificial process is not only violent, but also (and at the same time) confining or regulatory.

> [S]acrifice designates, precisely, the watershed on the basis of which the social and the symbolic are instituted: the thetic that *confines* violence to a single place, making it a signifier. Far from unleashing violence, sacrifice shows how representing that violence is enough to stop it and to concatenate an order. Conversely, it indicates that all order is based on representation: what is violent is the irruption of the symbol, killing substance to make it signify. (RLP 72–73/RPL 75, emphasis added)

The sacrifice characteristic of the thetic moment instituting symbolism confines semiotic violence to a single place, making semiotic violence a signifier, which tends to be on the way to a unified signified. It is important to provisionally note at this point that the language Kristeva uses here—"making it [i.e., semiotic violence] a signifier"—echoes her description of mimesis: mimesis is dependent on a subject of enunciation who does not theologize (and therefore repress) the semiotic *chora*, but instead "raises the *chora* to the status of a signifier" (RLP 57/RPL 57). This similarity of wording raises the question of the proximity of sacrifice and mimesis.

Although sacrifice exemplifies the ahistorical structural law of symbolism, it simultaneously ensures the concrete relation of this ahistorical logical phase to social history. Therefore, "the *same* sacrificial structure takes *different forms* depending on the development of the relations of production and productive forces" (RLP 74/RPL 76). As such, the "sacrificial object" (or "victim") representing the thetic (i.e., representing the fact that language irrupts as the murder or sacrifice of something) varies depending on the society's degree of economic development.

The Question of Sacrifice

Although, Kristeva argues, social anthropology does not yet seem to have systematically studied the history of the different forms of structure of sacrifice, it does make a significant advance by associating the sacrificial with the social. She notes that in *Sacrifice: Its Nature and Function* (1899), Henri Hubert and Marcel Mauss write that sacrifice has a "social function because sacrifice is concerned with social matters" (NFS 137/SNF 102; see RLP 74n109/RPL 250n94). Kristeva writes:

> It is only from this position bordering on the social that sacrifice can be viewed not only as an imposition of social coherence but also as its outer limit. On the other side of this boundary is the a-symbolic, the dissolution of order, the erasing of differences, and finally the disappearance of the human in animality. In this light one might well reread Robertson Smith, who ascribes to rites the function of maintaining the community between man and animal. (RLP 74/ RPL 76)

Claude Lévi-Strauss, however, questioned this association of the sacrificial with the social. In *The Savage Mind* (1962), he opposed totemism and sacrifice (as modes of classification).

social	**individual**
language	**speech**
(spiritual, ordered, intelligible)	(embodied, chaotic, unintelligible)
totemism	**sacrifice**
	("a private discourse wanting in good sense")

Totemic classification correlates differences between natural species and differences between social groups. Totemism represents differences within each series as discontinuous (which is necessary for order and intelligibility insofar as Lévi-Strauss relies on a structural model of language as a system of discontinuous operations within which continuity means unintelligibility). Sacrifice, on the contrary, represents differences within each series as continuous. In sacrifice (echoing the work of Hubert and Mauss) the series of natural species "plays the part of an intermediary between two polar terms, the sacrificer and the deity, between which there is initially no homology nor even any sort of relation," except the one established through the victim "by means of a series of successive identifications" (PS 297/SM 225). Sacrifice establishes relations of continuity (not resemblance) and is therefore a metonymic system. Yet in order to establish a relation (between the sacrificer and the deity), the metonymic chain must be ruptured. Sacrifice is a disrupted metonymy; that is, it is the formation of a (metonymic) relation through rupture (murder). "Metonymy and rupture, such is the logic of this 'relation' which is not yet an 'is,' but prepares the way for it to be posited" (RLP 75/RPL 77). The deity and the human being establish a relation within the violent sacrificial process itself. In fact, Kristeva seems to argue that this disrupted metonymy not only establishes the (metonymic) relation (between the sacrificer and the deity), it sets a deity (as a transcendental signified) in place. This is, according to Kristeva, the theologization of the thetic. It is not as though there is a pre-existing deity and a pre-existing human being that are then brought into relation by means of the violent sacrificial process. The violent sacrificial process itself establishes the relation insofar as it posits a deity and a human being (which regulate semiotic violence). Having set a deity in place, this disrupted metonymy expects as a reward an answer from the deity. The rupture (murder) is, furthermore, followed by a "compensatory continuity" (prayer).

> In this way, the entire circuit of symbolic communication between two hierarchized discursive agencies is established (gift—reward—symbolic praise), a circuit on which symbolic economy is based. In this way, sacrifice stages the *advent* of this economy, its *emergence* from the ecological continuum, and the *socialization of this ecology*. (RLP 75/RPL 77)

Sacrifice establishes relations of continuity where there are none, which introduces unintelligibility. For Lévi-Strauss, sacrifice "represents a private discourse wanting in good sense" (PS 302/SM 228). But it cannot be said, Kristeva responds, that totemism is true and sacrifice is false.

> Sacrifice would be false only if its role were to classify; it occupies, instead, the other side of symbolism. Rather than present symbolic functioning as an already existing system, it reproduces the process of its production. In its metonymic logic, its broken continuity, and its symbolic relation to a dominant agency, sacrifice resembles not language but the unconscious, which is the unspoken precondition of linguistic systematization. (RLP 75/RPL 77–78)

In fact, the violent sacrificial process (disrupted metonymy) is at the margin of the social code insofar as the violent sacrificial process reproduces not only the foundation of that code (i.e., the process of the symbolic system's production), but also what the code represses (i.e., semiotic violence) (RLP 76/RPL 78).

Sacrifice presents the confining or regulating aspect of the thetic instituting symbolism. "Sacrifice presents only the legislating aspect of the thetic phase: sacred murder merely points to the violence that was *confined* within sacrifice so as to found social order" (RLP 76/RPL 78). The instituting of the symbolic effected by the violent sacrificial process tends to be on the way to a unified signified. The murder at the origin of social order indicates that the establishment of the symbolic system "*tends* to prohibit jouissance, but at the same time, permits it" (RLP 76/RPL 78, emphasis added). Therefore, *jouissance* is "not so much forbidden as *regulated*" (RLP 76/RPL 78, emphasis added).

Mimesis is another "event" in the social order that may be viewed as the counterpart of the thetic moment instituting symbolism. But through, with, and despite the confining of semiotic violence by sacrifice, a certain practice accompanies sacrifice, which deploys the expenditure (*dépense*) of semiotic violence

(RLP 77/RPL 79). Mimesis and poetic language indicate the filtering of *jouissance* into language (insofar as it is not so much forbidden as regulated).

Mimesis, as Kristeva uses the word, is not the imitation of an object. It is internally dependent on a subject of enunciation who (unlike the transcendental ego) does not tend to repress the semiotic *chora*, but instead "raises the *chora* to the status of a signifier, which may or may not obey the norms of grammatical locution" (RLP 57/RPL 57). Mimesis is not the imitation of an object, but instead a reproduction of the trajectory of its enunciation. Said otherwise, it departs from denotation (in Frege's sense) and confines itself to meaning (RLP 57n84/RPL 248n72). It is the constitution of an enigmatic connoted mimetic object. The connoted mimetic object is enigmatic insofar as it may or may not obey the norms of grammatical locution.

> Poetic mimesis maintains and transgresses thetic unicity by making it undergo a kind of anamnesis, by introducing into the thetic position the stream of semiotic drives and making it signify. This telescoping of the symbolic and the semiotic pluralizes signification or denotation: it pluralizes the thetic doxy. (RLP 60–61/RPL 60)

Mimesis and poetic language therefore question the very principle of the ideological because they interrupt the unicity of the thetic and prevent its theologization. They tend to pluralize the unicity of the thetic doxy; that is, they tend to prevent monotheism. Mimesis and poetic language recognize both the necessity and the pretensions of theology; that is, they may appear as an argument complicitous with dogma, but they also set in motion what dogma represses (RLP 61/RPL 61). It is important to point out, therefore, that mimesis and poetic language do not disavow the thetic, "instead they go through its truth (signification, denotation) to tell the 'truth' about it" (RLP 61/RPL 60). Kristeva puts the latter use of the term *truth* in quotation marks to indicate that it no longer refers to denotative truth (in Frege's sense). "This 'second truth,'" she writes, "reproduces the path which was cleared by the first truth (that of *Bedeutung*) in order to posit itself" (RLP 61/RPL 60). The path that was cleared by the first truth in order for the first truth to institute its very position is, I would argue, sacrifice. Recall that sacrifice is the confining or regulating of semiotic violence that institutes the symbolic. As such, mimesis is the reproduction of this violent sacrificial process.

The filtering of semiotic violence into the symbolic—which is a transgression of position—is not only a reproduction of the violent sacrificial process, but (to be more precise) "a *reversed reactivation* of the contradiction that instituted this very position" (RLP 68/RPL 69, emphasis added). The filtering of semiotic violence into the symbolic is a "reversed reactivation" of the contradiction that instituted the very position that is being transgressed by the filtering. If the contradiction that instituted the thetic is the contradictory violent sacrificial process, then the "reversed reactivation" of the contradiction that institutes the thetic characteristic of the symbolic order is a "reversed reactivation" of sacrifice.

Earlier it was pointed out that it is as if the violent sacrificial process, which is a represented or focused violence that confines or regulates the death drive characteristic of semiotic violence, "tips the scales" in favor of the regulating process of stases, which is the instituting of the symbolic law. With the "*reversed reactivation*" characteristic of mimesis, it is as if mimesis "tips the scales" back in favor of the continuous rupturing movement of drives (as opposed to the regulating process of stases). But insofar as mimesis does not disavow the thetic, this reversal or "tipping of the scales" back in favor of the continuous rupturing movement of drives effects a dwelling in the thetic moment (rupture and/or boundary) itself, which is suspended between the semiotic and the theological. With mimesis, in other words, the "scales are tipped" back to the point of tension that Kristeva names a "new dialectic."

> [A]lthough semiotic functioning can be defined as the articulation of facilitations and stases that mean nothing, this mechanism must immediately be considered within the signifying chain instituted by the thetic. Without this new *dialectic*, a description of this functioning might eventually be related to the semiotic *chora* preceding the mirror stage and the Oedipal stage, but not to a signifying practice that is anti-Oedipal to the extent that it is anti-thetic, para-doxical.
>   Ultimately, such a dialectic lets us view signifying practices as asymmetrically divided—neither absolutizing the thetic into a possible theological prohibition, nor negating the thetic in the fantasy of a pulverizing irrationalism. (RLP 79–80/RPL 81–82)

The "reversed reactivation" of the contradiction that institutes the thetic characteristic of the symbolic order—which is a "reversed reactivation" of sacrifice—leaves one suspended between the semiotic and the theological or ideological.

What makes the poet an artist is what makes him or her comparable to the scapegoat, but at the same time it is what radically distinguishes him or her from sacrificial murderers and victims (i.e., scapegoats). The poet is comparable to the scapegoat insofar as the poet's practice "sets itself up as a *substitute* for the initially contested thetic" (RLP 70/RPL 71, emphasis added). The "initially contested thetic" refers to the thetic understood as "rupture and/or boundary" (RLP 41/RPL 43). But whereas the scapegoat is murdered as a means to an end (i.e., for the sake of the symbolic that tends toward the unicity of theological or ideological truth, which in turn represses the semiotic), art "*takes on* murder and moves through it" (RLP 69/RPL 70, emphasis added). Art "*assumes* murder insofar as artistic practice considers death the inner boundary of the signifying process" (RLP 69/RPL 70, emphasis added). What makes the poet an artist (and not merely a scapegoat) is the assumption or interiorization of the violent sacrificial process that institutes the symbolic by regulating or confining semiotic violence. "In other words, it is as if death becomes *interiorized* by the subject of such a practice; in order to function, he must make himself the *bearer* of death" (RLP 69/RPL 70, emphasis added). The poet, according to Kristeva, is not merely a scapegoat inasmuch as the poet's practice, setting itself up as a substitute for the initially contested thetic, does not allow his or her function to become harnessed (as is the case with economical sacrifice, which is the domain of theologizing religion). Kristeva thinks that the "truest" truth is not the unicity of theological or ideological truth, but the thetic moment (rupture and/or boundary) instituting symbolism, which is situated between the semiotic and the symbolic. The poet, "after the fact" of the institution of the symbolic, assumes or interiorizes death itself in order to situate him- or herself at the thetic moment (rupture and/or boundary) between the semiotic and the symbolic. The poetic practice, as the assumption of death, dwells in this moment. The poet dwells with this rupture, at this boundary. The poet "is" the subject in process/on trial (*en procès*). The "truth" of this moment is articulated by a "new dialectic."

Nancy on Bataille and the Mimicking of Sacrifice by Art

In "The Unsacrificeable" (1990), Nancy argues that Bataille's step from sacrifice to mimesis—a step remarkably similar to the step made by Kristeva—remains inscribed within the economical logic of sacrifice. In order to situate Nancy's comments on Bataille's step from sacrifice to mimesis (and their relevance to the work of Kristeva), it will be necessary to outline the preceding sections of Nancy's essay.

Nancy begins by outlining a genealogy of sacrifice. He traces the "mimetic rupture" of ancient sacrifice effected by the traditional philosophical and Christian versions of sacrifice. The sacrifices of Socrates and Christ are an appropriation of the self in its own negativity. They describe a necessary passage through death, an appropriation of death, in which death is sublated into a means of access to a supreme moment of transcendent truth. Although Bataille sought to break free of the traditional philosophical and Christian versions of sacrifice, Nancy argues that Bataille does no more than repeat their fundamental gesture. Rather than effect the revelation of truth that sublates its negation, Bataille interprets sacrifice as effecting the revelation of the "nothingness" of death itself. In both cases, however, sacrifice is thought as revelation.

Four characteristics are required by and presented by the ontotheology of the traditional philosophical and Christian versions of sacrifice: (1) this sacrifice is self-sacrifice, (2) this sacrifice is unique, and it is accomplished for all, (3) this sacrifice is inseparable from its being the unveiled truth of all sacrifices, or of sacrifice in general, and (4) the truth of this sacrifice sublates the sacrificial moment of sacrifice itself (I 73–78/U 22–24). Nancy calls this final characteristic of Western sacrifice "trans-appropriation." "Trans-appropriation" refers to the appropriation of the Self in its own negativity, that is, the *appropriation*, by means of the *trans*gression of the finite, of the infinite truth of the finite. Sacrifice is dialectically sublated in its finite functions and its exteriority (I 79/U 25). Yet despite this interiorization, spiritualization, and dialecticization of sacrifice, a fascinated gaze remains fixed on the sacrificial cruelty of the ancient (external and finite) sacrifice. The ancient sacrifice is at the heart of the modern sacrifice (I 80/U 25).

Western sacrifice is, therefore, suspended between the simulacrum (the mimesis of ancient sacrifice, i.e., the interiorization, spiritualization, and dialecticization of sacrifice in which the subject is *not* truly destroyed) and nothingness (the postulation of self-sacrifice in which the subject is destroyed). This is the impasse of sacrifice. Art comes to "supplement" this impasse of sacrifice. "[O]ut of this double impasse," Bataille writes, "arises a sense of the moment of art, which, putting us on the track of utter extinction—leaving us suspended there for a time—proposes to man a ravishing without repose" (AEC 485; see I 88/U 29). There is here, Nancy argues, a "ravishing" insofar as art preserves one "suspended" on the edge of extinction or nothingness, which is a way of recognizing a new form of simulacrum (I 88/U 29). But even though the "ravishing" here is limited to a new form of the simulacral, it (at the same time) only matters if it is not simulated. The "ravishing" only matters if it accedes to the effective exercise of an effective cruelty, at least with respect to the intense agitation of an emotion that accedes to extinction or nothingness. The very title of Bataille's essay suggests as much: "Art, exercise in cruelty." Art thus matters, Nancy writes, only if it continues to send one back to the sacrifice it supplements.

Here is a step beyond sacrifice by mimesis that is not beyond sacrifice. Bataille writes, "[T]he movement [of art] places him without difficulty at the height of the worst and, reciprocally, the painting of the horror reveals the opening towards the entirety of the possible" (AEC 486; see I 89/U 29). Art lets one commune, by means of a *trans*gression that is still effective, "with the enjoyment of an instantaneous *appropriation* of death" (I 90/U 29, emphasis added). This thought, therefore, "continues to be measured by the logic and the desire of an infinite '*trans-appropriation*'" (I 90/U 29–30, emphasis added). The supplementation of sacrifice by mimesis—that is, art's mimicking of sacrifice—should be a true suppression of sacrifice. For Bataille (according to Nancy), art mimics (or sets aside the horror of . . . ; see I 90/U 29) sacrifice in order to preserve one "suspended" on the edge of extinction or nothingness in order to gain "access without access to a moment of *disappropriation*" (I 90/U 30, emphasis added). The supplementation of sacrifice by mimesis should be a true suppression of sacrifice, but art maintains the sacrificial moment (by its emotion "at the height of the worst"), and sacrificial logic does not leave off reappropriating (transappropriating) this access without access to a moment of disappropriation. Sacrifice (by definition) appropriates death (the finite moment of sacrifice), and "it is by appropriating death that sacrifice escapes the truth of the moment of disappropriation" (I 90/U 30). Sacrificial logic, according to Nancy, appropriates the "nothingness" of death. The "nothingness" of death thereby becomes a "supreme moment" of revelation, rather than a moment of dis-appropriation.

Sacrifice Is Obliged to Mimic Itself

Recall that, for Kristeva, what makes the poet an artist (and not merely a scape-goat) is the assumption or appropriation of the violent sacrificial process that institutes the symbolic by regulating or confining semiotic violence. The poet, "after the fact" of the institution of the symbolic, appropriates death itself in order to situate him- or herself at the thetic moment. But now one can see that, like Bataille's work (which Kristeva draws upon), the radicality of Kristeva's work is at risk (despite her intentions) of being reinscribed back into the tradition.

For Kristeva, as for (Nancy's reading of) Bataille, art lets one commune, by means of a transgression that is still effective, with the enjoyment of an instantaneous appropriation of death. Art mimics sacrifice in order to preserve one "suspended" on the edge of nothingness. But art maintains the sacrificial moment, and sacrificial logic does not leave off reappropriating (trans-appropriating) death.

Despite Kristeva's intentions, mimesis is still governed by a traditional notion of sacrifice as the revelation of truth. The "new dialectic" articulates nothing more than a new truth. It is a "truth" that no longer refers to denotative truth (in Frege's sense). But it is a "truth" nonetheless, as she herself remarks. Kristeva's work must be incessantly corrected. I would argue that sacrifice must not be mimicked by the poet (in order to reveal the "truth" that is the "new dialectic"). Sacrifice is obliged, rather, to mimic itself in a gesture that infinitely postpones the revelation of a theologized truth (whether this truth is the unicity of traditional doxy or the plurality of the "new dialectic" that is likewise vulnerable to theologization). With this mimesis—that is, with this sacrifice of sacrifice—one finds it necessary (yet impossible) to dwell at the thetic moment (rupture and/or boundary) between the semiotic and the symbolic. As such, the critique of the very principle of the ideological or theological is necessary (yet impossible). The "critique" can only be accomplished as an incessant task. Only at the moment of the sacrifice of sacrifice, if only for a moment, is one suspended between the semiotic and the symbolic. Yet this critical position occurs in the atemporal temporality of the moment.

3

Bataille

The Hegelian Dialectic, Death, and Sacrifice

Nancy's reading of Bataille in the previous chapter sets the stage for a more detailed reading of Bataille, whose reading of sacrifice is at risk of being misread if his anthropological, philosophical, sociological, theological, and economic readings of sacrifice are not read within the horizon of an obsessional sacrifice of sacrifice. Bataille's obsession with sacrifice is a response to the question of death. I argue that a reading of Bataille's reading of sacrifice must be attentive to the sacrifice of sacrifice characteristic of the question of death, that is, the irreducible undecidability of the double meaning of death articulated by that moment when death as possibility turns into death as impossibility.

Bataille's "Hegel, Death and Sacrifice" (1955)—an essay written within the horizon of the work of Kojève—must be read, I would argue, as a response to the following "fundamental text" of the preface of Hegel's *Phenomenology of Spirit* (1807):

> Death, if that is what we want to call this non-actuality, is of all things the most dreadful, and to hold fast what is dead requires the greatest strength. Lacking strength, Beauty hates the Understanding for asking of her what it cannot do. But the life of Spirit is not the life that shrinks from death and keeps itself untouched by devastation, but rather the life that endures it and maintains itself in it. It wins its truth only when, in utter dismemberment, it finds itself. It is this power, not as something positive, which closes its eyes to the negative, as when we say of something that it is nothing or is false, and then, having done with it, turn away and pass on to something else; on the contrary, Spirit is this power only by looking the negative in the face, and tarrying with it. This tarrying with the negative is the magical power that converts it into being. (PG 27/PS 19)

This is likewise a fundamental text for Blanchot's "Literature and the Right to Death" from *The Work of Fire* (1949). Given that Bataille's response to this Hegelian text turns, I would argue, on "fiction," it would perhaps be helpful to explore Blanchot's response to the same text, a response that turns on "literature."

Blanchot and Literature

Literature begins, Blanchot writes, "at the *moment* when literature becomes a question" (LDM 293/LRD 300, emphasis added). This question—"the 'question' that seeks to pose itself in literature, the 'question' that is its essence" (LDM 311/ LRD 322)—is posed *to* language *by* language that has become literature. This question *is* "an irreducible *double meaning*" (LDM 330/LRD 344): death as possibility and as impossibility. "[L]iterature," Blanchot writes in the concluding sentence of the essay, "is the form in which this double meaning has chosen to show itself behind the meaning and value of words, and the question it asks is the question asked by literature" (LDM 331/LRD 344). This question is what Blanchot, in *The Space of Literature* (1955), calls "double death."

The following remarks on "Literature and the Right to Death" are limited to a reading of "Revolution," which marks the first instance of Blanchot's irreducibly ambiguous reading of the following passage from the preface to Hegel's *Phenomenology of Spirit*: "[T]he life of Spirit is [. . .] the life that endures it [i.e., death] and maintains itself in it" (PG 27/PS 19). Literature begins at the moment when it becomes a question, that is, at the moment when an initial reading of this passage, which reads death as possibility, turns into a reading of this passage that reads death as impossibility. Revolution is what Blanchot calls one of a writer's temptations. A writer's temptations are those decisive moments *in* the work or production of the *Phenomenology of Spirit*, those "decisive moments *in* history" (LDM 309/LRD 318, emphasis added), which *seem* (at least on a first reading) to describe the very process of literary creation, the destructive act of transformation that is a step into the next shape of the dialectical progression. But these decisive moments are fraught with ambiguity. They are decisive moments *in* the work of the *Phenomenology of Spirit* when work is discovered to be at a certain distance *from* that work.

Blanchot reads the experience of the writer alongside that moment of the *Phenomenology of Spirit* titled "Absolute Freedom and Terror." In the writer, Blanchot writes, "negation [. . .] wishes to realize itself" (LDM 308/LRD 318). Blanchot continues:

> It is at this point that he encounters those decisive moments in history when everything seems put in question, when law, faith, the State, the world above, the world of the past—everything sinks effortlessly, without work, into nothingness. The man knows he has not stepped out of history, but history is now the void, the void in the process of realization; it is *absolute* freedom which

has become an event. Such periods are given the name Revolution. At this moment, freedom aspires to be realized in the *immediate* form of *everything is possible, everything can be done.* (LDM 309/LRD 318)

The fabulous moment in history when one experiences his or her *"own* freedom as *universal* freedom" (LDM 309/LRD 318, emphasis added) ushers in the Reign of Terror, for the decision to allow the universality of freedom to assert itself completely in him or her negates the particular reality of his or her life (LDM 310/LRD 320). The meaning of the Reign of Terror is this: every citizen has a "right to death." Every citizen has a right to death because it is with death that absolute freedom is realized. But it is precisely at this decisive moment *in* history that death as possibility turns into death as impossibility. At this decisive moment Blanchot introduces, for the first time in his work, the distinction between death as possibility and death as impossibility.

> Death as an event no longer has any importance. During the Reign of Terror individuals die and it means nothing. In the famous words of Hegel, "It is thus the coldest and meanest of all deaths, with no more significance than cutting off a head of cabbage or swallowing a mouthful of water" [PG 320/PS 360]. Why? Isn't death the achievement of freedom—that is, the richest moment of meaning? But it is also only the empty point in that freedom, a manifestation of the fact that such a freedom is still abstract, ideal (literary), that it is only poverty and platitude. (LDM 310/LRD 320)

At this decisive moment *in* the *Phenomenology of Spirit, in* history, death as possibility, as the "richest moment of meaning," is discovered to be at a certain distance *from* the *Phenomenology of Spirit, from* history. It is discovered to be interrupted, or said otherwise, to be weakened—death as impossibility. It is at this decisive moment *in* history that a reading of the following passage from the preface to the *Phenomenology of Spirit* becomes irreducibly ambiguous: "[T]he life of Spirit is [. . .] the life that endures it [i.e., death] and maintains itself in it." Blanchot writes, "Literature contemplates itself in revolution, it finds its justification in revolution, and if it has been called the Reign of Terror, this is because its ideal is indeed that moment in history, that moment when 'life endures death and maintains itself in it' in order to gain from death the possibility of speaking and the truth of speech. This is the 'question' that seeks to pose itself in literature, the 'question' that is its essence" (LDM 311/LRD 321–322).

Literature begins at the moment when it becomes a question, that is, at the moment when an initial reading of the passage "life endures death and maintains itself in it" that reads death as possibility, turns into a reading of this passage that reads death as impossibility. Literature "is," for Blanchot, the very production of the ambiguous step/not beyond (*le pas au-delà*). What "appears" in this production of a step/not beyond is an irreducible ambiguity of being and nothingness (LDM 327, 331/LRD 340, 344). Literature "is" the very production of a trace of that which withdraws from (or, said otherwise, which infinity approaches) revelation — the "not yet" of death as impossibility, the "not yet" of the approach of death.

The Irreducible Aporia of Death

Literature, I would argue, "is" not unlike what Bataille calls "fiction" in "Hegel, Death and Sacrifice." A consideration of fiction in this essay first requires a consideration of sacrifice and its connection to the Hegelian text in question. Bataille begins the second (and final) part of the essay (titled "Sacrifice") by stating that he will not speak of the *explicit* interpretation of sacrifice offered in that part of the *Phenomenology of Spirit* devoted to religion because "it strays from the essential" and is (in Bataille's opinion) of less interest than the *implicit* representation of sacrifice offered in the preface of that work (HMS 335/HDS 18). Bataille says that the human being revealed and founded human truth by sacrificing, which makes of the human being (in the words of Heidegger) a Being-towards-death, or (in the words of Kojève) "death which lives a human life" (HMS 335/HDS 18). Bataille continues:

> [T]he problem of Hegel is given in the action of sacrifice. In sacrifice, death, on the one hand, essentially strikes the corporeal being; and on the other hand, it is precisely in sacrifice that "death lives a *human* life" [Kojève]. It should even be said that sacrifice is the precise response to Hegel's requirement, the original formulation of which I repeat:
> "Spirit attains its truth only by finding itself in absolute dismemberment. It does not attain that (prodigious) power by being the Positive that turns away from the Negative . . . no, Spirit is that power only in the degree to which it contemplates the Negative face to face [and] dwells with it . . ." [PG 27/PS 19]. (HMS 335/HDS 18)

This passage from the preface of Hegel's *Phenomenology of Spirit* immediately follows the passage in question in Blanchot's "Literature and the Right to Death." Sacrifice is the "precise response" to the Hegelian requirement that Spirit attain its truth only in finding itself in absolute dismemberment insofar as sacrifice, according to Bataille, responds to what one could call the irreducible aporia of death. The irreducible aporia of death: the richest moment of meaning (death) is simultaneously the moment of the impoverished meaninglessness of absolute dismemberment. Bataille writes it this way:

> In order for Man to reveal himself ultimately to himself, he would have to die, but he would have to do it while living — watching himself ceasing to be. In other words, death itself would have to become (self-) consciousness at the very moment that it annihilates the conscious being. [. . .] Thus, at all costs, man must live at the moment that he really dies, or he must live with the impression of really dying. (HMS 336–337/HDS 19–20)

Bataille describes an aporetic moment: One must appropriate death at the very moment that appropriation is impossible, that is, at the moment of ex-propriation. It is important to note that Hegel reads this aporetic moment *not* as an aporia, but rather as a contradiction. It is "sacrifice" that is, according to Bataille, adequate to this moment of the irreducible aporia (*not* contradiction) of death. It is sacrifice as response to this aporia, however, that is the blind spot of Hegelian interpretation of *Aufhebung*.

The Hegelian interpretation of *Aufhebung* is the *presentation* or *recognition* of the identity (the "at the same time") of contradictories. The contradictories are identified *as* a contradiction. This recognition effects the step into the next shape of the dialectical progression. For Hegel, death is productive insofar as one appropriates it. In order to appropriate death, it would be necessary (in the words of Bataille) for one to die, but one would have to do it while living— watching oneself ceasing to be. "In other words, death itself would have to become (self-) consciousness *at the very moment* that it annihilates the conscious being" (HMS 336/HDS 19, emphasis added). The presentation or recognition of the identity (the "at the same time") of these contradictories effects the step into the next shape of the dialectic.

Derrida on Hegel and Aufhebung

Hegel, according to Bataille, "did not know to what extent he was right" (HMS 339/HDS 22). It is just that while *seeming* to put everything at stake at the moment of death, Hegel in fact restricts the stakes of the wager. He restricts the absolute expenditure of death to an economy that expects a return on its investment. In "From Restricted to General Economy: A Hegelianism without Reserve" (1967) from *Writing and Difference* (1967), Derrida points out that the Hegelian interpretation of *Aufhebung* is just that: an interpretation. The Hegelian text *interprets itself*; that is, each proposition of the Hegelian text is an interpretation submitted to an interpretive decision (EREG 381/RGE 260). The horizon within which all Hegelian interpretive decisions are made is the necessity of logical continuity. In interpreting negativity as the productivity of labor, Hegel restricts the stakes of his interpretive wager to logic, history, meaning, etc. But Hegel's own interpretation can, by definition, be reinterpreted (EREG 382/RGE 260). Derrida writes:

> The notion of *Aufhebung* (the speculative concept par excellence, says Hegel, the concept whose untranslatable privilege is wielded by the German language) is laughable in that it signifies the *busying* of a discourse losing its breath as it reappropriates all negativity for itself, as it works the "putting at stake" into an *investment*, as it *amortizes* absolute expenditure; and as it gives meaning to death, thereby simultaneously blinding itself to the baselessness of the nonmeaning from which the basis of meaning is drawn, and in which this basis of meaning is exhausted. (EREG 377–378/RGE 257)

The notion of the *Aufhebung* is laughable insofar as Bataille—unlike Hegel, whose revolution in thought consists in taking the negative *seriously*, in giving meaning to its labor—does *not* take the negative seriously. To be indifferent to the comedy of the *Aufhebung* (as Hegel was) is to blind oneself to the experience of the absolute sacrifice of logic, history, meaning, etc. The blind spot of Hegelianism is the moment at which death is not restricted to the productivity of labor, but rather is an expenditure without reserve. The preface to the *Phenomenology of Spirit* reads, Spirit "wins its truth only when in absolute dismemberment, it finds itself" (PG 27/PS 19). If this "dismemberment" is *indeed* absolute dismemberment, then one cannot guarantee a return on one's investment.

Bataille is not indifferent to the comedy of the *Aufhebung*. He is not blind to the experience of absolute expenditure. He is attentive to the moment of absolute dismemberment integral to the Spirit's attainment of truth. As such, at the same time that Bataille recognizes the *necessity* that "death itself would have to become (self-) consciousness at the very moment that it annihilates the conscious being" (HMS 336/HDS 19), he recognizes the *impossibility* of this very necessity. With this recognition, Bataille recognizes what Derrida will later thematize as the aporias of time and death.

Derrida and the Aporia of Time

The aporias of time and death are central to Derrida's reading of Hegel. Although they were thematized after Derrida's reading of Bataille, they are foreshadowed in that reading. In *"Ousia* and *Grammē*: Note on a Note from *Being and Time"* (1968) from *Margins of Philosophy* (1972), Derrida describes the aporia of time. The "now" by definition is *present*. It *is* what cannot coexist with (another) itself, with itself (as another), because the other itself is already at a different time, is already a different now. The identity of the now is constituted by the impossible coexistence with an other now. "The now, presence in the act of the present, is constituted as the impossibility of coexisting with an other now, that is, with an other-the-same-as-itself. The now *is* (in the present indicative) the impossibility of coexisting *with itself*: with itself, that is, with an other self, an other now, an other same, a double" (OeG 63/OaG 55). This impossibility has meaning only at the moment of the possible coimplication of nows, that is, only at the moment of the minimal distance of a now from itself. "The impossibility of coexistence can be posited as such only on the basis of a certain coexistence, of a certain *simultaneity* of the nonsimultaneous, in which the alterity and identity of the now are maintained together in the differentiated element of a certain same" (OeG 63/OaG 55). For time to be time, the "at the same time" of contradictories is necessary, that is, the "at the same time" of (1) the impossibility of the *coexistence* of a now with itself, and (2) the *coimplication* of nows; that is, the fact that each now supersedes the previous now (for time to pass) at the same time as retaining the past now and future now (for time to be recognized as the passage of time). The minimal distance of a now from itself (characteristic of *coimplication*) is necessary for the "appearance" of the impossible *coexistence* of a now with itself. *But*, this necessity calls into question the identity of the now; that is, it calls into question the impossible *coexistence* of a now with itself. *Therefore*, these contradictories must be "at the same time," yet cannot be "at the same time." It is *necessary*, yet *impossible*, for these contradictories to be "at the same time." The *im*possible coexistence of two nows (i.e., the fact that one can*not* think the "at the same time" of two nows) has meaning only on the basis of the *possibility* of the coimplication of several "present" nows (i.e., the fact that one *can* think the "at the same time" of two nows), one called "past" and another called "future." The *possibility* of the coimplication of nows (i.e., the superseding and retaining of "present" nows) is nothing but the *impossibility* of the coexistence of nows. "Time is a name for this impossible possibility" (OeG 63/OaG 55). Time is the name for this "not yet."

Derrida and the Aporia of Death

Death is *also* a name for this impossible possibility, for this "not yet." In *Aporias: Dying—Awaiting (One Another at) the "Limits of Truth"* (1994), Derrida describes the aporia of death. For Heidegger, death is a paradoxical possibility insofar as it is "the possibility of the absolute impossibility of Dasein" (SZ 250/ BT 294). According to one reading of this phenomenological description, it is *possible* (and necessary) for Dasein to appropriate this possibility (i.e., this "possibility of impossibility"). But, according to another equally appropriate reading, if this possibility (of impossibility) is *indeed* impossible, then it is *not possible* for Dasein to appropriate this possibility (of impossibility). Turning what is at the very heart of the possibility of the existential analysis of death (i.e., the appropriation of death) against the very possibility of the existential analysis, Derrida writes, "If death, the most proper possibility of *Dasein*, is the possibility of its impossibility, death becomes the most improper possibility and the most expropriating, the most inauthenticating one" (AM 337/AD 77). The point Derrida is making is that the impossibility (or disappearance) of death "appears" *only within* possibility, or to be more precise, it "appears" *only within* the interruption of possibility. That is, one sees the ruination of the step that would complete the existential analysis *in the performance of the step itself*. One sees the unworking of the "work" *in* (paradoxically) the "working" of the work.

The Aporia of Time/Death "Is" the Aporia of Dialectic

It is important to point out that the aporias of time and death are aporetic, not contradictory. The contradictories of an aporia can*not* be *presented* or *recognized* "at the same time." The truth of contradiction (to speak Hegelese) is aporia. The "not yet" of the aporia interrupts the "at the same time" of contradictories (see AE 9/OB 7, and EL 22–23/SL 30–31). Recall that the Hegelian interpretation of *Aufhebung* is the *presentation* or *recognition* of the identity (the "at the same time") of contradictories. The contradictories are identified only *as* a contradiction. This recognition effects the step into the next shape of the dialectical progression. The "not yet" of the aporia interrupts the *presentation* or *recognition* of the identity (the "at the same time") of contradictories insofar as it is discovered that the moments of the aporia are *not* "at the same time"; they can*not* be *presented* or *recognized as* a contradiction. *The aporia of time/death "is" the aporia of dialectic. Just as* time is the name for the necessity (yet impossibility) of the contradictories of time (the *impossible coexistence* of a now with itself and the *possible coimplication* of nows) being "at the same time," and *just as* death is the name for the necessity (yet impossibility) of the contradictories of death (the *possible appropriation* of death and the *impossible appropriation* of death) being "at the same time," *so also* is dialectic the name for the necessity (yet impossibility) of the contradictories of dialectic being "at the same time."

For Hegel, death is productive insofar as one appropriates it. But, while *seeming* to put everything at stake at the moment of death, Hegel in fact restricts the stakes of the wager to the appropriation of death. He restricts the absolute expenditure of death to an economy that expects a return on its investment. "It does not suffice to risk death if the putting at stake is not permitted to take off, as chance or accident, but is rather invested as the work of the negative" (EREG 383/RGE 261; on this "permitted to take off," see: "Now death being in the program, since I must *actually* risk it [i.e., must *actually* permit it to take off], I can always lose the profit of the operation" [Gf 158/Ge 139], and *Aporias*: "if the impossibility of the 'as such' is *indeed* the impossibility of the 'as such,' . . ." [AM 336/AD 75, emphasis added], i.e., is *indeed* permitted to take off). The preface to the *Phenomenology of Spirit* reads, Spirit "wins its truth only when in absolute dismemberment, it finds itself" (PG 27/PS 19). If this "dismemberment" is *indeed* absolute dismemberment (i.e., is "permitted to take off"), then one cannot guarantee a return on one's investment. Bataille is attentive to the moment of absolute dismemberment integral to the Spirit's attainment of truth. Bataille permits the moment of absolute dismemberment to take off. As such, at the same time that Bataille recognizes the *necessity* that "death itself would have to become (self-) consciousness at the very moment that it annihilates the conscious being" (HMS 336/HDS 19), he recognizes the *impossibility* of this very necessity.

Fiction

Bataille recognizes the *impossibility* of this very necessity in his recognition of the aporias of time and death. As such, he recognizes that to be conscious at the moment of death requires spectacle, representation, or fiction. What follows is a passage cited earlier, now *supplemented* with the language that indicates Bataille's recognition of an aporia:

> In order for Man to reveal himself ultimately to himself, he would have to die, but he would have to do it while living—watching himself ceasing to be. In other words, death itself would have to become (self-) consciousness at the very moment that it annihilates the conscious being. In a sense, this is what takes place (what at least is on the point of taking place, or which takes place in a fugitive, ungraspable manner) by means of a subterfuge. In the sacrifice, the sacrificer identifies himself with the animal that is struck down dead. And

so he dies in seeing himself die, and even, in a certain way, by his own will, one in spirit with the sacrificial weapon. But it is a comedy! [. . .] Thus, at all costs, man must live at the moment that he really dies, or he must live with the impression of really dying.

This difficulty proclaims the necessity of *spectacle*, or of *representation* in general, without the practice [alternate translation: repetition] of which it would be possible for us to remain alien and ignorant in respect to death, just as beasts apparently are. Indeed, nothing is less animal than fiction, which is more or less separated from the real, from death [alternate translation: nothing is less animal than the fiction, more or less removed from reality, of death]. (HMS 336–337/HDS 19–20)

Derrida argues, "Only the accent on simulacrum and subterfuge interrupt[s] the Hegelian continuity of this text" (EREG 379/RGE 258). This accent on simulacrum, that is, this accent on spectacle, representation, or fiction, testifies to Bataille's recognition of an aporia. To be conscious at the moment of death requires (by definition) a minimal distance from the moment of death, a minimal distance that is spectacle, representation, or fiction. This minimal distance from the moment of death is the interval of the aporia of time, the interval of the "not yet" of the approach of death. Sacrifice (like time and death) is *a* name for this impossible possibility, for this expenditure without reserve. To be indifferent to the comedy of the *Aufhebung* (as Hegel was) is to blind oneself to the experience of death as expenditure without reserve, to blind oneself to the experience of the sacred. Bataille writes:

[O]ne cannot say that Hegel was unaware of the "moment" of sacrifice; this "moment" is included, implicated in the whole movement of the *Phenomenology*—where it is the Negativity of death, insofar as it is assumed, which makes a man of the human animal. But because he did not see that sacrifice in itself bore witness to the *entire* movement of death, [. . .] he did not know to what extent he was right. (HMS 338–339/HDS 21–22)

Sacrifice bears witness to the *entire* movement of death; that is, it bears witness to death not only as the most proper possibility (insofar as it is appropriated), but also as expenditure without reserve. Through sacrifice (which is the mime of the absolute risk of death), experience simultaneously produces (according to Derrida's reading of Bataille) "the risk of absolute death, the feint through which this risk can be lived, the impossibility of reading a sense or a truth in it, and the laughter which is confused, in the simulacrum, with the opening of the sacred" (EREG 378/RGE 257). But if "sacrifice" is the "experience" that is the mime/simulacrum of the risk of death (insofar as it is the "experience" of being at a minimal distance from death, the "not yet" of the approach of death), then it is simultaneously withdrawn from experience, insofar as the moment of the risk of death cannot (properly speaking) be experienced. In naming this impossible possibility, the term "sacrifice" slides to name that which cannot be experienced. This "experience," this "spectacle," this "representation," this "fiction" is therefore *not* (properly speaking) an experience, a spectacle, a representation, or a fiction. Sacrifice is a name for the atemporal temporality of the moment of interruption, a name for the "not yet" of the approach of death. Sacrifice is a name for philosophy's (and Hegel's, as the philosopher *par excellence*) blind spot, that is, a name for philosophy's condition of (im)possibility.

Derrida and a Way of Rereading Nancy on Bataille

Sacrifice, according to Derrida's reading of Bataille, is subject to a "mutation of meaning" in which its meaning *slides* from the traditional interpretation of the word to what I would argue is a self-reflective sacrifice of sacrifice. The interruption of the *presentation* or *recognition* of the identity (the "at the same time") of contradictories (which is the Hegelian interpretation of the *Aufhebung*) discerns, according to Derrida, two forms of writing (EREG 389/RGE 265). One form of writing—"minor writing"—seeks to maintain itself in non-meaning (EREG 389, 393/RGE 265, 268). The other from of writing—"major writing"—seeks to constitute itself as the possibility of absolute expenditure or erasure. Within this "major writing," which exceeds the *logos* of meaning and of presence, apparently unchanged concepts such as sacrifice will be subject to a mutation of meaning as they *slide toward* non-meaning. "To blind oneself to this rigorous precipitation, this pitiless sacrifice of philosophical concepts, and to continue to read, interrogate, and judge Bataille's text *from within* 'significative discourse' is, perhaps, to hear something within it, but it is assuredly not to read it" (EREG 392/RGE 267). This pitiless sacrifice of philosophical concepts sacrifices (perhaps first and foremost) the concept of sacrifice. What Derrida describes is, I would argue, a pitiless sacrifice of sacrifice. Contrary to what is the case in "minor writing," this exceeding or transgression of the meaning of sacrifice is not "an access to the immediate and indeterminate *identity* of a nonmeaning, nor is it an access to the possibility of *maintaining* nonmeaning" (EREG 393/RGE 268). What is called for is *not* a phenomenological *epochē*, which, as a reduction *to* meaning, is carried out in the name of and in sight of meaning. "Sovereign transgression is a reduction of this reduction: not a reduction to meaning, but a reduction of meaning" (EREG 393–394/RGE 268). Rather than being an access to the immediate and indeterminate *identity* of a non-meaning, or an access to the possibility of *maintaining* non-meaning, sovereign transgression is a sacrifice *of* the sacrifice that gives access to the immediate and indeterminate *identity* of a non-meaning, or a sacrifice *of* the sacrifice that gives access to the possibility of *maintaining* non-meaning. Sovereign transgression is a sacrifice of sacrifice. These two forms of writing considered by Derrida serve to correct Nancy's reading of Bataille in "The Unsacrificeable" (1990). Nancy argues, in effect, that Bataille interprets sacrifice as an access to the immediate and indeterminate *identity* of a non-meaning, or an access to the possibility of *maintaining* nonmeaning (EREG 393/RGE 268). In *both* the traditional philosophical and Christian versions of sacrifice, *and* (Nancy's reading of) Bataille's version of sacrifice, sacrifice is thought as revelation. Sacrificial logic does not leave off reappropriating (trans-appropriating) this access without access to a moment of disappropriation. Sacrifice (by definition) appropriates death (the finite moment of sacrifice), and "it is by appropriating death that sacrifice escapes the truth of the moment of dis-appropriation" (I 90/U 30). Sacrificial logic, according to Nancy, appropriates the "nothingness" of death. The "nothingness" of death thereby becomes a "supreme moment" of revelation, rather than a moment of dis-appropriation. This is to interpret Bataille's work as "minor writing," insofar as it interprets it as a writing that seeks to maintain itself in non-meaning. What is called for, I would argue, is an attentiveness to the "mutation of meaning" characteristic of what Derrida calls "major writing." What is called for is an attentiveness to the pitiless sacrifice of sacrifice in the work of Bataille.

Blanchot and Literature/Bataille and Fiction

Blanchot, like Derrida, *reads* sacrifice as *gliding* from the traditional interpretation of the word to what I would argue is an obsessive self-reflective sacrifice of sacrifice. Sacrifice is, according to Blanchot, an "obsessive notion" for Bataille. Its meaning would be deceptive, according to Blanchot, if it did not "glide continuously from the historical and religious interpretation to the infinite exigency it exposes itself to in what opens it to the others and separates it violently from itself" (CI 30/UC 15). I would argue that the infinite exigency that sacrifice exposes itself to is the obsessively self-reflective sacrifice of itself. I would argue that the meaning of sacrifice glides "continuously from the historical and religious interpretation to the infinite exigency it exposes itself to in what opens it to the others and separates it violently from itself" precisely insofar as one is attentive to the necessarily obsessive character of sacrifice. Sacrifice sacrifices itself. This obsessive self-reflection (which echoes the work of Levinas) opens sacrifice to others and separates it violently from itself.

Insofar as sacrifice is the "experience" that is the mime/simulacrum of the risk of death (insofar as it is the "experience" of being at a minimal distance from death, the "not yet" of the approach of death), it is (in the aporetic sense outlined earlier) "fiction." Fiction, like sacrifice, glides continuously from its traditional interpretation. Fiction, in Bataille's "Hegel, Death and Sacrifice," is governed, I would argue, by a "logic" similar to the one that governs literature in the work of Blanchot. Both fiction and literature glide continuously from the traditional interpretation to the infinite exigency it exposes itself to in what opens it to the others and separates it violently from itself. Both fiction and literature are governed by the "logic" of approach, by the "logic" of the minimal distance of the "not yet."

Blanchot, Freud, Girard, and Community

The fact that sacrifice, for Bataille, is an obsessive sacrifice of sacrifice that opens sacrifice to others and separates it violently from itself serves to correct a too-quick association of this reading of sacrifice with either a crude reading of Freud's reflections on the origin of society or Girard's reading of sacrifice as integral to the origin of community. Blanchot writes:

> In *Théorie de la Religion*, it is stated: "to sacrifice is not to kill, but to abandon and to give." To link oneself with Acéphale [a secret community of which Bataille was a member] is to abandon and to give oneself: *to give oneself wholly to limitless abandonment.* This is the sacrifice that founds the community by undoing it, by handing it over to time the dispenser, time that does not allow the community nor those who give themselves to it, any form of presence, thereby sending them back to a solitude which, far from protecting them, disperses them or dissipates itself without their finding themselves again or together. (CI 30/UC 15)

Freud hypothesizes the sacrificial murder of the leader of a horde to explain the passage from the primal horde to the regulated society. Girard offers the most contemporary example of this traditional sacrificial logic: guilt is projected onto a scapegoat whose sacrifice allows for the establishment of social peace by localizing violence, with the victim thereby acquiring an aura of sanctity. But Blanchot points out in "The Negative Community" from *The Unavowable Community* (1983) that though death is present in Acéphale, sacrificial murder eludes it. Blanchot writes, "[T]he victim is consenting, a consent that is not enough, as the only one who can give death is the one who, giving it, would die at the same time, that is, could *substitute* himself for the voluntary victim" (CI 32n1/UC 58n7, emphasis added). The only one who can give death is the one who would die *in the very giving* of death, which would mean the impossible possibility of giving death. The only one who can give death is the one who dies in the giving, thereby substituting him or herself for the voluntary victim. The only one who can give death is the one who cannot give death, insofar as he/she dies *in place* of the other. This is what Blanchot calls "mortal substitution" (CI 24/UC 11). One is called to read this aporia within the horizon of the work of Levinas (as it is read by Blanchot). The phrase "mortal substitution," echoing the work of Levinas, is a description of "me" *not* as my ownmost self in the possibility of being-towards-death, *but* as essentially one who dies for the other. In "mortal substitution," one is (in Levinas's words) nothing but "for the other." In *The Writing of the Disaster* (1980), Blanchot reads this substitution of the "other *in place* of me" in the aporetic structure of responsibility:

> *My* responsibility for the Other [*Autrui*] presupposes an overturning such that it can only be marked by a change in the status of "me," a change in time and perhaps in language. Responsibility, which withdraws me from my order— perhaps from all orders and from order itself—responsibility, which separates me from myself (from the "me" that is mastery and power, from the free, speaking subject) and reveals the other [*autre*] *in place* of me, requires that I answer for absence, for passivity. It requires, that is to say, that I answer for the impossibility of being responsible—to which this responsibility without measure has always already consigned me by holding me accountable and also

discounting me altogether. (ED 45–46/WD 25, translation modified; the phrase *"responsabilité sans mesure"* was omitted)

Responsibility requires that I respond, that I answer for what I do, say, and give, as irreplaceable singularity, *and* it requires that I am exposed to ex-propriation, to anonymity, that I forget or efface myself, that I be (in Levinas's words) nothing but "for the other." On the one hand responsibility holds *me* accountable, and on the other hand, responsibility *discounts* me insofar as it requires that I be *selfless*. Said in the language of Levinas (though perhaps not necessarily in a way he would say it), *at the moment* that my death comes first (death as possibility), the death of the other comes first (death as impossibility). Only death as possibility turning into death as impossibility is adequate to this aporia of responsibility. Responsibility reveals (aporetically) the singularity of the "me," and *at the same time* the other *in place* of me (i.e., the substitution of me for the other).

Continuing with the theme of the role Bataille's obsessive sacrifice of sacrifice plays in the origin of community, Blanchot writes: "The community cannot found itself on the bloody sacrifice of two of its members alone, called upon (scapegoats of a sort) to expiate for all" (CI 32n1/UC 58n7). Blanchot is here commenting on an economic reading of sacrifice, which is a reading of sacrifice that expects a return on its investment of blood. Blanchot's "work" is at a certain distance from this reading insofar as he writes, "Each person should have to die for all, and it is in the death of all that each person would determine the community's destiny" (CI 32n1/UC 58n7). The community's destiny is to be founded *in* the death of *all* members of the community, which is accomplished by *each* (and every) person (*not* merely the scapegoats) dying *for all* (i.e., dying *for* the founding of the community). Here (paradoxically) is a community founded on radical anonymity and passivity (i.e., on being nothing but "for the other"). The community's destiny is the impossibility of community. The community is founded in (made possible by) the impossibility of community. The possibility of the community is *at the same time* its impossibility. As radical anonymity and passivity, being nothing but "for the other" (giving oneself for the other) is *not* a project. If it were, it would break the law of the group: "But to give oneself, as a project, the execution of a sacrificial death means to break the law of the group [i.e., Acéphale, the secret community of which Bataille was a member] whose first requirement is to renounce creating a *work* (even though it be the work of death) and whose essential project excludes all projects" (CI 32n1/UC 58n7). Blanchot concludes, "From this follows the passage to *a completely different kind of sacrifice*, a sacrifice that would no longer be the *murder* of one person or of all persons, but gift and abandonment, the infinite of abandonment" (CI 32n1/ UC 58n7, emphasis added). This completely different kind of sacrifice is, I would argue, an obsessive sacrifice of sacrifice that opens sacrifice to others and separates it violently from itself. It is precisely this kind of sacrifice, this kind of "dying for," that Blanchot is referring to when he writes that to link oneself with

The Question of Sacrifice

Acéphale is to give oneself wholly to limitless abandonment, which is the sacrifice that founds the community by undoing it (CI 30/UC 15).

Žižek on Bataille

The fact that sacrifice, for Bataille, is an obsessive sacrifice of sacrifice that opens sacrifice to others and separates it violently from itself serves also to correct Žižek's reading of Bataille. In *The Indivisible Remainder* (1996), Žižek argues that Bataille's "subject" is not yet the pure void (the transcendental point of the double, self-relating negativity characteristic of the "sacrifice of the sacrifice"), but a positive force of a pre-Newtonian universe of balanced circular movement. As such, the self-relating negativity of the subject can express itself only in an "irrational," excessive, non-economical expenditure that interrupts the balanced circular movement of nature. According to Žižek, what Bataille fails to take into consideration is that the subject no longer needs "real," material sacrifice, since its very existence already entails the most radical double, self-relating sacrifice; that is, it already entails the sacrifice of the very core of its being (IR 124–125). I would argue, however, that Bataille's work is *not* fundamentally governed by a need for a "real," material sacrifice. Sacrifice, according to Derrida's reading of Bataille, is subject to a "mutation of meaning" in which its meaning *slides* from the traditional interpretation of the word toward non-meaning. Sacrifice, according to Blanchot's reading of Bataille, would likewise be misread if it did not glide continuously from the traditional interpretation to "the infinite exigency it exposes itself to in what opens it to the others and separates it violently from itself" (CI 30/UC 15). The infinite exigency that sacrifice exposes itself to is (I have argued) the obsessively self-reflective sacrifice of itself. Both Derrida's and Blanchot's readings of Bataille move continuously (I have argued) to a self-reflective sacrifice of sacrifice. Blanchot quotes the following passage from Bataille's *Theory of Religion* (1973): "To sacrifice is not to kill but to relinquish and to give" (TdR 310/ToR 48–49; see CI 30/UC 15). To sacrifice, according to Blanchot's reading of this passage, is *"to give oneself wholly to limitless abandonment"* (CI 30/UC 15). With this possible allusion to the work of Levinas, one can detect here a sacrifice of the very core of one's being that is not unlike the "sacrifice of the sacrifice" described by Žižek.

Bataille's obsession with sacrifice is incessantly at risk of being misread unless it is read within the horizon of an obsessional sacrifice of sacrifice. This question of sacrifice is a response to the question of death.

4

Nietzsche

The Eternal Return of Sacrifice

Sacrifice is to be overcome. What could be more obvious to a reader of the work of Nietzsche? And yet, is it that obvious? A careful reading of the work of Nietzsche will reveal that in the attempt to step beyond sacrifice, one becomes inextricably implicated in the move of nihilistic sacrifice. Sacrifice returns, eternally.

In *Beyond Good and Evil* (1886), Nietzsche traces a genealogy of sacrifice — quoted by Bataille in *Inner Experience* (1954) — that anticipates the work of *On the Genealogy of Morals* (1887).

> There is a great ladder of religious cruelty with many rungs; but three of them are the most important. At one time one sacrificed [*opferte*] human beings to one's god, perhaps precisely those human beings one loved best — the sacrifice of the first-born [*Erstlings-Opfer*] present in all prehistoric religions belongs here, as does the sacrifice [*Opfer*] of the Emperor Tiberius in the Mithras grotto on the isle of Capri, that most horrible of all Roman anachronisms. (JGB 72/BGE 63)

This first rung of the great ladder of religious cruelty almost certainly refers, among other things, to the *Akedah*: the binding of Isaac. God says to Abraham, "Take your son, your only son Isaac, whom you love, and go to the land of Moriah, and offer him there as a burnt offering on one of the mountains that I shall show you" (Gen. 22:2, NRSV). Nietzsche also refers to Emperor Tiberius. In the waning years of his life, Tiberius (42 B.C.E.–37 C.E.), the second Roman emperor, built a dozen villas ringing Capreae (now called Capri, near Naples), with prisons, underground dungeons, torture chambers, and execution places. Nietzsche continues up (down?) the ladder.

> Then, in the moral epoch of mankind, one sacrificed [*opferte*] to one's god the strongest instincts one possessed, one's 'nature'; the joy of *this* festival glit-

> ters in the cruel glance of the ascetic, the inspired 'anti-naturalist'. (JGB 72/
> BGE 63)

This second rung of the great ladder of religious cruelty is characterized by the "anti-naturalist" nihilism of *ressentiment*, the bad conscience, and the ascetic ideal. The third (and last) rung of the great ladder of religious cruelty puts one at the threshold of the death of God.

> Finally: what was left to be sacrificed [*opfern*]? Did one not finally have to sacrifice [*opfern*] everything comforting, holy, healing, all hope, all faith in a concealed harmony, in a future bliss and justice? Did one not have to sacrifice [*opfern*] God himself and out of cruelty against oneself worship stone, stupidity, gravity, fate, nothingness? To sacrifice [*opfern*] God for nothingness — this paradoxical mystery of the ultimate act of cruelty was reserved for the generation which is even now arising: we all know something of it already. — (JGB 72/ BGE 63; see EI 152/IE 131)

To sacrifice God for nothingness reveals the concealed truth of sacrifice itself. To sacrifice God is to sacrifice the very reason of sacrifice, insofar as sacrifice is understood as a sacrifice to God for the redemption of sin (i.e., for the redemption of every kind of distancing relationship between God and human beings). To sacrifice God is to sacrifice economical sacrifice. To sacrifice God is to sacrifice the sacrifice that pays, that gives a return on one's investment of suffering. In *On the Genealogy of Morals*, Nietzsche reveals the previously concealed truth of sacrifice to be *"a will to nothingness, an aversion to life, a rebellion against the most fundamental presuppositions of life"* (GdM 430/GoM 163). It is revealed to be nihilistic insofar as it negates (sacrifices) this life in favor of a transcendent world that remunerates sacrifice. The genealogist reveals a nihilistic evaluation at the heart of sacrifice. I would argue that the "paradoxical mystery" of the ultimate sacrifice outlined in the genealogy of sacrifice in *Beyond Good and Evil* — that is, the sacrifice of economical sacrifice — *momentarily* reveals the previously concealed truth of sacrifice *and* the sacrifice without reserve, sacrifice for no reason, sacrifice for nothingness. To be more precise, I would argue that it momentarily reveals the concealed truth of sacrifice *as* sacrifice without reserve, sacrifice for no reason, sacrifice for nothingness.

The Stroke of Genius on the Part of Christianity

Nietzsche's genealogy of the Christian concepts of responsibility and justice is concerned with economics: credits, debts, speculation, and calculation. In the "Second Essay" of *On the Genealogy of Morals*, Nietzsche writes, " '[E]verything has its price; *all* things can be paid for' — the oldest and naïvest moral canon of *justice*, the beginning of all 'good-naturedness,' all 'fairness,' all 'good will,' all 'objectivity' on earth" (GdM 322/GoM 70). A few pages later, Nietzsche takes into account that which *exceeds* this justice, this economy of exchange: mercy. But instead of crediting this *excess* to pure goodness, to giving without reserve, he reveals in the self-destruction of justice (by means of mercy) a ruination of this pure goodness, a sacrifice of this giving without reserve. And insofar as one understands this giving without reserve as a sacrifice, one could say that Nietzsche reveals a sacrifice of the sacrifice of giving without reserve. He reveals a sacrifice of sacrifice.

> The justice which began with, "everything is dischargeable, everything must be discharged," ends by winking and letting those incapable of discharging their debt go free: it ends, as does every good thing on earth, by *overcoming itself* [sich selbst aufhebend]. This self-overcoming of justice [*Diese Selbstaufhebung der Gerechtigkeit*]: one knows the beautiful name it has given itself— *mercy* [Gnade]; it goes without saying that mercy remains the privilege [*Vorrecht*] of the most powerful man, or better, his—beyond the law [*sein Jenseits des Rechts*]. (GdM 325/GoM 72–73)

According to Derrida in *The Gift of Death* (1992), Christian justice *denies* itself (i.e., it *overcomes* itself in becoming mercy, giving without reserve) and so *conserves* itself in what seems to exceed it (i.e., mercy). Justice remains what it supposedly ceases to be: a cruel economy of debts and credits involving sacrifice (DM 105–106/GD 113–114). In its self-overcoming (i.e., in its becoming mercy), justice remains a *privilege*. It remains the "beyond the law" or super-law of the powerful person.

This same sacrifice of sacrifice is, according to Nietzsche, taken to an extreme point in the sacrifice of Christ, the creditor, for the debtor.

> [S]uddenly we stand before the paradoxical and horrifying expedient that afforded temporary relief for tormented humanity, that stroke of genius on the part of Christianity [*jenem Geniestreich des Christentums*]: God himself sacrifices [*opfernd*] himself for the guilt of mankind, God himself makes payment to himself, God as the only being who can redeem man from what has become unredeemable [*unablösbar*] for man himself—the creditor [*der Gläubiger*] sacrifices [*opfernd*] himself for his debtor [*seinen Schuldner*], out of *love* (can one credit that [*sollte man's glauben*]?), out of love for his debtor!— (GdM 347/ GoM 92; concerning another perspective on these passages from Nietzsche's *On the Genealogy of Morals*, Derrida refers the reader to CP 282/PC 263– 265)

One way to read Derrida's reading of this passage is the following: Derrida argues that the attribution of the "stroke of genius" to Christianity is based on a thaumaturgical or miraculous secret, like "a ruse that depends on a special know-how" (DM 106/GD 115). What is this miraculous secret? I would argue (in a merely provisional way that will call for further explanation) that it is the aporia of the irreducible experience of the belief of the believer suspended between *knowing* (that one is redeemed) and *not knowing* (for certain that one is redeemed). Derrida continues: If (on the basis of this miraculous secret) one were able to attribute the "stroke of genius" to Christianity, then one would have to envelop *another* secret within it. This *other* secret confers on the name "God" *the responsibility for* what remains more secret than ever. This *other* secret is God's knowing/not knowing, which is responsible for what remains more secret than ever: the believer's special know-how, the believer's knowing/not knowing. God's knowing/not knowing is responsible for the believer's knowing/not knowing, which is the (unshareable) secret shared by the Christian community through time and space. "To share a secret is not to know or to reveal the secret, it is to share we know not what: nothing that can be determined" (DM 78/GD 80). What is this *other* secret? What is God's knowing/not knowing that is responsible for the miraculous secret of the believer's special know-how, the believer's knowing/not knowing?

The Christian believer is redeemed only if God *knows* that God sacrificed, insofar as it is necessary for there to be a witness to the sacrifice in order for the sacrifice to be credited to Christianity's otherwise unredeemable account. But if God *knows*, then the sacrifice without reserve necessary to redeem what has become unredeemable is ruined or sacrificed. In order for God to redeem what has become unredeemable, it is necessary that God's sacrifice be a sacrifice without reserve, which requires that God must sacrifice *without* knowing that he sacrificed. The *other* secret (mentioned earlier) is God's knowing (that God sacrificed) while at the same time not knowing (that God sacrificed). Paradoxically, for the "stroke of genius" to "work" it is necessary (yet impossible) that God both know and not know (at the same time).

Paradoxically, Christianity has to *believe* that God sacrificed *without* God's *knowing* (in order for the sacrifice to be a sacrifice without reserve, a sacrifice capable of redeeming what has become unredeemable), while *knowing* (in order for there to be a witness to the sacrifice, in order for the sacrifice to be credited to Christianity's otherwise unredeemable account). If God *knows*, then the sacrifice without reserve is sacrificed (and the belief of the debtor is empty), and if God does *not know*, then the debtor's account cannot be credited (and the belief of the debtor is empty). The belief of the debtor is *not* empty only when it is suspended (like God) between knowing and not knowing. Believing is being suspended (as God is suspended) between knowing and not knowing. Here one sees that God's knowing/not knowing is responsible for the believer's knowing/ not knowing. God's knowing/not knowing is responsible for the aporia of the irreducible experience of the belief of the believer suspended between *knowing* (that one is redeemed) and *not knowing* (for certain that one is redeemed).

The irreducible experience of belief is an aporia, it is "that which remains more secret than ever" (DM 106/GD 115). Here there is the necessity, yet impossibility, of knowing and not knowing being *at the same time*. The "not yet" characteristic of the aporia interrupts the *presentation* of the identity (the "at the same time") of contradictories insofar as it is discovered that the moments of the aporia are *not* "at the same time"; they can*not* be *presented as* a contradiction. The "not yet" of the aporia interrupts the "at the same time" of contradictories (see AE 9/OB 7, and EL 22–23/SL 30–31). *Believing* is the name for the necessity (yet impossibility) of the contradictories of believing (knowing and not knowing) being "at the same time."

The irreducible experience of belief is the believing—the knowing/not knowing—suspended *between* the credit of the creditor *and* the credence (or faith) of the believer (or debtor). The believing is suspended between credit and faith insofar as there is a *"disconnect"* between what is usually thought of as an *assured connection* between credit and faith. Rather than being assured of re- demption, believing is suspended, insofar as it is discovered that *both* the credit of the creditor *and* the faith of the believer unwork themselves.

Paradoxically, for the "stroke of genius" to work, it has to unwork itself; that is, God can only credit the account of the debtor by sacrificing without knowing (which makes the crediting impossible) and the believer can only have faith without knowing (which makes confidence in an assured redemption impossi- ble). The believer's faith in redemption is not empty *only if*, at the same time, the believer cannot count on redemption. Believing is suspended in the "not yet" of credit and the "not yet" of faith.

The irreducible experience of belief is, I would argue, the aporia of the believing suspended *between* the sacrifice of the (economical) sacrifice—which requires not knowing—and the sacrifice of the (aneconomical) sacrifice—which comes with knowing.

In the wake of his consideration of the irreducible experience of the aporia of belief, Derrida writes:

> How can one *believe* this history of *credence* or *credit*? That is what Nietzsche asks, *in fine*, what he asks himself or has asked by another, by the specter of his discourse. Is this a false or counterfeit question, a rhetorical question as one says in English? For what makes a rhetorical question possible can some- times disturb the structure of it.
>
> As often happens, the call of or for the question, and the request that echoes through it, takes us further than the response. The question, the re- quest, and the appeal *must* indeed have begun, since the eve of their awak- ening, by receiving accreditation from the other: by being believed. Nietzsche must indeed believe he knows what believing means, unless he means it is all make-believe [*à moins qu'il n'entende le faire accroire*]. (DM 107/GD 115)

Nietzsche asks, "Can one credit that?" or (according to Derrida's paraphrase) "How can one *believe* this history of *credence* or *credit*?" The question *must* have begun by *already* being believed. Said otherwise, the question Nietzsche asks implies a negative judgment with respect to belief (i.e., he means it is all make- believe), and *at the same time*, presupposes (Derrida argues) that Nietzsche *al- ready* believes he knows what believing means. Nietzsche's believing is suspended *between* believing it is all make-believe (i.e., *not* knowing what believing means) *and* believing he *knows* what believing means. As such, Nietzsche's believing is no different from the ("true") Christian believer's believing. They are both apor- etic. In both cases, the irreducible experience of belief is the irreducible expe- rience of knowing and not knowing.

Blanchot and *le pas au-delà* (the step/not beyond) Nihilism

This step beyond economical sacrifice that is not beyond economical sacrifice is also inscribed in the final pages of the "Third Essay" of Nietzsche's *On the Genealogy of Morals*. At a certain moment in history, Nietzsche writes, the will to truth is revealed in its truth. When Christian truthfulness asks itself, "What is the meaning of all will to truth?" it will bring about its own destruction through an act of self-overcoming. In the "Second Essay," Nietzsche writes that justice "ends, as does every good thing on earth, by *overcoming itself* [sich selbst aufhebend]" (GdM 325/GoM 73). Echoing this earlier consideration of the self-overcoming of justice (*Diese Selbstaufhebung der Gerechtigkeit*), Nietzsche writes, "All great things bring about their own destruction through an act of self-overcoming [*Selbstaufhebung*]: thus the law of life will have it, the law of the necessity of 'self-overcoming' [,*Selbstüberwindung*'] in the nature of life—the lawgiver himself eventually receives the call: '*patere legem, quam ipse tulisti*' ['submit to the law you yourself proposed']" (GdM 428/GoM 161). This necessary act of self-overcoming, this *Aufhebung* that is at the threshold of a step beyond nihilism, is "weakened" by the very work of *On the Genealogy of Morals*. In response to the question, "What is the meaning of all will to truth?," the final dramatically climactic lines of the work answer: "[W]*hat* is expressed by all that willing which has taken its direction from the ascetic ideal" is "*a will to nothingness*, an aversion to life, a rebellion against the most fundamental presuppositions of life; but it is and remains a *will*! . . . And, to repeat in conclusion what I said at the beginning: man would rather will *nothingness* than *not* will—" (GdM 430/GoM 162–163). The willing that has taken its direction from the sacrifice, the saying "No" characteristic of the ascetic ideal, is revealed as a will to nothingness. It is revealed as nihilistic. Here is a moment in history when history is revealed in its truth. Here is a momentary revelation of the previously concealed truth of sacrifice *and* the sacrifice without reserve, sacrifice for no reason, sacrifice for nothingness. To be more precise, I would argue that it is the momentary revelation of the concealed truth of sacrifice *as* sacrifice without reserve, sacrifice for no reason, sacrifice for nothingness. Here is *also* the prophesying of the extreme form of nihilism: the overman as the one who maintains this pure essence of will in willing nothingness. The overman reveals the truth of economical sacrifice *and* sacrifices economical sacrifice. The overman reveals the truth of economical sacrifice *as* the sacrifice of economical sacrifice. But this *Aufhebung* that is a step beyond nihilism insofar as it reveals a concealed evaluation as the truth of history *repeats* the evaluative move characteristic of nihilism, thereby reinscribing the step beyond nihilism into the not beyond. The genealogist becomes inextricably implicated in the nihilistic sacrifice of the ascetic priest. The genealogist, therefore, produces or performs an interminable step/not beyond (*le pas au-delà*), a step beyond that eternally returns.

Although the eternal return remains merely implicit in the structure of *On the Genealogy of Morals*, Nietzsche explicitly draws a connection between the eternal return and nihilism in one of the notes of what was to be *The Will to Power: Attempt at a Revaluation of All Values*—a text that Nietzsche refers to as a "work in progress" (GdM 427/GoM 160) in the final pages of *On the Genealogy of Morals*.

> Let us think this thought in its most terrible form: existence as it is, without meaning or aim, yet recurring inevitably without any finale of noth-ingness: *"the eternal recurrence."*
>
> This is the most extreme form of nihilism: the nothing (the "meaning-less"), eternally! (NF 217/WP 35–36)

This passage tells one that the extreme form of nihilism is precisely where the possibility of coming to an end—that is, the possibility of maintaining the pure essence of will in willing nothingness—turns into the impossibility of coming to an end. In *The Infinite Conversation* (1969), Blanchot writes:

> Until now we thought nihilism was tied to nothingness. How ill-considered this was: nihilism is tied to being. Nihilism is the impossibility of being done with it and of finding a way out even in that end that is nothingness. It says the impotence of nothingness, the false brilliance of its victories; it tells us that when we think nothingness we are still thinking being. Nothing ends, everything begins again; the other is still the same. Midnight is only a dissim-ulated noon, and the great Noon is the abyss of light from which we can never depart. (EI 224/IC 149)

This weakening of negation—which is also experienced at those decisive mo-ments in the *Phenomenology of Spirit* (1807), in history, when negation is dis-covered to be at a certain distance from the *Phenomenology of Spirit*, from his-tory—will have profound consequences.

> [I]f we will grant that all modern humanism, the work of science, and plan-etary development have as their object a dissatisfaction with what is, and thus the desire to transform being—to negate it in order to derive power from it and to make of this power to negate the infinite movement of human mas-tery—then it will become apparent that this sort of weakness of the negative, and the way in which nothingness unmasks itself in the being that cannot be negated, lays waste at one stroke to our attempts to dominate the earth and to free ourselves from nature by giving it a meaning—that is, by denaturing it. (EI 225/IC 149)

The desire to transform being by negating it, fueled by a dissatisfaction with what is, is interrupted by the weakness of the negative. Nihilism is the impossibility of being done with the being with which one is dissatisfied and of finding a way out even in that end that is nothingness. One can never definitively go beyond.

This production of a step/not beyond is likewise traced in *Thus Spoke Zar-athustra* (1883–1885). Zarathustra prophesies the overman as the overcoming of the nihilistic evaluations of human beings. The overman, insofar as he maintains the pure essence of will in willing nothingness, is the pure form of nihilism. Blanchot writes:

The Question of Sacrifice

> [H]is [i.e., the overman's] essential trait, the will, would make him, in his pure rigor and his harshness, the very form of nihilisim for, according to Nietzsche's clear statement, *"the will would rather will nothingness than not will"* [GdM 430/GoM 163]. The overman is he in whom nothingness makes itself will and who, free for death, maintains this pure essence of will in willing nothingness. This would be nihilism itself. (EI 222/IC 148)

At this moment, the overman, like Dasein in the act of authentic (*eigentlich*), resolute, determinate, and decided assumption of death, is "free for death" (see SZ 266/BT 311). This would be the extreme point or extreme form of nihilism. But in *Thus Spoke Zarathustra*, as in *On the Genealogy of Morals*, this step beyond is equivocal. Immediately following his announcement of the eternal return in "On the Vision and the Riddle," Zarathustra encounters a young shepherd gagging on a heavy black snake. In "The Convalescent," Zarathustra's remarks are reminiscent of this encounter: "The great disgust with man—*this* choked me and had crawled into my throat; and what the soothsayer said: 'All is the same, nothing is worth while, knowledge chokes.' A long twilight limped before me, a sadness, weary to death, drunken with death [*eine todesmüde, todestrunkene Traurigkeit*], speaking with a yawning mouth. 'Eternally recurs the man of whom you are weary, the small man'" (ASZ 270/TSZ 219). Zarathustra's disgust arises, Blanchot writes, from his understanding that

> he will never definitively go beyond man's insufficiency, or that he will only be able to do so, paradoxically, by willing his return [*retour*]. But what does this return [*retour*] mean? It means what it affirms: that the extreme point of nihilism is precisely there where it reverses itself [*se renverse*], that nihilism is this very turning itself [*le retournement même*], the affirmation that, in passing from the No to the Yes, refutes nihilism, but does nothing other than affirm it, and henceforth extends it to every possible affirmation [a footnote here reads: "Hence one can conclude that nihilism identifies itself with the will to surmount it *absolutely*" (EI 225n1/IC 451n9).]. (EI 225/IC 149–150)

In the attempt to step beyond nihilism, that is, in the attempt to negate (or sacrifice) nihilism, one *repeats* the negation characteristic of nihilism. One becomes inextricably implicated in the move of nihilistic sacrifice. The sacrifice of *the sacrifice characteristic of nihilism*, that is, the sacrifice of sacrifice, can only take place as the impossibility (or eternally postponed possibility) of its realization. One, therefore, performs an incessant step beyond that eternally returns.

Ressentiment and the Action Characteristic of Jesus' Evangelic Practice

An irreducibly paradoxical genealogy, similar to the one traced in *On the Genealogy of Morals*, is traced by Nietzsche in *The Anti-Christ* (1895). Nietzsche begins his genealogy with a people whose national self-confidence (DA 191–192/

66

TA 135–136) is so great that it needs a god to whom it can express its gratitude in the form of sacrifice.

> A people which still believes in itself still also has its own God. In him it venerates the conditions through which it has prospered, its virtues — it projects its joy in itself, its feeling of power on to a being whom one can thank for them. He who is rich wants to bestow; a proud people needs a God in order to *sacrifice* [opfern]. . . . Within the bounds of such presuppositions religion is a form of gratitude. One is grateful for oneself: for that one needs a God. — Such a God must be able to be both useful and harmful, both friend and foe — he is admired in good and bad alike. The *anti-natural* castration of a God into a God of the merely good would be totally undesirable here. (DA 180/TA 126)

"God" here is merely the name of the projection of a people's own affirmation of itself onto a being whom it can thank for the conditions through which it prospered. This "God" is fundamentally "a word [*Wort*] for every happy inspiration of courage and self-reliance" (DA 192/TA 136). This "God" is a God before whom one affirms this world, rather than before whom one denies this world. It is a God before whom sacrifice is a form of gratitude, rather than a means of redemption.

The good conscience of this national self-affirmation resembles the noble morality considered in the "First Essay" of Nietzsche's *On the Genealogy of Morals*. Noble morality "develops from a triumphant affirmation of itself." Noble morality "acts and grows spontaneously" (GdM 284–285/GoM 36–37), while the action of slave morality is fundamentally reaction against the noble. With the Jews there begins the slave revolt in morality, which involves a radical revaluation or inversion of their enemies' values, that is, a reaction or imaginary revenge against the noble mode of valuation (GdM 281–282/GoM 33–34).

> In my *Genealogy of Morals* I introduced for the first time the psychology of the antithetical concepts of a *noble* morality and a *ressentiment* morality, the latter deriving from a *denial* [aus dem Nein] of the former: but this latter corresponds totally to Judeo-Christian morality. To be able to reject all that represents the *ascending* movement of life, well-constitutedness, power, beauty, self-affirmation on earth, the instinct of *ressentiment* here become genius had to invent *another* world from which that *life-affirmation* would appear evil, reprehensible as such. (DA 190/TA 135)

In both Judaism and Christianity (albeit in different forms), the instinct of *ressentiment* is predicated on denial or sacrifice. *Ressentiment* is a denial or sacrifice of this world, with the simultaneous invention of *another* world "beyond" this world. The chasm between these two worlds opened up by this denial or sacrifice is accompanied by a feeling of guilty indebtedness from which one attempts to redeem oneself through sacrifices. These sacrifices were progressively interiorized until they took on the form of the asceticism of self-sacrifice:

> [A]n ascetic life is a self-contradiction: here rules a *ressentiment* without equal, that of an insatiable instinct and power-will that wants to become master not over something in life but over life itself, over its most profound, powerful, and basic conditions; here an attempt is made to employ force to block up the wells of force; here physiological well-being itself is viewed askance, and especially the outward expression of this well-being, beauty and joy; while pleasure is felt and *sought* in ill-constitutedness, decay, pain, mischance, ugliness, voluntary deprivation, self-mortification, self-flagellation, self-sacrifice [*Selbstopferung*]. (GdM 381/GoM 117–118)

This progressive interiorization of sacrifice culminating in ascetic self-sacrifice testifies to the progressive abstraction from natural life.

Jewish morality, which does not venerate the conditions through which a nation has prospered, is not an affirmation of life, but rather has "become abstract [*abstrakt*], become the antithesis of life" (DA 192/TA 136). Christian morality invents "an even *more abstract* [*einer noch* abgezogneren] form of existence" than the one conditioned by the social hierarchy of Jewish ecclesiastical teaching (DA 195/TA 139). A people characterized by national self-confidence "perishes if it mistakes *its own* duty for the concept of duty in general. Nothing works more profound ruin than any 'impersonal' duty, any sacrifice [*Opferung*] to the Moloch of abstraction [*Abstraktion*]. — Kant's categorical imperative should have been felt as *mortally dangerous!*" (DA 175/TA 122). Access to acting *from* duty (i.e., from respect for the law, as opposed to *according to* duty) involves, according to Kant, a sacrifice of the "pathological" interests. The unconditionality of respect for the law involves a sacrifice of everything that links one's sensibility to calculation, that is, to the conditionality of hypothetical imperatives. "If a rational creature could ever reach the stage of thoroughly liking to do all moral laws, it would mean that there was no possibility of there being in him a desire which could tempt him to deviate from them, for overcoming such a desire always costs the subject some sacrifice [*Aufopferung*] and requires self-compulsion [*Selbstzwang*], i.e., an inner constraint to do that which one does not quite like to do" (KPV 83–84/CPR 86). In *The Gift of Death*, Derrida echoes certain Nietzschean concerns regarding this sacrifice that requires self-compulsion when he points out that Kant closely links sacrifice to debt and duty, which are never separable from the guilt (*Schuldigkeit*) from which one can never be acquitted (DM 88–89/GD 92–93). This unredeemable situation described by Kant found its genesis, according to Nietzsche, in the "stroke of genius" on the part of Christianity. Though the sacrifice of the Christian God afforded temporary relief for tormented humanity from what had become unredeemable, it is merely that: *temporary*. Christ's sacrifice merely replaces one unredeemable debt with another unredeemable debt.

The advent of the Christian God was accompanied by the greatest feeling of guilty indebtedness (GdM 346/GoM 90), which in turn called for the greatest degree of the redemptive asceticism of self-sacrifice. "The Christian faith is from the beginning sacrifice [*Opferung*]: sacrifice [*Opferung*] of all freedom, all pride, all self-confidence of the spirit, at the same time enslavement and self-mockery, self-mutilation" (JGB 64/BGE 57). In *On the Genealogy of Morals*, Nietzsche argues that Jesus of Nazareth was this seduction of *ressentiment* in "its most uncanny and irresistible form" (GdM 282/GoM 35). But in *The Anti-Christ*, the genealogy has changed. While Nietzsche still maintains that Jewish morality and Christian morality are moralities of *ressentiment*, he writes that Jesus is a "free spirit" (DA 202/TA 144) who is characterized by "the freedom from, the superiority *over* every feeling of *ressentiment*" (DA 211/TA 153). The "glad tidings" of Jesus are, according to Nietzsche, an interruption of the Judeo-Christian morality of *ressentiment*. This momentary interruption was preceded by the Jewish form of *ressentiment* and was followed by the Christian form of *ressentiment*.

This interruption (by the "glad tidings" of Jesus) was preceded by Jewish ecclesiastical teaching. The Jews, in revenge on their enemies, had "separated their God from themselves and raised him on high" (DA 212/TA 153). There now exists a will of God as to what human beings are to do and not to do. With the introduction of this lie of a "moral world-order," the concept of God is falsified. The ruling power of the will of God is now expressed as punishment and reward commensurate with one's degree of obedience to that will. The priest exists as the perpetrator of this lie.

> For one must grasp this: every natural custom, every natural institution (state, administration of justice, marriage, tending of the sick and poor), every requirement presented by the instinct for life, in short everything valuable *in itself*, becomes utterly valueless, *inimical* to value through the parasitism of the priest (or the "moral world-order"): a sanction is subsequently required—a *value-bestowing* power is needed which denies [*verneint*] the natural quality in these things and only by doing so is able to *create* a value. . . . The priest disvalues, *dissanctifies* nature: it is only at the price of this that he exists at all.—Disobedience of God, that is to say of the priest, of "the Law," now acquires the name "sin." (DA 194–195/TA 138)

The priest creates value only through the denial of the natural quality of things. With the Jews, a priestly people embodying the most deeply repressed priestly vengefulness, there begins the slave revolt in morality (GdM 281–282/GoM 34). This revolt begins when "*ressentiment* itself becomes creative and gives birth to values: the *ressentiment* of natures that are denied [*versagt*] the true reaction, that of deeds, and compensate themselves with an imaginary revenge" (GdM 284/GoM 36). *Ressentiment* is predicated on denial or sacrifice. *Ressentiment* is a denial or sacrifice of natural life, with the simultaneous invention of a supernatural life. The chasm between these two types of "life" opened up by this denial or sacrifice is (especially with the advent of the Christian God) accompanied by a feeling of guilty indebtedness from which one attempts to redeem oneself through sacrifices. One sought redemption from any kind of distancing relationship with God—that is, from "sin," the priestly name for the bad conscience or feeling of guilty indebtedness (DA 203/TA 145, GdM 407/GoM 140) — through sacrifices. The priest is everywhere indispensable for the redemption of "sin" through sacrifice.

If *ressentiment* is predicated on denial or sacrifice, then the action characteristic of Jesus' evangelic practice is a denial of this denial, a sacrifice of this sacrifice.

> In the entire psychology of the "Gospel" the concept guilt and punishment is lacking; likewise the concept reward. "Sin," every kind of distancing relationship between God and man, is abolished — *precisely this is the "glad tidings."* Blessedness is not promised, it is not tied to any conditions: it is the *only* reality. (DA 203/TA 145)

The consequence of this reality is lived as a new practice. Jesus is distinguished not by belief, but by a different mode of acting. Nietzsche lists Jesus' true evangelic practices: he does not resist (either by words or in his heart) the one who does him evil, he makes no distinction between foreigner and native, or between Jew and non-Jew, he is not angry with anyone, he does not disdain anyone, and "he entreats, he suffers, he loves *with* those, *in* those who are doing evil to him" (DA 203, 205/TA 145–146, 148). The life of Jesus was a denial of Jewish ecclesiastical teaching.

> The life of the redeemer was nothing else than *this* practice — his death too was nothing else. . . . He no longer required any formulas, any rites for communicating with God — not even prayer. He has settled his accounts with the whole Jewish penance-and-reconciliation doctrine; he knows that it is through the *practice* of one's life that one feels "divine," "blessed," "evangelic," at all times a "child of God." It is *not* "penance," *not* "prayer for forgiveness" which leads to God: *evangelic practice alone* leads to God, it *is* God! — What was *abolished* with the Evangel was the Judaism of the concepts "sin," "forgiveness of sin," "faith," "redemption by faith" — the whole of Jewish *ecclesiastical* teaching was denied [*verneint*] in the "glad tidings." (DA 203–204/TA 146)

Jesus denied (*geleugnet*) any chasm between God and human beings (DA 213/TA 154). As a consequence of this denial, the whole of Jewish ecclesiastical teaching was denied (*verneint*). He denied an economic conception of sacrifice, that is, any sacrifice performed in the name of bridging any distancing relationship between God and human beings. Jesus likewise denied the denial of the world that sets up a chasm between God and human beings. Jesus "never had any reason to deny [*verneinen*] 'the world', he had no notion of the ecclesiastical concept 'world.' . . . *Denial* [*Das* Verneinen] is precisely what is totally impossible for him" (DA 202/TA 145). Jesus denied the denial characteristic of nihilism. He denied the nihilistic sacrifice that produces this chasm, as well as the sacrifices performed in the name of bridging this chasm. Jesus denied denial; he sacrificed sacrifice. This sacrifice of sacrifice steps beyond sacrifice, at the same time as it *repeats* what it steps beyond. Jesus' action is (in Blanchot's words) the step/not beyond (*le pas au-delà*) sacrifice.

Jesus' action suspends him, if only for a moment, between the apparent world and the "real" world. Jesus' "world" is *not* beyond the apparent world (as is the case with St. Paul, according to Nietzsche). But Jesus' "world" is likewise, according to the "logic" of "How the 'Real World' at Last Became a Myth," *not* the apparent world, for the apparent world only makes sense in relation to a real world. The extreme moment of this "History of an Error" from *Twilight of the Idols, or How to Philosophize with a Hammer* (1889) reads:

> We have abolished the real world: what world is left? the apparent world perhaps? . . . But no! *with the real world we have also abolished the apparent world!*
>
> (Mid-day; moment of the shortest shadow; end of the longest error; zenith of mankind; INCIPIT ZARATHUSTRA.) (GD 75/TI 41)

Jesus' world is nothing but the "not yet" characteristic of the step/not beyond the apparent world, nothing but the "not yet" of being suspended, if only for a moment, between the apparent world and the real world. Nietzsche describes this suspension in the "not yet," I would argue, as nothing but the pure transposition characteristic of the inner world of metaphor.

> The concept, the *experience* "life" in the only form he knows it is opposed to any kind of word, formula, law, faith, dogma. He [i.e., Jesus] speaks only of the inmost thing: "life" or "truth" or "light" is his expression for the inmost thing—everything else, the whole of reality, the whole of nature, language itself, possess for him merely the value of a sign, a metaphor. (DA 202/TA 144)

> If I understand anything of this great symbolist it is that he took for realities, for "truths," only *inner* realities—that he understood the rest, everything pertaining to nature, time, space, history, only as signs, as occasion for metaphor. (DA 204/TA 146)

This inner world of metaphor is the "not yet" of *any* world; it is the denial of *every* reality. It is the denial of the denial of the apparent world, the sacrifice of the sacrifice of the apparent world.

Insofar as Jesus denies *every* reality, and insofar as he maintains the pure essence of will in willing nothingness, and insofar as he is the extreme form of nihilism, is Jesus an overman? Recall that for Blanchot, the overman embodies the step/not beyond (*le pas au-delà*) nihilism.

This interruption of Judaism by the "glad tidings" of Jesus was followed by the *ressentiment* of St. Paul. It was followed by the Pauline perversion of the evangelic practice. Jesus abolished every kind of distancing relationship between God and human beings and proclaimed that it is through his evangelic practice alone that one feels at all times a "child of God" (DA 203–204/TA 145–146). Jesus taught the equal right of everyone to be a child of God. But this teaching fell prey to *ressentiment*. The enraged reverence of the "theologian" possessed by *ressentiment* could "no longer endure that evangelic equal right of everyone to be a child of God which Jesus had taught, and their revenge consisted in *exalting*

The Question of Sacrifice

Jesus in an extravagant fashion, in severing him from themselves: just as the Jews, in revenge on their enemies, had previously separated their God from themselves and raised him on high" (DA 212/TA 153). The *one* God and the *one* Son of God are both, according to Nietzsche, products of *ressentiment*. St. Paul perverted this "evangelic equal right of everyone to be a child of God [*evangelische Gleichberechtigung von Jedermann zum Kind Gottes*]" into "the doctrine 'equal rights for all' [*der Lehre 'gleiche Rechte für Alle'*]" (DA 215/TA 156) by shifting the center of gravity of life *out* of life into the "Beyond" and perpetuating the great lie of personal immortality, the great lie that everybody (as an immortal soul) is equal (*gleichen*) to everybody else (DA 215/TA 155–156).

St. Paul was, according to Nietzsche, an apostle of *ressentiment*. With St. Paul, the unevangelic feeling of revengefulness again came uppermost (DA 212/TA 153). St. Paul embodied the antithetical type to the "bringer of glad tidings." He was the genius of hatred. "*What* did this dysangelist not sacrifice [*Opfer*] to his hatred!" (DA 214/TA 154). If Jesus' action can be interpreted as the sacrifice of economical sacrifice, then St. Paul could be interpreted as sacrificing this sacrifice of economical sacrifice. St. Paul restored economical sacrifice. The unreasonable sacrifice of Jesus was replaced by the reasonable sacrifice of St. Paul. St. Paul thirsted for reasons — "reasons relieve" (GdM 407/GoM 140).

> —And now an absurd problem came up: "How *could* God have permitted that?" For this question the deranged reason of the little community found a downright terrifyingly absurd answer: God gave his Son for the forgiveness of sins, as a *sacrifice* [Opfer]. All at once it was all over with the Gospel! The *guilt sacrifice* [Schuldopfer], and that in its most repulsive, barbaric form, the sacrifice [*Opfer*] of the *innocent man* for the sins of the guilty! What atrocious paganism! — For Jesus had done away with the concept "guilt" itself — he had denied [*geleugnet*] any chasm between God and man, he *lived* this unity of God and man as *his* "glad tidings." . . . And *not* as a special prerogative! — From now on there is introduced into the type of the redeemer step by step: the doctrine of a Judgement and a Second Coming, the doctrine of his death as a sacrificial death [*Opfertode*], the doctrine of the Resurrection with which the entire concept "blessedness," the whole and sole reality of the Evangel, is juggled away — for the benefit of a state *after* death! (DA 212–213/TA 153–154)

The *ressentiment* of Judaism, interrupted by the "glad tidings" of Jesus, was replaced by the *ressentiment* of St. Paul.

Sacrifice can only sacrifice itself over and over (in an eternal return of the same) because what it seeks to overcome (the nihilistic revelation of truth that sublates sacrifice's negation) makes this sacrifice of itself both *necessary* and *useless*. The truth is eternally postponed in a *necessary* sacrificial gesture that can only sacrifice itself, thereby rendering itself *useless*. In the attempt to step beyond nihilism, that is, in the attempt to negate (or sacrifice) nihilism, one *repeats* the negation characteristic of nihilism. This sacrifice of (nihilistic) sacrifice can only take place as (perform itself as) the impossibility (or eternally postponed possibility) of its realization. One, therefore, performs an incessant step beyond that eternally returns. Sacrifice (without reserve) *remains* as a spectral presence insofar as sacrifice infinitely approaches (or withdraws from) revelation.

5

Levinas

On Resorting to the Ethical
Language of Sacrifice

The fact that sacrifice can only sacrifice itself over and over in an eternal return of the same, making it both necessary and useless, helps to correct a too-easy reading of Levinas. One frequently hears the following: Levinas is a Continental philosopher concerned with ethics. His ethics can be described by beginning with the subject, which he describes not as a free independent thinking thing, but as always already subject to the other, always already for-the-other. This for-the-other characteristic of Levinas's ethics gets read, in turn, in a variety of ways. For example, one sometimes reads that a symptom of the interruption of the independence of the same by the face of the other is a feeling of guilt in the same. Or that the for-the-other is an indication of a natural benevolence. On other occasions, it is read as a divine instinct. This reading is supported by an appeal to Levinas's reading of Descartes's *Meditations*, where he says that the idea of the infinite other is not an idea originating in me, but rather put in me by God. Continuing in this religious vein, one also reads the for-the-other interpreted as a tendency to sacrifice. Sacrifice is a word used with increasing frequency by Levinas after *Totality and Infinity: An Essay on Exteriority* (1961). It is a word loaded with an enormous amount of baggage, particularly for feminists, who (understandably) see its use as a call to an unquestioning selflessness that is often debilitating and demeaning. All of these readings of the for-the-other characteristic of Levinas's ethics are at best too easily read, and at worst misleading. In *Otherwise than Being or Beyond Essence* (1974), Levinas writes, "The for-the-other characteristic of the subject can be interpreted neither as a guilt complex (which presupposes an *initial* freedom), nor as a natural benevolence or divine 'instinct,' nor as some love or some tendency to sacrifice" (AE 160/OB

124). Despite this caution regarding the word sacrifice, Levinas writes the following in "Language and Proximity" from *En découvrant l'existence avec Husserl et Heidegger* (2nd ed. 1967): "The I, the non-interchangeable par excellence, is, in a world without play, what in a permanent sacrifice substitutes itself for others and transcends the world" (LeP 234/LaP 124). The question therefore arises: How is one to read "sacrifice" in the work of Levinas?

For Levinas, sacrifice (like responsibility) requires, paradoxically, both singularity and being nothing but "for the other." Sacrifice is sacrifice without reserve. But Levinas is careful to point out that this sacrifice is *not* an *action* performed *by* the same *for* the other. Sacrifice is not something the same does in response to the face of the other. In being torn up from oneself in the core of one's unity, the unity of oneself "is sacrificed rather than sacrificing itself" (AE 64/OB 49–50); that is, sacrifice is imposed on this existence (AE 64/OB 50). Levinas insists that he is *not* describing a "will for sacrifice" (AE 70/OB 55) or an "ethics of sacrifice" (MP 229/DF 216). How, therefore, is one called to read sacrifice in the work of Levinas? I would argue that one is obliged to necessarily, yet impossibly, read it in the following manner: Sacrificing sacrificing sacrificing.

The "Not Yet" of Approach from Which Comes Ethical Language

Before considering this paradoxical phrase, it is necessary to explore why Levinas's work necessarily resorts to ethical language. Levinas's consideration of his resorting to an ethical language is found primarily in "Language and Proximity" and *Otherwise than Being* (Chapter IV: "Substitution"). In a note in Chapter IV of *Otherwise than Being*, Levinas writes:

> This chapter [i.e., Chapter IV: "Substitution"] was the germ of the present work. Its principal elements were presented in a public lecture at the Faculté Universitaire Saint-Louis in Brussels, on November 30, 1967. That talk was a continuation of the lecture "Proximity" given the prior day, and which was substantially the same text as the study entitled "Langage et Proximité" subsequently published in the second edition of our book *En découvrant l'existence avec Husserl et Heidegger* (Paris: Vrin, 1967). The two lectures "La Proximité" and "La Substitution" were given the general title "Au-delà de l'Essence." The text of the second lecture published in the *Revue Philosophique de Louvain* (August, 1968) represented a finished version of the lecture. (AE 125n1/OB 193n1)

The ethical language Levinas resorts to "does not proceed from a special moral experience, independent of the description developed until then" (LeP 234/LaP 124; see AE 154/OB 120). I would argue that the "description developed until then" refers to those moments in the work of Levinas when philosophy encounters what can only be described as paradoxical. What makes these moments paradoxical is that one finds both the necessity, yet the impossibility, of thinking the two aspects of the paradox *at the same time*. To neither of these aspects (which

The Question of Sacrifice

reveal themselves in turn) does the last word belong (TeI 139/TaI 165). There is a necessary (yet illogical) alternation between the two aspects of the paradox. Said otherwise, each aspect of the paradox is, in effect, "not yet," insofar as each aspect is the condition of the possibility of the other aspect; they mutually found one another (TeI 19/TaI 48). Paradoxically, one could write that the constituted becomes *within constitution* the condition of the constituting (TeI 101/TaI 128). As such, the "description developed until then" refers to those moments in the work of Levinas that describe the irreducibly paradoxical "not yet" of approach (articulated by the paradoxical *necessity* to continue with the phenomenological description when continuing is experienced as *impossible*). The ethical language resorted to "comes from the very meaning of approach" (LeP 234/LaP 124), and not vice versa. "Ethical language alone succeeds in being equal to the paradox in which phenomenology is abruptly thrown" (LeP 234/LaP 124; see AE 155/ OB 121). "Ethical language," as it is referred to here, does not proceed from a moral experience, but from that moment when philosophy encounters the paradoxical. Ethical language "comes from the very meaning of approach" and, as such, "succeeds in being equal" to the paradoxical "not yet" of approach.

Reading Descartes's Meditations

What is this irreducibly paradoxical "not yet" of approach from which comes the ethical language to which Levinas resorts? A response to this question calls for the description of a few instances of the moment in Levinas's work when philosophy encounters the paradoxical. These are moments when comprehension is called into question. Comprehension is called into question by what Levinas calls critique. In the opening sections of *Totality and Infinity*, Levinas makes a distinction between knowledge or theory understood as comprehension and the critical essence of knowing. In its comprehension of being, knowledge or theory is concerned with critique. Discovering the arbitrary dogmatism of its free exercise, knowing calls itself into question. The critical essence of knowing turns back at every moment to the origin of this arbitrary dogmatism of its free exercise (TeI 13/TaI 43). The essence of knowing does not consist in grasping an object, but in being able to call itself into question. Knowing "can have the world as its theme, make of it an object, because its exercise consists, as it were, in taking charge of the very condition that supports it and that supports even this very act of taking charge" (TeI 57/TaI 85). Knowledge or theory seems, therefore, to be characterized by an ambiguity—two distinct movements. The movement of comprehension is inverted at every moment by the movement of critique. However, these two movements are not *merely* opposed to one another. Although oriented in inverse directions, and therefore opposed, they nevertheless call for being thought at the same time. "Knowing becomes knowing of a fact only if it is *at the same time* [*en même temps*] critical, if it puts itself into question, goes back beyond its origin—in an unnatural movement to seek higher than one's own origin, a movement which evinces or describes a created freedom" (TeI 54/TaI

82–83, emphasis added). In this unnatural movement of critique, knowledge goes back beyond its *own* origin, that is, back beyond an origin in which it is justified by itself. "Knowledge as a critique, as a tracing back to what precedes freedom, can arise only in a being that has an origin prior to its origin" (TeI 57/TaI 85). The *moment* when comprehension is called into question by critique is what Levinas calls "ethics."

In his reading of Descartes's *Meditations on First Philosophy* (1641), Levinas describes two paradoxical moments: the moment in the Third Meditation when the constituted (i.e., the infinite) becomes the condition of the constituting (i.e., of the constituting performed by the *cogito*), and the moment (read *into* Descartes's *Meditations* by Levinas, though in a way arguably consistent with Descartes's logic) when the refutation of the doubt arising from the evil genius is in turn called into doubt. The profundity of the Third Meditation lies, for Levinas, in "[t]he ambiguity of Descartes's first evidence, revealing the I and God in turn without merging them, revealing them as two distinct moments of evidence mutually founding one another" (TeI 19/TaI 48). This paradoxical "double origin" of the *cogito* and the infinite is performed in a reading that progresses from the First Meditation to the discovery of the infinite in the Third Meditation. "If, in a first movement, Descartes takes a consciousness to be indubitable of itself by itself, in a second movement—the reflection on reflection—he recognizes conditions for this certitude" (TeI 186/TaI 210). In a second movement—that is, "after the fact" (*après coup*, TeI 25/TaI 54), or in the critical reflection on the reflection characteristic of comprehension—Descartes recognizes conditions for the certitude of comprehension. The critical essence of knowing leads—according to Levinas's reading of Descartes's *Meditations*—beyond the knowledge of the *cogito* (TeI 58/TaI 85). It penetrates beneath knowledge understood as comprehension, beneath knowledge which takes itself to be indubitable of itself by itself. He recognizes the "condition" of the certitude characteristic of the first movement, the condition of what was initially taken to be "indubitable of itself by itself," an absolute origin. Descartes discovers in the Third Meditation a paradoxical preoriginary origin: the infinite. The performance of this reading is the production of a trace of the *infinition* of the infinite, of the infinite *as* interrupting the thought that thinks it.

For Levinas, Descartes's *Meditations* is characterized by "two times" (TeI 29/TaI 58) or "movements" (TeI 186/TaI 210): the chronological order (in which the *cogito* is the cause of the idea of the infinite) and the "logical" order (in which the infinite is the cause of the *cogito*). The comprehension characteristic of the chronological order is called into question by the critique characteristic of the "logical" order.

> The being infinitely surpassing its own idea in us—God in the Cartesian terminology—subtends the evidence of the *cogito*, according to the third *Meditation*. But the discovery of this metaphysical relation in the *cogito* constitutes chronologically only the second move of the philosopher. That there could

> be a chronological order distinct from the "logical" order, that there could be several moments in the progression, that there is a progression—here is separation. For by virtue of time this being is not *yet* [*n'est pas* encore]—which does not make it the same as nothingness, but maintains it at a distance [*à distance*] from itself. It is not all at once [*n'est pas d'un seul coup*]. Even its [i.e., the *cogito's*] cause, older than itself, is still to come. The cause of being is thought or known by its effect *as though* it were posterior to its effect. (TeI 24–25/TaI 54)

The *cogito* and God are maintained in the interval of the "not yet" (or the "not all at once," or the "still to come"). It is this interval, I would argue, that Levinas calls dead time (*le temps mort*). Dead time marks the moment in comprehension when comprehension finds itself at a distance from itself, when comprehension is not yet. An attentive reading of Descartes's *Meditations* obliges one to critique or sacrifice (and, *at the same time*, to recognize) comprehension. At the moment of the discovery of the infinite, that is, at the moment of critique or sacrifice (if only for a moment), what is critiqued (that is, comprehension) retains all of its value *in* the very critique. Referring to these passages, Levinas writes, "Thus already theoretical thought [. . .] articulates separation. Separation is not *reflected* in thought, but *produced* by it" (TeI 25/TaI 54, emphasis added). Separation is produced by thought in that one effects a progression through the two movements of the *Meditations*, in that one effects a performance of a reading of the *Meditations*. But what is reflected upon in this effectuation is not the unambiguous appearance of something, as is usually the case in production (which ambiguously conveys both effectuation of being and being brought to light or appearing; TeI XIV/TaI 26). For what is produced in this effectuation is an inversion of order with respect to the chronological order and the "logical" order. What is produced in this effectuation is the double origin of the *cogito* and God: the ambiguity of Descartes's first evidence, revealing the *cogito* and the infinite as two distinct moments of evidence mutually founding one another (TeI 19/TaI 48). To borrow a phrase from another context in *Totality and Infinity*, one could write that the constituted becomes within constitution the condition of the constituting (TeI 101/TaI 128). What is produced in this effectuation is not something that appears unambiguously, but rather an irreducible ambiguity, a trace of what infinitely approaches (or withdraws from) revelation, of what is not yet. The performance of the two movements of Descartes's *Meditations* is a production of a trace of the not yet of the subject and the not yet of the infinite. The performance of these two movements is the production of a trace of the subject *as* interrupted and the infinite *as* interrupting. It is the production of a trace of dead time, of the "not yet" of approach. Here one sees a productionless production. Here one sees the unworking of the work of comprehension.

One also sees the unworking of the work of comprehension in Levinas's reading of the evil genius in Descartes's *Meditations*. Descartes concludes, in the wake of the pathway of doubt that seems to leave everything doubtful, that the exercise of doubt itself is beyond doubt; that is, he has no doubt that he doubts. But taking the *cogito* as the first certitude constitutes, according to Levinas, an arbitrary halt that is not justified of itself since it can likewise be cast into doubt. This alternation between doubt and refutation of doubt is the spiraling movement of descent toward the *il y a*. Levinas outlines here, I would argue, two movements not wholly unlike those outlined with respect to the *cogito* and the infinite. In both cases, dead time marks the moment when the *cogito* finds itself at a distance from itself. In this particular case, it is as if the certitude of the *cogito*—which is characteristic of the first movement—were not yet, as if every attempt to realize it were interrupted *in* the very attempt. At this moment, if only for a moment, what is doubted, what is critiqued (i.e., comprehension, specifically, the process of doubting) retains all of its value *in* the very negation, which effects a refutation of doubt. Here again one is obliged to critique or sacrifice (and, *at the same time*, to recognize) comprehension, if only for a moment. Dead time, therefore, marks the alternation between doubt and refutation of doubt that is a spiraling movement of descent toward the *il y a*. In each of these two cases, one encounters a moment of an irreducibly paradoxical alternation between two alternatives: between the *cogito* and the infinite, and between the *cogito* and the doubt arising from the evil genius. (For a more detailed consideration of Levinas's reading of Descartes's *Meditations*, see my *Death and Responsibility: The "Work" of Levinas*.)

As important as Descartes's *Meditations* is to the work of Levinas, there are two issues that must be taken into consideration. First, it is loaded with a great deal of philosophical presuppositions that must be acknowledged. In "Philosophy and the Idea of Infinity" (1957) from *En découvrant l'existence avec Husserl et Heidegger* (2nd ed. 1967), Levinas writes that his reading of Descartes's *Meditations* retains "only the *formal* design of the structure it outlines" (PeI 171/PaI 53). In "God and Philosophy" (1975) from *Of God Who Comes to Mind* (1986), Levinas writes, "Descartes maintains a substantialist language here [i.e., in the *Meditations*], interpreting the immeasurableness of God as a superlative way of existing. But for us his unsurpassable contribution does not lie here. It is not the proofs of God's existence that matter to us here, but rather the breakup of consciousness" (DP 104–105/GP 62–63). With respect to the proof of God's existence, Levinas writes, "[T]here perhaps is not much sense to proving an existence by describing a situation prior to proof and to the problems of existence" (TeI 20/TaI 49). By conceiving God "ethically" as the interruption (rather than ontologically as the ground) of consciousness, Levinas seeks to transform the Cartesian text. There still remains the question of the degree to which the Cartesian text can be transformed. Second, it maintains a distinction between the infinite and the doubt arising from the evil genius associated with the *il y a*. The phrase *relation without relation* is used by Levinas to articulate the fact that one term of the relation (that is, the infinite) absolves itself from the relation, or, said otherwise, merely leaves a trace of itself in the irreducibly paradoxical double origin of the *cogito* and the infinite that Levinas inextricably weaves in *Otherwise than Being* into the couple skepticism and refutation of skepticism (AE 195–218/ OB 153–171). This weaving of the double origin of the *cogito* and the infinite *and* the couple skepticism and refutation of skepticism weaves the two readings of Descartes's *Meditations* in *Totality and Infinity*—the reading of the infinite and the reading of the evil genius—ever more tightly. It is as though the two readings of Descartes's *Meditations* in *Totality and Infinity* become indistinguishable in *Otherwise than Being*.

Both of these issues—the philosophical presuppositions of Descartes's argument and the distinction between the infinite and the doubt arising from the evil genius associated with the *il y a*—are addressed by Levinas, I would argue, in what he regards as the necessary deformalization or concretization of this reading (TeI 21/TaI 50) in a phenomenological description of the irreducibly paradoxical body. One is obliged to deformalize or concretize the formal description of the paradoxical moments in Levinas's reading of Descartes's *Meditations*.

The Body and the (Non-)Sense in Sensibility

Another paradoxical moment in Levinas's work is his phenomenological description of the body. "The body naked and indigent identifies the *center* of the world it perceives, but, *conditioned* by its own representation of the world, it is thereby as it were torn up from the center from which it proceeded, as water gushing forth from rock washes away that rock" (TeI 100/TaI 127). The constituted becomes within the constitution (characteristic of representation) the condition of the constituting. The surplus over meaning (characteristic of the elemental) is not a meaning in its turn, now thought as a condition. This would reduce the elemental to another correlate of representation. On the contrary, the elemental conditions the very representation that would think it as a condition (TeI 101/TaI 128). The body is the effectuation of this perpetual inversion of order. The body is the very reverting of the subject that represents into a "living from . . ." that is sustained by what the representing subject claims to constitute by giving it meaning.

> The body is a permanent contestation of the prerogative attributed to consciousness of "giving meaning" to each thing; it lives as this contestation. The world I live in is not simply the counterpart or the contemporary of thought and its constitutive freedom, but a conditioning and an antecedence. The world I constitute nourishes me and bathes me. It is aliment and "medium" [«*milieu*»]. The intentionality aiming at the exterior changes direction in the course of its very aim by becoming interior to the exteriority it constitutes, somehow comes from the point to which it goes, recognizing itself past in its future, lives from what it thinks. (TeI 102/TaI 129)

If one persists, as Levinas does here, in using the language of intentionality, one runs up against a paradox. It is as though intentionality aiming at an exterior inverts direction *in the course* of its aim. This incessant inversion that is the production of an irreducibly paradoxical double origin of the independence of representation and the dependence of being steeped in the elemental formally parallels, I would argue, Levinas's reading of Descartes's *Meditations*. That is, these two aspects of the body—lived body and physical body—articulate two movements not formally unlike the two movements of Descartes's *Meditations*.

> Life is a body, not only lived body [*corps propre*], where its self-sufficiency emerges, but a cross-roads of physical forces, body-effect. In its deep-seated fear life attests this ever possible inversion of the body-master into body-slave, of health into sickness. *To be a body* is on the one hand *to stand* [se tenir], to be master of oneself, and, on the other hand, to stand on the earth, to be in the *other*, and thus to be encumbered by one's body. (TeI 138/TaI 164)

Here Levinas seems to make a distinction between standing, detached from its concrete conditions (which articulates the independence of the I of representation), and "standing on the earth, in the other" (which articulates the dependence upon the elemental).

> To be at home with oneself in something other than oneself, to be oneself while living from something other than oneself, to live from . . . , is concretized in corporeal existence. "Incarnate thought" is not initially produced as a thought that acts on the world, but as a separated existence which affirms its independence in the happy dependence of need. It is not that this equivocation amounts to two successive points of view on separation; their simultaneity constitutes the body. To neither of the aspects which reveal themselves in turn does the last word belong. (TeI 139/TaI 164–165)

This irreducible paradox of the body—which articulates the not yet of the lived body and the not yet of the physical body that is "a sector of an elemental reality" (TeI 140/TaI 165)—is, according to Levinas, consciousness. "Consciousness does not fall into a body—is not incarnated; it is a disincarnation—or, more exactly, a postponing of the corporeity of the body" (TeI 140/TaI 165–166), the not yet of the physical body, the not yet of complete dependence upon the elemental. To describe consciousness as postponement is—as is the case in Levinas's description of the *cogito* in Descartes's *Meditations* as not yet or not all at once—to describe it as always already in relation to the other. Consciousness, therefore, is produced in the effectuation of a double origin.

> To be conscious is to be in relation with *what is*, but as though the present of *what is* were not yet [*n'était pas encore*] entirely accomplished and only constituted the *future* of a recollected being. To be conscious is precisely to have time—not to exceed the present time in the project that anticipates the future, but to have a distance [*une distance*] with regard to the present itself, to be related to the element in which one is settled as to what is not yet [*n'est pas encore*] there. All the freedom of inhabitation depends on the time that, for the inhabitant, still always remains. (TeI 140/TaI 166)

Insofar as consciousness names that *moment in* the intentionality of the lived body when intentionality finds itself at a distance *from* itself, the term *consciousness* undergoes slippage. It names the irreducibly paradoxical body as the "site" of a moment when a rigorous phenomenological description becomes a paradox, when it becomes impossible. This not yet, which names the moment when a rigorous phenomenological description becomes a paradox, is dead time. Dead time—articulated by the irreducibly paradoxical body—is ambiguous. The body, as the site of the relationship with the other (*autre/Autrui*), is the site of enjoyment, exposure to violence, and responsibility. Or, said in the language of *Otherwise than Being*, the body is the site of enjoyment, the by-the-other (or nonsense), and the for-the-other (or sense). (For a more detailed consideration of Levinas's reading of the body as the site of enjoyment, the by-the-other, and the for-the-other, see my *Death and Responsibility: The "Work" of Levinas*.)

Ethical Language as Response *to What Exceeds Philosophy*

These excursus into Levinas's reading of Descartes's *Meditations* and Levinas's concretization of that reading in the phenomenological description of the irreducibly paradoxical body were a response to the question: What is the irreducibly paradoxical "not yet" of approach from which comes the ethical language to which Levinas resorts? A response to this question calls for the description of a few paradoxical moments in Levinas's work, and the preceding description of Levinas's reading of Descartes's *Meditations* and Levinas's concretization of that reading in the phenomenological description of the irreducibly paradoxical body are instances of such moments. These are instances of moments in the work of Levinas when philosophy encounters what can only be described as the necessary, yet illogical, alternation characteristic of the paradox in which philosophy finds itself abruptly thrown: the irreducibly paradoxical alternation between the *cogito* and the infinite, between the *cogito* and the doubt arising from the evil genius, and between the lived body and the physical body. These are instances of moments in the work of Levinas that describe the necessity, yet impossibility, of thinking the two aspects of the paradox at the same time. Each aspect of the paradox is characterized not by presence, but by the irreducibly paradoxical "not yet" of approach. Each aspect of the paradox is not yet. When Levinas writes that the ethical language to which he resorts "does not proceed from a special moral experience, independent of the description developed until then," he is referring to the preceding descriptions (among others) of his reading of Descartes's *Meditations* and his concretization of that reading in the phenomenological description of the irreducibly paradoxical body.

This necessary, yet illogical, alternation characteristic of the paradox in which philosophy finds itself abruptly thrown betrays that which exceeds philosophy. It betrays what Levinas calls the *otherwise than being*. This betrayal is a betrayal of saying. "The *otherwise than being* is stated in a saying that must also be unsaid in order to thus extract the *otherwise than being* from the said in which it already comes to signify but a *being otherwise*" (AE 8/OB 7). The unsaying of the said is cast by Levinas in terms of conveying and betraying. As soon as the otherwise than being is conveyed, it is betrayed in the said that conveys it. "A methodological problem arises here, whether the pre-original element of saying (the anarchical, the non-original, as we designate it) can be led to betray itself by showing itself in a theme (if an an-archeology is possible), and whether this betrayal can be reduced; whether one can at the same time know and free the known of the marks which thematization leaves on it by subordinating it to ontology" (AE 8/OB 7). Playing on the ambiguity of the term *betray*, which designates both to mislead and to reveal, Levinas wonders whether in the inevitable betrayal of the saying conveyed in the said, the saying can be led to betray itself. He wonders whether the betrayal can be reduced, or said otherwise, whether the saying's betraying itself can be highlighted, freed from the marks of thematization. He wonders whether it can be clandestinely caught in the act or listened in upon, so to speak. It can, Levinas insists, if one is attentive to the paradoxical trace of "the pre-original element of saying" inscribed in the said, inscribed, for example, in Descartes's *Meditations* or in the phenomenological description of the irreducibly paradoxical body. On the one hand, saying is the *way* the otherwise than being is said, the *way* the reduction of the betrayal is produced. But this is not the preoriginal element of saying. It is, rather, that element of saying which is merely a particular form of the said, specifically, the way something (including the preoriginal element of language) is said. On the other hand, saying is the preoriginal, an-archical or excessive element of language that exceeds language. It is that which is otherwise than being. But as excessive it inevitably is betrayed in the said. However, it is, as was noted earlier, betrayed in a particular *way*. Saying, as the excessive element of language that exceeds language, leaves a trace of itself in an "ambiguous or enigmatic way of speaking" (AE 9/OB 7), in the form of an irreducible paradox. *Saying on the one hand is the trace of saying on the other hand.* Saying "is produced out of time or in two times without entering into either of them, as an endless critique, or skepticism, which in a spiralling movement makes possible the boldness of philosophy, destroying the conjunction into which its saying and its said continually enter" (AE 57/OB 44). This passage echoes Levinas's reading of Descartes's *Meditations* as well as the phenomenological description of the irreducibly paradoxical body. The description of that which exceeds philosophy obliges one to remain with the description when the description becomes a paradox, when it becomes impossible. The ethical language is a *response* to that which exceeds philosophy.

The Aporetic Meaning of Ethical Language

Ethical language comes from the meaning of approach and, as such, succeeds in being equal to the paradoxical "not yet" of approach. The economical meaning of *sacrifice* and *responsibility*—as they have been inherited from the tradition—undergoes slippage at a certain moment in history and is "experienced" as aporetic. Said otherwise, at a certain moment in history they are experienced at a certain distance from themselves. They are experienced as possible at the moment they are impossible. They are experienced as approach, as "not yet."

Sacrifice and responsibility require that I respond, that I answer for what I do, say, and give, as irreplaceable singularity, and they require that I am exposed to ex-propriation, to anonymity, that I forget or efface myself, that I be (in Levinas's words) nothing but "for the other." In other words, sacrifice and responsibility require—using words of Blanchot that echo Heidegger's analysis of death as possibility of the impossibility of Dasein—that I answer for the impossibility of sacrifice, for the impossibility of being responsible, which makes me always already guilty or irresponsible. The more I sacrifice or the more I am responsible, the more irresponsible I am, because (on the one hand) sacrifice and responsibility hold me accountable, and (on the other hand) sacrifice and responsibility discount me (insofar as they require that I be selfless, that I be nothing but "for the other"). Only the aporia of death—that moment when death as possibility turns into death as impossibility—is adequate to the aporias of sacrifice and responsibility, insofar as death as possibility gives irreplaceable singularity and death as impossibility gives the ex-propriation, the anonymity, that is a forgetting or effacement of oneself.

The possibility of the ethical language of sacrifice and responsibility having the predominantly economical meaning that they have inherited from the tradition *is* its impossibility. Ours is the moment in history when they are experienced as aporetic.

Rather than a work to be accomplished, or an action to be performed, sacrifice and responsibility (at a certain moment in history) are experienced as aporetic, and as such are experienced as otherwise than merely an imperative. They become calls to action that call themselves into question. They become works that unwork themselves in the very performance of the work. They are experienced as coming from the meaning of approach.

Responsibility and Sacrifice

The ethical language of *this* responsibility is without reserve; that is, it is experienced as aporetic, as impossible at the moment it is possible. Responsibility is without reserve. As such, the ethical language of responsibility is always to have one degree of responsibility more. Levinas writes, "To be oneself, the state of being a hostage, is always *to have one degree of responsibility more*, the responsibility for the responsibility of the other" (AE 150/OB 117, emphasis added). This formulation is often a stumbling block for many readers of Levinas's work. I would argue that the reason it is often a stumbling block is that responsibility in the work of Levinas is too easily read; that is, it is understood as the *action* performed *by* the same *for* the other. A note to this passage reminds the reader that responsibility necessarily involves one movement more. One has "to catch sight of a suffering of suffering" in responsibility without reserve. This element of suffering *for nothing* in suffering "is not a purifying fire of suffering," but rather "the passivity of suffering which prevents its reverting into suffering assumed, in which the for-the-other of sensibility, that is, its very sense, would be annulled. This moment of the 'for nothing' in suffering is the surplus of non-sense over sense by which the sense of suffering is possible" (AE 150n21/OB 196n21). For the sense of the for-the-other to be maintained—that is, that it *not* be the phenomenal action of responsibility and, therefore, the domestication of the anarchy of responsibility without reserve—there necessarily has to be a suffering of suffering, that is, a suffering *for nothing*, a suffering that is non-sense.

The ethical language of *this* sacrifice is without reserve; that is, it is experienced as aporetic, as impossible at the moment it is possible. Sacrifice (like responsibility) is without reserve. Levinas reads this sacrifice without reserve alongside saying: "[S]aying remains, in its activity, a passivity, more passive than all passivity, for it is a sacrifice without reserve, without holding back, and in this non-voluntary—the sacrifice of a hostage designated who has not chosen himself to be hostage, but possibly elected by the Good, in an involuntary election not assumed by the elected one" (AE 18–19/OB 15). It is a work that unworks itself in the very performance of the work. It is experienced as coming from the meaning of the "not yet" of approach.

> Of itself saying is the sense [*sens*] of patience and pain. In saying suffering signifies in the form of *giving*, even if the price of signification is that the subject run the risk [*courait le risque*] of suffering without reason. If the subject did not run this risk [*ne courait pas ce risque*], pain would lose its very painfulness. Signification, as the one-for-the-other in passivity, where the other is not assumed by the one, presupposes the possibility of pure non-sense invading and threatening signification. Without this folly at the confines of reason, the one would take hold of itself, and, in the heart of its passion, recommence essence. How the adversity of pain is ambiguous! The for-the-other (or sense) turns into by-the-other [*Le pour-l'autre (ou le sens) va jusqu'au par-l'autre*], into suffering by a thorn burning the flesh, but *for nothing* [*pour rien*]. It is only in this way that the *for-the-other* [*pour-l'autre*], the passivity more passive still than any passivity, the emphasis of sense [*sens*], is kept from being *for-oneself* [*pour-soi*]. (AE 64–65/OB 50)

The "by-the-other" is necessarily, yet impossibly, to be read alongside the "for-the-other." The non-sense of the *il y a* (AE 208/OB 163) is a *modality* of the for-the-other (AE 208–209/OB 164). The suffering "for-the-other" is necessarily, yet impossibly, a passivity of suffering, a suffering *for nothing*, non-sense. This prevents the suffering from being a *virtuous* suffering, a self-edifying suffering. Such a self-edifying suffering would be a suffering that would no longer be (that would be blind to) the suffering of the aporia of sacrifice. This aporia of sacrifice would be stilled. The fact that the demonic is a modality of infinite goodness is what makes (true) sacrifice possible. With self-edifying suffering, an ethics of good conscience reinstalls itself; that is, rather than being for-the-other, one would be for-oneself. Therefore, the "for-the-other" is necessarily, yet impossibly, *to have one degree of sacrifice more*. The "for-the-other" must necessarily, yet impossibly, be a sacrifice of sacrifice. It must necessarily, yet impossibly, be a sacrifice *for nothing*, a sacrifice for no reason, no goal. It must necessarily, yet impossibly, be a non-sensical sacrifice. Sacrifice without reserve is impossible, but it is necessary to justify the phenom-

The Question of Sacrifice

enal action of sacrifice (see AE 176/OB 138). The phenomenal action of sacrifice only has meaning given sacrifice without reserve. The phenomenal action of sacrifice only has meaning given that sacrifice sacrifices itself.

Obsession

It is now possible to appreciate what is involved in my argument that sacrifice in the work of Levinas must, of necessity, be read as "sacrificing sacrificing sacrificing." Is this phrase the mere repetition of the same word? Is it a repetition that has, perhaps, an obsessional quality to it? Is the same word repeated time after time after time, making up nothing more than the fragment of something (perhaps a sentence), or more likely, a fragmented thought? Sacrificing sacrificing sacrificing. Or is this phrase a rigorously constructed thought? That is to say, is it saying sacrificing (understood in a nominal sense) sacrificing (understood in a verbal sense) sacrificing itself? What is "sacrifice" doing? Sacrificing. What is "it" sacrificing? Itself *as* sacrificing. Sacrificing sacrificing itself *as* sacrificing. Sacrificing sacrificing sacrificing. There is here an irreducible ambiguity of an obsessional thought *and* of a clear rigorous thought. Or, to be more precise, there is here a clear rigorous thought that is, at the same time, fragmented by an obsessional repetition. There is, to be even more precise, an obsessional alternation *between* the clear rigorous thought *and* the obsessional repetition.

What, exactly, is an obsession? Mental health workers routinely assess what they refer to as the "thought content" of a client. Some of the possible distinctions available to the worker are ruminations, delusions, and obsessions. *Ruminations* (or preoccupations) are an excessive concern with something. It is important to note that with ruminations the thinking process does *not* appear strange to the client, and he/she does not generally try to stop the ruminations. *Delusions* are false beliefs strongly held in spite of invalidating evidence. One could argue that delusions are similar to ruminations insofar as the thinking process in either case does *not* appear strange to the client, and he/she does *not* generally try to stop them. *Obsessions* are a persistent and disturbing intrusion of, or anxious and inescapable preoccupation with, ideas or feelings, especially if these ideas or feelings are *known* to be unreasonable. Therefore, unlike ruminations and delusions, clients find these obsessive thought processes to be both odd and painful. Obsessions are unique among the three distinctions of thought content insofar as it is a thought that one realizes is unreasonable. It is an irrational thought that one realizes one should take leave of, yet one is unable to take leave of it. It is a paradoxical thought that one necessarily yet impossibly desires to step beyond. In an obsessed existence, one finds oneself at a certain distance from oneself. Obsession is, I would argue, the trace of the not yet of consciousness.

Obsession comes to play an increasing role in the work of Levinas, beginning particularly with "Language and Proximity," where he thematizes his resorting to an ethical language. In an obsessed existence, according to Levinas, consciousness is faced with an incessant presence of what "contests its own presence" (LeP

86

230/LaP 120), of a "non-repose itself, restlessness" (LeP 230/LaP 120). In an obsessed existence, consciousness is faced with the infinite/*il y a*, the description of which is nothing other than the anarchical description of the restless and uprooted vigilance of obsessed existence itself. In fact, all the infinite/*il y a* "is" is the restless and uprooted vigilance of obsessed existence with which consciousness finds it necessary, yet impossible, to remain. All the infinite/*il y a* "is" is the trace it leaves in the obsessional alternation or repetition (AE 115n31/OB 193n31).

The obsessional alternation *between* the clear rigorous thought *and* the obsessional repetition characteristic of the phrase "sacrificing sacrificing sacrificing" is meant to echo the "logic" of the phrase "saying saying saying" in the following passage:

> For subjectivity to signify unreservedly, it would then be *necessary* that the passivity of its exposure to the other not be immediately inverted into activity, but expose itself in its turn; a passivity of passivity is *necessary*, and in the glory of the Infinite ashes from which an act could not be born anew. Saying is this passivity of passivity and this dedication to the other, this sincerity. Not the communication of a said, which would immediately cover over and extinguish or absorb the said, but saying holding open its openness, without excuses, evasions or alibis, delivering itself without saying anything said. *Saying saying saying* itself [*Dire disant le dire même*], without thematizing it, but exposing it again. Saying is thus to make signs of this very signifyingness of the exposure; it is to expose the exposure instead of remaining in it as an act of exposing. (AE 181–182/OB 142–143, emphasis added)

In order for sacrifice to be (true) sacrifice, it is necessary (echoing the concluding words of the preceding quotation) that sacrifice sacrifice the sacrificing instead of remaining in it as an act of sacrifice. This sacrifice of sacrifice is impossible, but it is necessary to justify the phenomenal action of sacrifice (see AE 176/OB 138). The phenomenal action of sacrifice only has meaning given sacrifice without reserve. The phenomenal action of sacrifice only has meaning given that sacrifice sacrifices itself.

When Levinas writes that the ethical language to which he resorts "does not proceed from a special moral experience, independent of the description developed until then," he is referring to the preceding descriptions (among others) of his reading of Descartes's *Meditations* and his concretization of that reading in the phenomenological description of the irreducibly paradoxical body. These moments in the work of Levinas describe the irreducibly paradoxical "not yet" of approach (articulated by this paradoxical necessity to continue with the phenomenological description when continuing is experienced as impossible) from which comes the ethical language of for-the-other (which interrupts the presence of for-oneself) to which Levinas resorts. This necessarily obsessive and illogical alternation characteristic of the paradox in which philosophy finds itself abruptly thrown betrays that which exceeds philosophy; that is, it is a trace of that which exceeds philosophy. The ethical language of sacrifice (like responsibility) comes from the meaning of approach and, as such, succeeds in being equal to approach. The economical meaning of sacrifice—as it has been inherited from the tradition—undergoes slippage at a certain moment in history and is experienced as aporetic. As such, it is experienced as possible at the moment it is impossible. The possibility of the ethical language of sacrifice having the meaning inherited from the tradition *is* its impossibility. Sacrifice is experienced as coming from the meaning of the "not yet" of approach. Said otherwise, at a certain moment in history it is experienced at a certain distance from itself. Rather than a work to be accomplished, or an action to be performed, sacrifice is experienced as aporetic, and as such is experienced as otherwise than merely an imperative. It becomes a call to action that calls itself into question. It becomes a work that unworks itself in the very performance of the work. Sacrificing sacrificing sacrificing.

6

Irigaray

The Sacrifice of the Sacrifice of Woman

Like the chapters that precede it, this chapter on Irigaray considers the necessity, yet uselessness, of the sacrifice of sacrifice, but specifically within the context of her concern with how sacrifice is relevant to women. The consideration of the work of Irigaray looks back to some of the themes considered in the chapter on Nietzsche (the risk of belief characteristic of sacrificing sacrifice) and the chapter on Levinas (the "night of the world" characteristic of the *il y a*), and it looks forward to some of the themes that will be considered in the chapter on Lacan/Žižek (the sacrifice of sacrifice as *separation* from, rather than *alienation* in/by, the symbolic order) and the chapter on Derrida (the work of mourning and the risk of belief characteristic of sacrificing sacrifice).

   Irigaray states that "[m]ost of our societies have been built on sacrifice" (FSA 89/WSM 75). Numerous instances of social space existing only through immolation are offered by the work of Girard, notably *Violence and the Sacred* (1972) and *Things Hidden since the Foundation of the World* (1978). However, Irigaray points out, Girard writes very little about how his work is relevant to women. In "Belief Itself" and "Women, the Sacred, Money"—both from *Sexes and Genealogies* (1987)—Irigaray is concerned with, among other things, inquiring into how sacrifice is relevant to women. In "Women, the Sacred, Money," Irigaray writes, "It would seem to me to be more appropriate to inquire whether, under the sacrificed victim, another victim is often *hidden*" (FSA 90/WSM 76, emphasis added). Several questions will guide her inquiry into this issue: Who is the *other* victim hidden under the sacrificed victim? What would it mean to reveal this other victim hidden under the sacrificed victim? One of the problems with a superficial reading of these essays is that Irigaray is too easily understood as merely saying that woman is the hidden victim of sacrifice and that one is called to reveal this hidden victim, acknowledge the violence associated with sacrificial rites perpetuated against women (and men), and promote other rites (associated with women) that promote a nonsacrificial way of communing with the divine. While all of these points play an important role in Irigaray's inquiry into how sacrifice is relevant to women, I will argue that a more radical reading of "Belief Itself" and "Women, the Sacred, Money" is necessary. This more radical reading—which provides the condition of the possibility (and, paradoxically, the condition of the impossibility) of those points—is opened up, I would argue, when one reads "Belief Itself" and "Women, the Sacred, Money" alongside the work of Lacan and Žižek. What is called for is attending to the atemporal temporality of the moment of *the sacrifice of the sacrifice* that inevitably gets concealed by sacrificial societies.

In "Belief Itself" and "Women, the Sacred, Money," Irigaray considers (among other things) the symbolic economy of Christianity. In particular she is concerned with the sacrifice of the Eucharist. Within this particular symbolic economy—which is characterized by God the Father and (within Catholicism) "Father" (i.e., the priest)—woman is perceived as mother. "In effect, the women in attendance [at the sacrifice of the Eucharist] must be mothers, mothers of sons, whereas *the other*, the woman lover, is kept away from the scene" (CM 58/ BI 46). Not only is woman perceived only in this limiting role as mother, but also her natural fertility is sacrificed by the socially constructed fertility of the sacrificial culture of the Father. The sacrificial economy of the Father sacrifices the mother. This sacrifice of the natural fertility of woman leads to an economic superstructure that has no respect for the infrastructure of natural fertility. This is what prompts Irigaray to consider the specific symbolic economy of Christianity from the perspective of (the socially constructed fertility of) the Father and (the natural fertility of) the mother. And yet, it is a too-easy reading of not only the perception (within the symbolic economy of Christianity) of woman as mother, but also the very perception of woman (whether mother or not) that *the sacrifice of sacrifice* will call into question.

The Revelation of the Hidden Victim of Sacrifice as a *New* Sacrifice

Irigaray's inquiry into the hidden victim of sacrifice in "Women, the Sacred, Money" begins with a consideration of the reduction of Christianity to the sacrificial element. Drawing on her *Marine Lover of Friedrich Nietzsche* (1980), which in turn draws on the work of Nietzsche, Irigaray argues that the crucifixion is an accidental rather than an essential aspect of Christianity. Though the cross is accepted by Jesus (in faithfulness to his incarnation), it forms no part of his gospel that the flesh has been redeemed. It signals, on the contrary, the way that certain powers refused that gospel. The Eucharist, which is often understood as either a *repetition* of the sacrifice of Jesus or as a memorial (*anamnesis*) of the *singular* sacrifice of Jesus, is understood by Irigaray to mean "I am going to be immolated, I give you something other than my flesh to share together—fruits of the earth that I have blessed and sanctified—before the sacrifice occurs, so that my body returns to life and is not dead when you consume it in my absence" (FSA 92/WSM 78; see CM 39n3/BI 26n3). According to this interpretation, one would err in understanding the Eucharist as either a repetition of or a memorial of the sacrifice of Jesus, rather than as inaugurating a new way of sharing with the divine. The fact that women are excluded from the priesthood that performs this eucharistic sacrifice prompts Irigaray to ask, "Therefore, could it not be argued that the hidden sacrifice is in fact this *extradition*, this ban on women's participation in religious practice, and their consequent exile from the ultimate sources of social decision making?" (FSA 92/WSM 78). One could conclude that Irigaray's inquiry into the other victim hidden under the sacrificed victim that builds social space reveals woman as the hidden victim and sacrifice as the manner of hiding. Under eucharistic sacrifice is hidden another sacrifice: the sacrifice of woman. This, in turn, prompts Irigaray to ask, "*Could it be that the sacrifice of natural fertility is the original sacrifice?*" (FSA 95/WSM 80). Anticipating Nancy Jay's argument in *Throughout Your Generations Forever: Sacrifice, Religion, and Paternity* (1992) that sacrifice is a remedy for having been born of woman, Irigaray seems to be contrasting the natural fertility of woman with the socially constructed fertility of a male sacrificial culture, "a system of values that prizes sacrifice above all" (FSA 99/WSM 85; see Wolff and Resnick's *Economics: Marxian versus Neoclassical*, 244–253). This sacrifice of the natural fertility of woman leads to an economic superstructure that has no respect for the infrastructure of natural fertility. The currency of this economic superstructure is an "unsecured" currency insofar as sacrificial cultures perpetuate the unconsidered destruction of the only guarantees of exchange value: the products of the natural fertility of the earth and their possible reproduction (FSA 95/WSM 80–81). "Under the sacrifice of animal or human is hidden the sacrifice of the plant and the disappearance of the goddesses of natural fertility" (FSA 95/WSM 81). Recall that, according to Irigaray's interpretation of the Eucharist, it is not animals but fruits of the earth (bread and wine) that are blessed and sanctified by Jesus, and it is the gift of these blessed and sanctified fruits of the natural fertility of the earth that inaugurates a new way of sharing with the divine.

Another aspect of this hidden sacrifice of woman is the lack of recognition that the infrastructure of natural fertility functions for free. "No social body can be constituted, developed, or renewed without female labor [*travail*]" (FSA 100/ WSM 86), that is, without the labor of work and the labor of giving birth. This failure to recognize (this hiding of) the sacrifice of woman establishes the sacrificial rite or rhythm, which "overlays the natural rhythms with a different and *cumulative* temporality that dispenses and prevents us from attending to the moment" (FSA 91/WSM 77).

What is called for? To reveal the hidden sacrifice of woman. "To reveal that murder has been committed means not killing but rather putting an end to the hidden crime, aggression, and sacrifice" (FSA 101–102/WSM 87). This revelation would involve the acknowledgment of a crime. To acknowledge to someone that one is a criminal is a way to make one conscious of the self and to allow the other to be. This changes the economy of consciousness insofar as the master, or masters, are doubled into two sexes (at least). "What is sacrificed," Irigaray writes, "is henceforward the all-powerfulness of both one and the other" (FSA 102/WSM 87). There is here (paradoxically) a doubling of the masters of the economy of consciousness.

This revelation of the hidden sacrifice of woman (and, more specifically, the hidden sacrifice of natural fertility) may seem relatively straightforward, but Irigaray is, I would argue, inviting the reader to radically rethink his or her understanding of these all-too-easily understood words: revelation, sacrifice, and woman. I would argue that read alongside the logic of Lacanian psychoanalysis (and Žižek's reading of the work of Lacan), one can see that Irigaray returns these words to the reader in a way that opens up a different understanding of each of them. One could say that Irigaray disturbs the traditional discourses on revelation, sacrifice, and woman on one level while at the same time reinforcing their most extreme ramifications.

The revelation of the hidden sacrifice of woman calls (paradoxically) for a sacrifice. "What is sacrificed," Irigaray writes, "is henceforward the all-powerfulness of both one and the other" (FSA 102/WSM 87). The revelation of the hidden sacrifice of woman would, therefore, ultimately involve a *new* sacrifice.

> This new sacrifice opens things up whereas the old immolation habitually led to the creation of a *closed* world through *periodic exclusion* [i.e., through periodic hiding of the sacrifice of woman]. This new sacrifice, if sacrifice it be rather than a discipline, means that the individual or the social body gives up narcissistic self-sufficiency. (FSA 102/WSM 87)

This new sacrifice is a recognition that rather than being closed off, we are always already open to the other. This new sacrifice *"means recognizing that we are still and have always been open to the world and to the other because we are living, sensible beings, subject to the rhythms of time and of a universe whose properties are in part our own, different according to whether we are men or women"* (FSA 102/WSM 87). Is this new sacrifice the sacrifice *of* the revealed sacrifice of man that hides the sacrifice of woman? That is, is this new sacrifice the sacrifice of sacrifice? This seems to be an acknowledgment of the impossibility of merely stepping beyond sacrifice. It seems to be an acknowledgment of the step/not beyond sacrifice. What would this sacrifice of sacrifice give one to think about revelation, sacrifice, and woman?

The Risk of Belief

In "Belief Itself," Irigaray addresses not only what this sacrifice of sacrifice gives one to think about revelation, sacrifice, and woman, but also the fine risks associated with this sacrifice of sacrifice. In the essay, Irigaray relates a woman's message that came her way by way of the postal service: "At the point in the mass when they, the (spiritual) father and son, are reciting together the ritual words of the consecration, saying, 'This is my body, this is my blood,' I bleed" (CM 38/BI 25–26). Irigaray adds that the (spiritual) father and the son (the priest who performs the eucharistic sacrifice) celebrate the Eucharist together *in her absence*. They then distribute the consecrated bread and wine to the congregation to complete the communion service. The woman makes the connection between the ritual words of the consecration and her bleeding only after the fact. Though the woman is not alien to that aspect of the divine that finds an impoverished form in the celebration of this eucharistic sacrifice, she does not accept the men's current forms of belief. But, she adds (elliptically) that she loves the son.

Žižek and Safe Belief

Belief is safe, Irigaray argues, when "a sacrifice of a different body and flesh is made"; different, that is, from the body and flesh of Jesus sacrificed in the Eucharist. Belief is safe when it stands for confidence and loyalty, when it succeeds in making the other the other *of the same*, rather than giving up narcissistic self-sufficiency and being open to the other. Belief is safe when it makes one "forget the real" (CM 38/BI 26).

The Real, for Lacan, is the maternal Thing (*das Ding*), the incestuous object of enjoyment (*jouissance*). According to what Žižek calls the predominant reading of Lacanian psychoanalytic theory, the emergence of the subject into the symbolic order involves the primordial sacrifice of the maternal Thing. Lacan, drawing upon Hegel, writes, "[T]he symbol manifests itself first of all as the murder of the thing" (E 319/ES 104). The separation from the mother and the perception of lack (*manque*) is at once the constitution of the subject *as* want(ing)-to-be (*manque à être*) and the irruption of desire (of the incestuous Thing embodied initially in the mother). The subject finds its identity in a place where "it" is not, that is, *in* the symbolic Other. The subject emerges as alienated in/by the symbolic order; the subject, according to Lacan, is barred by language, alienated in/by the symbolic order, castrated (= alienated): hence Lacan's use of the matheme $ ("S" for subject, "/" for barred). The subject "is" as subordination to the Father's *prohibition* against the incestuous desire of the mother and the identification with the Father's *name* (the Law, the symbolic order). With this subordination to the authority of the No/Name of the Father (Lacan plays on the homophony of le "*non*" *du père* and le *nom du père*), the subject gives ground relative to his or her desire and thus contracts a guilt constitutive of the subject, for as Lacan writes in *The Ethics of Psychoanalysis* (1986; lectures delivered 1959–1960), "the only thing of which one can be guilty is of having given ground relative to one's desire" (EdP 368/EoP 319). One lives this alienation by striving (impossibly) to live up to an ideal (e.g., God). One lives this alienation by sacrificing for a cause (e.g., appeasing God and/or achieving salvation) in which one believes. This cause in which one believes gives "meaning" to the Law (the symbolic order) at the same time as it is the primordial sacrifice of the mother.

Žižek writes that belief involves being led along by the Law (without acknowledging its non-sensical character). One believes there is a "meaning" to the Law. One believes that it makes sense. The dead, senseless letter of the Law (i.e., the symbolic network, the unconscious) leads one unconsciously. In the following passage from *Pensées* (1670), Žižek argues that Pascal produces the very Lacanian definition of the unconscious: "For we must make no mistake about ourselves: we are as much automaton as mind. [. . .] Proofs only convince the mind; habit provides the strongest proofs and those that are most *believed*. It inclines the automaton, which leads the mind unconsciously along with it" (Pf 1219/Pe 274, emphasis added). Belief is being led along unconsciously; that is, it is being caught in the symbolic network. It is the lack of acknowledgment of its non-sensical, traumatic character.

> [F]or the Law to function "normally," [the] traumatic fact that "custom is the whole of equity for the sole reason that it is accepted" [which is "the mystic basis of its authority"; Pf 1150/Pe 46; see Derrida's "Force of Law: The 'Mystical Foundation of Authority' "]—the dependence of the Law on its process of enunciation or, to use a concept developed by Laclau and Mouffe, its radically *contingent* character—must be repressed into the unconscious, through the ideological, imaginary experience of the "meaning" of the Law, of its foundation in Justice, Truth (or, in a more modern way, functionality). (SOI 37–38)

For Law to function "normally," its non-sensical, traumatic character must be repressed. To be more precise, one must (in the words of Irigaray) "forget the real." The mother, the incestuous object of enjoyment, must be sacrificed. Safe belief is predicated on the sacrifice of the mother. Recall that Irigaray argues that belief in the sacrifice of the Eucharist is safe when it is accompanied by *another* sacrifice. Yet, Irigaray adds, this *other* sacrifice must be repressed. "[N]o one must ever see that, by means of the male twosome [i.e., the spiritual father and the priest son], *it is she who is being offered in partial oblation,* she who manages the communion between them and among the other men and women present" (CM 39/BI 26, emphasis added). Belief is safe only if the one in whom the community communes is hidden or subject to concealment. Safe belief serves to hide the sacrifice of woman, which sustains our cultural economy as a sacrificial economy (that is, an economy in which one lives alienation in/by the symbolic order by sacrificing for a cause in which one believes). Once this is revealed, according to Irigaray, there is no need to believe, at least insofar as it is usually understood: safe, standing for confidence and loyalty, for forgetting the real, and appropriating the other by making the other the other *of the same* (CM 38–39/BI 26).

Derrida, Freud, Lacan, and the Work of Mourning

Irigaray relates that she associated or joined (initially, without any interpretation) this woman's message that came her way by way of the postal service with Derrida's reading in *The Post Card: From Socrates to Freud and beyond* (1980) of the *fort-da* game of little Ernst as recorded in Freud's *Beyond the Pleasure Principle* (1920). The *fort-da* game is a game about gaining some sort of mastery over loss; specifically, it seeks to *master* rather than *mourn* the loss of the mother. As such, this mastery is integral to safe belief, insofar as it serves to merely *hide* the mother. Safe belief displaces the work of mourning.

Ernst, a good little boy greatly attached to his mother, had a wooden spool with a piece of string tied around it. He would very skillfully throw it onto a veiled bed so that it disappeared. Its disappearance was accompanied by a loud, long-drawn-out "o-o-o-o" accompanied by an expression of interest and satisfaction, which (according to Freud) represented the German word *fort* (gone, far-away). The reappearance of the wooden spool from "out of the bed" (effected by pulling on the string) was accompanied by a joyful *da* (there). This was the complete game: disappearance and return. Freud interprets the *fort-da* game as "related to the child's great cultural achievement—the instinctual renunciation (that is, the renunciation of instinctual satisfaction) which he had made in allowing his mother to go away without protesting" (JL 13/BPP 15). Freud argues that the child's efforts may be put down to "an instinct for mastery." Freud then connects this instinct for mastery associated with the *fort-da* game with the way Ernst handles his mother's death: "Now that she was really 'gone' ('o-o-o'), the little boy showed no signs of grief" (JL 14n1/BPP 16n1). It was as if the work of mourning his mother was displaced by the mastery associated with the *fort-da* game. The *fort-da* game seeks to master rather than mourn the loss of the mother. The *fort-da* game, by means of which Ernst believes that he can master her appearance-disappearance, will, according to Irigaray, undermine his language of beliefs. Once he believes he can master her appearance-disappearance, he is, according to Irigaray, most slave to his (safe) belief in his power and in the presence of his mother even when she is absent (CM 44/BI 31). Safe belief displaces the work of mourning.

Derrida brings to the reader's attention what Freud does not: the veil (with all of its sexual connotations). He refers to it as "the *hymen* of the *fort:da*" (CP 337/PC 316). But Derrida does not pursue this line of inquiry, merely remarking that he has "neither the time nor the taste for this task, which can be accomplished by itself or done without" (CP 330/PC 309). Irigaray, however, follows through on the task. The veil lies at the margin of a "loss" more primordial than either the temporary absence of the mother or permanent absence of the mother through death. It lies at the margin of the mother('s body). Recall that according to what Žižek calls the predominant reading of Lacanian psychoanalytic theory, the emergence into the symbolic order involves the primordial sacrifice (or renunciation) of the maternal Thing. According to Žižek, however, this is a misreading of Lacanian psychoanalytic theory. Recall that one lives alienation in/by the symbolic order by sacrificing for a cause (e.g., appeasing God and/or achieving salvation) in which one believes. This cause gives "meaning" to the Law (the symbolic order) at the same time as it is the primordial sacrifice of the mother. In this scene (from the perspective of the economy of the No/Name of the Father, the Law), both God and woman are fantasized as substantial alien Entities not immediately present in their givenness; they are, rather, "given" as lost. What distinguishes the two in this (patriarchal) fantasy is that the sacrifice *for* God is at the same time the sacrifice *of* woman. What is called for is the sacrifice of *this* sacrifice, which is a "going through the fantasy" (of God and woman, both understood as substantial alien Entities).

"Going through the fantasy," which is equivalent to the act of "subjective destitution," exculpates one from the guilt that constitutes the subject. Exculpating oneself from constitutive guilt involves, therefore, not sacrifice for a cause (which is a sacrifice within the symbolic order, governed by the economy of the No/Name of the Father, the Law), but the sacrifice of *this* sacrifice. This sacrifice of sacrifice, this repetition of sacrifice, involves not *alienation* in/by, but rather *separation* from, the symbolic order.

"Going through the fantasy," according to Žižek, produces (i.e., is the effectuation of the being of *and* the revelation of) the "true meaning" (or essence) of something. According to Žižek, the "true meaning" (or essence) of something—such as God the Father or woman (understood as "one of the names of the father"; IR 156–157)—is produced "after the fact" through a structurally necessary *delay*. One achieves the "true meaning" of something when one experiences this delay as the "essence" of the essence, the immanent interruption of the essence. One achieves the "true meaning" of something when one recognizes that what initially appears as an *impediment* to one's access to Truth is a *condition* of one's access to Truth (SOI 214). It is achieved with the vertiginous experience that Truth coincides with the path toward Truth (FTK 100). It is achieved with the vertiginous experience that the Truth is not given in advance and then appears, is rather *produced* in the advance toward Truth (FTK 171). The Truth is produced through the structurally necessary *misrecognition* of Truth, that is, through the structurally necessary illusion characteristic of what in psychoanalytic theory is called transference (the supposition of Truth behind the appearance) or *subjet supposé savoir* ("the subject supposed to know") (SOI 57, FTK 171). "The Truth arises from misrecognition" (Lacan; SOI 57). Recall that the substantial alien Entity (be it God or woman) is not immediately present in its givenness; it is, rather, "given" as lost. This deceives one into thinking that in the process of knowledge, one will discover some substantial-immediate otherness (some alien Entity) that was once immediately present. But, according to Žižek, the crucial insight occurs when one experiences that the substantial alien Entity only *comes to be* through being *left behind*; that is, its emergence coincides with its loss (FTK 167). The substantial alien Entity emerges, it comes to be what it is (i.e., its "essence" is "discovered"), only through being left behind, insofar as it is experienced that the loss of the givenness of the alien Entity "is" the "alien Entity"; that is, all the alien Entity "is" is loss. Or, said otherwise, the return to the immediacy *creates what it returns to* (IR 52), insofar as it is experienced that what is returned to is not some kind of substantial external kernel given in advance (albeit as lost) and excluded from knowledge, but rather the experience that the loss of the givenness of the alien Entity "is" the "alien Entity"; that is, all the alien Entity "is" is loss. Therefore, "one's own work" of knowledge is experienced ("after the fact," i.e., after the working of knowledge) as creating what is returned to. One experiences that there is no substantial alien Entity excluded from knowledge. All the mother('s body) "is" is loss.

The *fort-da* game seeks to master rather than mourn this primordial "loss" of the mother('s body). It *masters* the primordial "loss" of the mother('s body) by conceiving it as a substantial alien Entity excluded from knowledge, but potentially available. What would it mean to *mourn* the primordial "loss" of the mother('s body)? Since the work of Freud (and Abraham and Torok), the normal work of mourning is described as an interiorization of the other, an attempt to keep the other in me, in memory. But mourning is an unfaithful fidelity in that, according to Derrida's "Mnemosyne" from *Memoires for Paul de Man* (1986), mourning is where "*success fails*" and "*failure succeeds*" (Mf 54/Me 35). What does this mean? Faithful interiorization is unfaithful in that it effaces the radical otherness of the other; that is, it masters the other by making the other the other *of the same.* Unfaithful interiorization is faithful in that it respects the radical otherness of the other. This is what Derrida calls "ex-appropriation," that is, appropriation caught in a double bind (P 321). In mourning one is "obliged to harbor something that is greater and other" than oneself (Mf 54/Me 34). In *Aporias: Dying—Awaiting (One Another at) the "Limits of Truth"* (1994), Derrida argues that the self of *Jemeinigkeit*, like mourning, is structured by the irreducible ambiguity of the "death of the other" being both inside and outside "me" (AM 336/AD 76). "If *Jemeinigkeit*, that of *Dasein* or that of the ego (in the common sense, the psychoanalytic sense, or Levinas's sense) is constituted in its ipseity in terms of an originary mourning, then this self-relation welcomes or supposes the other within its being-itself as different from itself. And reciprocally: the relation to the other (in itself outside myself, outside myself in myself) will never be distinguishable from a bereaved apprehension" (AM 331/AD 61). Here one sees an ex-appropriation not unlike Lacan's description of *objet petit a.* A sublime object (*objet petit a*) is an ordinary everyday object "elevated to the level of *das Ding*" (SOI 194). For Lacan, *objet petit a* is that strange object that is radically interior and at the same time radically exterior. It is that strange object that is "in me more than me" (SOI 76–79, 95). It is in me as that which breaks me up (compare with Levinas's reading of the idea of the infinite in "God and Philosophy"). What would it mean to *mourn* the primordial "loss" of the mother('s body)? I would argue that it would mean the new sacrifice referred to by Irigaray in "Women, the Sacred, Money." It would mean the sacrifice *of* the revealed sacrifice of man that hides (and, therefore, masters) the sacrifice of woman. This sacrifice of sacrifice would be the (momentary) ex-appropriation of woman('s body) as *objet petit a.*

The Hidden Victim of Sacrifice: Woman('s Body)

Ernst's mother is, according to Irigaray, mastered or appropriated rather than mourned. With respect to the *fort-da* game, Irigaray asks, "Does she [i.e., Ernst's mother] stay the same once she has been thrown away, put at a distance, pulled back, brought near, in this way?" (CM 49/BI 37). Irigaray answers, "No." On her return, Ernst has appropriated her to his, or their—the men's—*own* language. On her return, she is mastered rather than mourned. Ernst only has to call her back and she will be re-present(ed) to him. Like safe belief that displaces the work of mourning (and to which Ernst is enslaved), the *fort-da* game is merely an appropriation of the other by making the other the other *of the same.* "This protects him from disappearing into her. This return annihilates that other return that might swallow him up, take him back into that first dwelling place inside her" (CM 49/BI 37). Like safe belief, the *fort-da* game protects him from the (patriarchal) fantasy of the mother('s body) understood as a substantial alien En-tity. What is this "other return" that might appropriate him? What is this "other return" that is annihilated by the *fort-da* game? What is this "other return" that is sacrificed by safe belief? This "other return" is, I would argue, a "going through the fantasy," which is equivalent to the act of "subjective destitution." This "other return" is the sacrifice of sacrifice, which produces (i.e., is the effectuation of the being of and the revelation of) the "true meaning" of the mother('s body). This return creates what it returns to (IR 52), insofar as it is experienced that what is returned to is not some kind of substantial external kernel given in ad-vance (albeit as lost) and excluded from knowledge, but rather the experience that the loss of the givenness of the mother('s body) "is" the mother('s body); that is, all the mother('s body) "is" is loss. The mother('s body) is nothing that can be presented in language.

> Thus the body that gives life never enters into language. Ernst, the son, *believes* perhaps that, in his first language game, he holds his mother. She has no place there. She subsists *before* language as the woman who gives her flesh and her blood, and *beyond* language as she who is stripped of a matrix/womb, a veil, an enclosure or a clearing in which she might live according to the horizon of her games, symbolizations, representations. She remains the elemental sub-strate of life, existing before all forms, all limit, all skin, and of heaven, visible beyond-horizon. (CM 58/BI 46, emphasis added)

Both the *fort-da* game and safe belief sacrifice the mother('s body) that is the substrate of life, that is, sacrifice the mother('s body) understood as "loss," as what cannot be presented in language. It is important to point out that this "body" that is the substrate of life is not the essence of woman (though it is perceived that way from the perspective of the economy of the No/Name of the Father, the Law). As existing before and beyond language, before all forms, before all limit, before all skin, it "is" only *as* return, only *as* approach. Following Žižek's reading, the mother('s body) is not a substantial alien Entity that is the essence of woman. It "is," rather, nothing but loss.

At this point in the essay, Irigaray explicitly joins the message of the woman who (absent from the celebration of the Eucharist) bleeds during the ritual words of the consecration with the *fort-da* game of little Ernst. She begins the passage by writing, "Both of them bleeding, the one openly, the other secretly" (CM 58/ BI 46). Both of them—both the son (which includes both Jesus and Ernst) and the woman—bleeding, the one (man) openly, the other (woman) secretly. The sacrifice of woman('s body) is hidden.

> Both of them bleeding, the one openly, the other secretly, but he and she remain bound to their functions as son and mother. Yet he puts her at a distance, seeking the society of the father [which includes both God the Father and Ernst's father]. Together he and the father organize the world, bless the fruits of the earth, identify them with their body and blood, and in this way effect the communion between the units of the people that have been neutered, at least apparently. (CM 58/BI 46)

This eucharistic celebration (reduced to the sacrificial element by identifying the fruits of the earth with the male body and blood) effects a communion between units of people that have been neutered insofar as the singularity of woman is hidden. The sacrifice of woman('s body) is hidden.

> No one must see that it is they, the wives and mothers, who are being offered up in communion here, who effect the communion, that, like the earth and its fruits, it is the body and the blood especially of virgin women that are being sacrificed to that intermale society. The duty to bear children, to be silent, to be in attendance but off on the side—all this wounds the flesh and the spirit of women, and there is no representation of that sacrifice. In fact, it is doubled in the duty women have to believe and to be practicing believers. Dogmas and rites appear as substitutions and veils that hide the fact that women's carnal and spiritual virginity is being sacrificed and traded. The sons are separated from their mothers and from the women who love them out of duty to their Fathers. (CM 58–59/BI 46–47)

The lack of representation of the sacrifice of woman('s body) is doubled: not only is the sacrifice of woman('s body) hidden, but insofar as woman has a duty to believe, she participates in the *hiding* of that hidden sacrifice.

Both the *fort-da* game and safe belief sacrifice the woman('s body) that is the substrate of life. The revelation of this body calls for the sacrifice of this sacrifice. The sacrifice of sacrifice produces (i.e., is the effectuation of the being of *and* the revelation of) woman('s body). But the necessary sacrifice of sacrifice that reveals woman('s body) returns all of these words—sacrifice, revelation, and woman—to the reader in a way that opens up a different understanding of each of them. As argued earlier, one could say that Irigaray disturbs the traditional discourses on revelation, sacrifice, and woman on one level while at the same time reinforcing their most extreme ramifications. Referring to woman('s body) — the elemental substrate of life that is the suspension of all meaning — from which the son separated and from whose return he protects himself by safe belief, Irigaray writes:

> This suspension of all meaning unveils the commerce that underlies meaning, and risks going back to a time when separation had not yet occurred, when there was as yet no attempt to rate this as more valuable than that. In this opacity, this night of the world, they discover the trace of vanished gods [see CM 61/BI 49], at the very point when they have given up their safety. Light shines on them once they have agreed that nothing shall ensure their protection, not even that age-old citadel of man — being [être] — not even that guarantor of the meaning or nonmeaning of the world — God.
>
> These prophets know that if anything divine is still to come our way it will be won by abandoning all control, all language, and all sense already produced, it is through risk, only risk, leading no one knows where, announcing who knows what future, secretly commemorating who knows what past. No project here. Only this refusal to refuse what has been perceived, whatever distress or wretchedness may come of it. (CM 64–65/BI 52–53)

How does the necessary sacrifice of sacrifice that produces woman('s body) return the words sacrifice, revelation, and woman to the reader in a way that interrupts a traditional understanding of these all-too-easily understood words?

Sacrifice traditionally has been interpreted in economic terms. It has been primarily understood as a passage through suffering and/or death that effects the revelation of truth. One gets a return on one's investment of suffering and/or death. It is a project with an expected result. Recall that one lives alienation in/by the symbolic order by sacrificing for a cause, which gives "meaning" to the Law (the symbolic order) at the same time as it is the primordial sacrifice of the mother. In this scene (from the perspective of the economy of the No/Name of the Father, the Law), both God and woman are fantasized as substantial alien Entities. What distinguishes the two in this (patriarchal) fantasy is that the sacrifice for God is at the same time the sacrifice of woman. What is called for is the sacrifice of this sacrifice. There is, as Irigaray writes, "no project here" because this new sacrifice — the sacrifice mentioned by Irigaray in "Women, the Sacred, Money," which I argue is the sacrifice of sacrifice — is both *necessary* and *useless*. With this new sacrifice, the truth is eternally postponed (there is "no project here" with an expected result) in a necessary sacrificial gesture (necessary in that the sacrifice of woman is to be sacrificed) that can only sacrifice itself, thereby rendering itself useless. With this new sacrifice, the truth is nothing but "still to come" (CM 65/BI 53). In fact, one could argue that for any sacrifice to genuinely be a sacrifice it has to be *an*economical. It has to sacrifice an economical understanding of itself. It has to be beyond calculation and expectation of a result, lest it be construed as self-serving.

Revelation traditionally has been interpreted in visual or epistemological terms. To reveal is to open up a view or to make something known (e.g., "I see what you mean"). To reveal is to make something present, either to the body's eye or the mind's eye. Though in the scene of primordial sacrifice both God and woman are fantasized as substantial alien Entities not immediately present, (patriarchal) fantasy expects the possibility of revelation. It supposes that God and woman exist (though hidden), waiting to be revealed. But the sacrifice of sacrifice is, as Irigaray writes, no traditional revelation. It is the "night of the world" that is the "suspension of all meaning." The sacrifice of sacrifice is a "going through the fantasy" (of God and woman, both understood as substantial alien Entities). This "night of the world" is also not unlike the separation from (rather than alienation in/by) the symbolic order. Irigaray writes that at the very moment of the suspension of all meaning—in this "night of the world"—one discovers "the trace of vanished gods." This proximity of the "night of the world" and the death of the divine is likewise established by Žižek with respect to the death of God described in Hegel's *Phenomenology of Spirit* (1807). Describing the separation from the symbolic order, Žižek writes:

> [T]he "death of God" involves the loss of the consistent "terrestrial" reality itself. [. . .] [T]he "death of God" is more akin to what the great texts of mysticism usually designate as the "night of the world": the dissolution of (symbolically constituted) reality.
>
> In Lacanian terms, we are dealing with the suspension of the big Other, which guarantees the subject's access to reality: in the experience of the death of God, we stumble upon the fact that "the big Other doesn't exist [*l'Autre n'existe pas*]" (Lacan). (ME 42)

This "night of the world" (or sacrifice of sacrifice) is a "going through the fantasy" (of God and woman). What is revealed is not the unambiguous appearance of something. What is revealed is not something that unambiguously appears, but rather what infinitely approaches (or withdraws from) revelation and merely leaves a trace of itself in an irreducible ambiguity. With this new sacrifice, the revelation of truth is nothing but "still to come."

Without neglecting the essential differences, the "night of the world" referred to by both Irigaray and Žižek is, if only for a moment, not unlike Levinas's description of the *il y a* in *Existence and Existents* (1947).

> When the forms of things are dissolved in the night, the darkness of the night, which is neither an object nor the quality of an object, invades like a presence. In the night, where we are riven to it, we are not dealing with anything. [. . .] What we call the I is itself submerged by the night, invaded, depersonalized, stifled by it. The disappearance of all things and of the I leaves what cannot disappear, the sheer fact of being in which *one* participates, whether one wants to or not, without having taken the initiative, anonymously. (DEE 94–95/EE 58)

This "night of the world" that is a risk leading one knows not where is not unlike the "not yet" in the work of Levinas. This not yet is dead time, which is articulated by the irreducibly paradoxical body. The body, as the site of the relationship with the other (*autre/Autrui*), is the site of enjoyment, the by-the-other (or non-sense), and the for-the-other (or sense). The non-sense of the *il y a* (AE 208/ OB 163) is a *modality* of the for-the-other (AE 208–209/OB 164). The suffering "for-the-other" is necessarily, yet impossibly, a suffering *for nothing*, non-sense. There is, as Irigaray writes, "[n]o project here." As such, it involves, as Irigaray writes, "risk, only risk, leading no one knows where, announcing who knows what future, secretly commemorating who knows what past." Levinas writes, "Of itself saying is the sense [*sens*] of patience and pain. In saying suffering signifies in the form of *giving*, even if the price of signification is that the subject run the risk [*courait le risque*] of suffering without reason. If the subject did not run this risk [*ne courait pas ce risque*], pain would lose its very painfulness" (AE 64/OB 50). If the subject did not run this risk, then the irreducible ambiguity of pain would become a virtuous suffering, a self-edifying suffering. With this self-edifying suffering, being for-the-other becomes for-oneself, and the pain of the aporia of sacrifice loses its very painfulness.

Recall that prior to this brief digression into the work of Levinas, three words—sacrifice, revelation, and woman—were being considered. It was asked: How does the necessary sacrifice of sacrifice that produces woman('s body) return the words sacrifice, revelation, and woman to the reader in a way that interrupts a traditional understanding of these all-too-easily understood words? Two of the three have been considered. The third remains.

Woman traditionally has been interpreted in essentialist terms. But one must be careful not to hypostatize woman as she is given to be understood by Irigaray. Recall that from the perspective of the economy of the No/Name of the Father, woman is fantasized as a substantial alien Entity not immediately present in her givenness; she is, rather, "given" as lost. But the sacrifice of sacrifice returns the word to the reader in a way that interrupts the traditional understanding of woman governed by the economy of the No/Name of the Father. Woman is not a substantial alien Entity that first exists and then reveals itself. Woman is nothing other than the exceeding of limits. This obviously echoes Lacan's controversial formula "Woman does not exist [*la femme n'existe pas*]." Žižek points out that "it is not that 'Woman doesn't exist' because, on account of patriarchal 'repression,' she is not allowed to express herself freely and constitute her full symbolic identity, but, rather, the other way around—patriarchal symbolic authority emerges in order to 'gentrify' the scandal of 'Woman doesn't exist,' to constrain the feminine subject to a determinate place in the symbolic structure" (IR 165). With emergence into symbolic order, the sacrifice of sacrifice—which produces (i.e., is the effectuation of the being of and the revelation of) woman('s body)—is gentrified into the sacrifice of woman('s body) understood as a substantial alien Entity of (patriarchal) fantasy. With regard to Lacan's "formulas of sexuation" in general, Žižek writes that "in Lacan, 'masculine' or 'feminine' is not a predicate providing positive information about the subject—that is, designating some of its phenomenal properties; rather, it is a case of what Kant conceives of as a purely negative determination which merely designates, registers, a certain limit—more precisely: a specific modality of how the subject failed in his or her bid for identity which would constitute him or her as an object within phenomenal reality" (ME 159). Following Žižek's reading, the mother('s body) is not a substantial alien Entity that is the essence of woman. It "is," rather, nothing but loss.

The *New* Sacrifice and the Risk of Belief

This point in the essay "Belief Itself"—this night of the world that is a risk leading no one knows where, announcing who knows what future, secretly commemorating who knows what past—is, I would argue, instructive for understanding what Irigaray referred to as the new sacrifice in "Women, the Sacred, Money." Recall that Irigaray states that this new sacrifice is a recognition that rather than being closed off, we are always already open to the other. This new sacrifice is, I would argue, the sacrifice of sacrifice. This new sacrifice is the sacrifice *of* the revealed sacrifice of man that hides the sacrifice of woman. The sacrifice of the sacrifice of woman reveals woman('s body) not as a substantial alien Entity— that is, not as a substantial alien Entity sacrificed/gentrified with the emergence of the patriarchal symbolic authority—but as the elemental substrate of life that never enters into language. What is revealed is woman('s body) as nothing but "still to come" (CM 65/BI 53). This new sacrifice involves risks. This risk is "belief *itself*" rather than the safe belief that succeeds in making the other the other *of the same*. The revealed sacrifice of man hides (and, therefore, masters) the sacrifice of woman. Safe belief displaces the work of mourning. Rather than a mastering of the primordial "loss" of woman('s body), belief itself is a mourning of the primordial "loss" of woman('s body). What would it mean to mourn the primordial "loss" of woman('s body)? It would mean the sacrifice *of* the revealed sacrifice of man that hides (and, therefore, masters) the sacrifice of woman. This sacrifice of sacrifice would be the momentary ex-appropriation of woman('s body) as *objet petit a*: "in me more than me." Belief itself is the "true meaning" (or essence) of belief that undermines the language of safe belief. There is no project here because this new sacrifice, which I argue is the sacrifice of sacrifice, is both necessary and useless. With this new sacrifice the truth is "still to come" (CM 65/BI 53). This new sacrifice, this sacrifice of sacrifice, "this refusal to refuse what has been perceived, whatever distress or wretchedness may come of it" (CM 65/BI 53), is the unworking of the work of sacrifice.

One is called, I would argue, not to relegate the category of "sacrifice" to the status of a contemporary anachronism, but to use the resources of this idea to interrupt the economics, epistemology, and sexism, characteristic of the traditional interpretation of sacrifice, and momentarily open it to other possibilities. What is called for is not retrieving what the tradition merely overlooked, such as an idyllic presacrificial time. What is called for is "going through" the tradition to retrieve what the tradition could only have overlooked, and which even now only reveals itself in an irreducibly ambiguous way.

The Question of Sacrifice

"Going through" the tradition will involve understanding the liturgy of the sacrifice *of* the Eucharist according to both senses of the genitive: the (economical) sacrifice that is a constitutive element of the liturgy of the Eucharist, and the sacrifice of this (economical) sacrifice, which interrupts sacrifice *in the very "doing" of the action.* This "new" sacrifice, this sacrifice of sacrifice (which is an interruption of the "work" of sacrifice), is an interruption of the (patriarchal) fantasy of God and woman, both understood as substantial alien Entities. "Going through" the tradition is "going through the fantasy." "Going through" the tradition—which is an interruption of the "work" of the sacrifice *of* the Eucharist—also reveals the necessary possibility that the Roman Rite is "impossible," that is, that it is not the sole appropriate form of liturgy. If it is structured by the "logic" of the sacrifice of sacrifice, then it necessarily has to be open to the possibility of its being called into question, of its being sacrificed. This will disturb this sacrifice on one level while at the same time reinforcing its most extreme ramifications.

7

Lacan/Žižek

The Repetition of the Sacrifice of the Sacrifice as an Ethical Act

For Lacan (as well as Kristeva and Irigaray), the status of the human being as a "being of language" is defined by a primordial sacrifice. According to what Žižek calls the predominant reading of Lacanian psychoanalytic theory, the emergence of the subject into the symbolic order involves "symbolic castration"; that is, it involves *the loss of the Real*, a primordial sacrifice of the Thing (*das Ding*), which is the incestuous Object of impossible/unattainable enjoyment (*jouissance*). As subjects of the symbolic order, subjects are characterized by constitutive and irreducible lack. Characterized as such, the subject is propelled by desire, a wanting-to-be reunited with the "lost" Thing, a wanting to come to rest in absolute *jouissance*. The aim of the psychoanalytic cure is the subject's heroic assumption of his or her constitutive lack, the endurance of the splitting that propels desire. But this reading of Lacanian psychoanalytic theory is a misreading. According to Žižek, the primordial sacrifice of the Thing (*das Ding*) does *not* simply involve *the loss of the Real*. The Real does *not* simply withdraw into the realm of the "impossible/unattainable" with the emergence into the symbolic order. The Real (as drive) is, according to Žižek, the "driving force" of desiring (IR 97). As the "driving force" of desiring, the Real is *not* an impossible/unattainable alien Entity. It "is," rather, *nothing but* loss, *nothing but* radical negativity, *nothing but* radical sacrifice, *nothing but* the sacrifice of sacrifice (*nothing but* a surplus that is the condition of the possibility and the condition of the impossibility of the symbolic order). As such, the primordial sacrifice (which is the emergence into the symbolic order) is not an act of exchange that ultimately pays. The subject gets "nothing" in exchange (and also gives nothing; see Copjec's *Read My Desire: Lacan Against the Historicists*, 65–116). Said other-

The Question of Sacrifice

wise, this sacrifice (renunciation) is a "pure" negative gesture of withdrawal; it is the sacrifice of the sacrifice, which constitutes the space of economic exchange (EYS 75), that is, of a sacrifice that pays.

Hegel and the Triad of Positing, External, and Determinate Reflection

The theoretical space of the work of Žižek is molded by three centers of gravity: Hegelian dialectics, Lacanian psychoanalytic theory, and contemporary criticism of ideology. It is the work of Lacan, however, that is (according to Žižek, quoting Marx) "the general illumination which bathes all the other colours and modifies their particularity," "the particular ether which determines the specific gravity of every being which has materialized within it" (FTK 2). In *The Sublime Object of Ideology* (1989) and in *For They Know Not What They Do: Enjoyment as a Political Factor* (1991), Žižek finds the Hegelian triad of positing, external, and determinate reflection in *Science of Logic* (1812–1816; 2nd ed. 1832; WL vol. 11, 249–257/SL 399–408) to be especially helpful in negotiating these three centers of gravity. Specifically, his thesis is that what is constitutive of the Hegelian notion of the "absolute" subject is the redoubling of reflection characteristic of determinate reflection (the "negation of the negation," or the "sacrifice of the sacrifice") by means of which the subject presupposes *itself* as positing its own substantial presuppositions (SOI 215, 229).

The Hegelian triad of positing, external, and determinate reflection can be briefly described as follows: the premise of positing reflection is that every immediate content can be reduced to something posited; that is, every immediate content can be mediated. But when reflection recognizes that its *own* reflective activity is excluded from this reflective recuperation characteristic of positing reflection, it (mis)perceives its own reflective activity in a hypostatized form; it presupposes itself in the form of a substantial-immediate otherness given in advance and *excluded* from reflective recuperation (which is why reflection here is "external"). One achieves determinate reflection when one recognizes that the substantial-immediate otherness (of external reflection) that (positing) reflection futilely attempts to recuperate *coincides with reflective activity itself* (IR 51). The reflective-recuperative return to the immediacy *creates what it returns to* (IR 52). This brief description of the Hegelian triad of positing, external, and determinate reflection calls, however, for a more detailed elaboration.

Positing reflection is the activity of the essence (as the pure movement of mediation, of self-referential negativity; SOI 225) that *presupposes the unmediated world of appearance* in order to *posit*(-mediate-sublate) the appearance as "mere appearance" (it posits-mediates-sublates the given immediacy insofar as it is thought *as* "mere appearance").

External reflection is the activity of the essence that *presupposes itself as a substantial-immediate otherness,* as its "own" other in the form of something given in advance (*reflects **itself*** in the presuppositions/appearances *as* a substantial-immediate otherness). One achieves external reflection when the essence not only *presupposes an otherness* (as is the case in positing reflection), but also *presupposes **itself*** in the form of an otherness *excluded* from the movement of reflection (which is why reflection here is "external," i.e., external reflecting does *not* concern the essence as the pure movement of mediation) (SOI 225). *"This self-fissure of the essence means that the essence is 'subject' and not only 'substance'* " (SOI 226). Essence is "substance" insofar as it is reflected in appearance *as* an alien Entity, given in advance, and *excluded* from the movement of reflection. Essence is "subject" insofar as it is split so that it can experience *itself* as an alien Entity. One could say (paradoxically), Žižek adds, that "the subject is *substance precisely in so far as it experiences itself as substance* (as some alien, given, external, positive Entity existing in itself)" (SOI 226). For "subject" is nothing but "substance" at a certain distance from itself, nothing but this distance from which substance can experience itself as some alien Entity. This self-fissure of the essence opens up the space in which essence can *appear* as distinct from itself, in which it can *appear* as "mere appearance." External reflection shows that one only gets positing (or *simple*) reflection if the essence is *always already* internally fissured.

Determinate reflection is the activity of the essence that *presupposes **itself*** *as positing* (SOI 228), *reflects **itself*** in the (substantial-immediate) presupposition (of external reflection) *as* positing (SOI 229) that presupposition.

As soon as one passes from positing to external reflection, one experiences a *redoubled* reflection, that is, a *reflection* that designates the relationship **between** (1) positing (or "*simple*") reflection, in which the appearance reflects the essence, which (as the pure movement of mediation, of self-referential negativity) *presupposes the unmediated world of appearance* in order to *posit*(-mediate-sublate) the appearance as "mere appearance," **and** (2) the essence insofar as it *presupposes **itself*** (and is, therefore, internally fissured) as a substantial-immediate otherness *excluded* from the movement of reflection. Said otherwise, one passes from external to determinate (or *redoubled*) reflection when one experiences the relationship between (1) and (2) *as (itself) that of reflection.* One passes from external to determinate (or *redoubled*) reflection when one experiences the substantial-immediate otherness (i.e., the alien Entity, given in advance, and *excluded* from the movement of reflection) as *not excluded* from the movement of reflection. One passes from external to determinate (or *redoubled*) reflection when one experiences the *image* of the substantial-immediate otherness as *nothing but* the inverse-alienated reflection of essence *as* pure movement of mediation, of self-referential negativity (SOI 227–228). This *image* is the *way* self-referential negativity appears. This is the *form* of its appearance.

Reflection is here *redoubled* insofar as it not only reflects ***itself** in appearance* *as* an alien Entity, given in advance, and *excluded* from the movement of reflection (and is, therefore, internally fissured, which one experiences as always already necessary for the "mere appearance" characteristic of "*simple*" reflection), but it also reflects *itself in itself*, that is, reflects *itself as reflecting* (this is the *redoubled* reflection characteristic of determinate reflection). This reflection of *itself in itself* is an immediacy that is not "mere appearance," but rather *essence itself* (as the pure movement of mediation, of self-referential negativity) *in the form of its otherness, in the form of a phenomenon that* (paradoxically) *(dis)embodies the fact that there is nothing beyond phenomena.* Here the presupposition is *not* simply posited by the essence, as was the case with "*simple*" (or positing) reflection. Here, essence *presupposes itself as positing* (SOI 228), *reflects itself* in the (substantial-immediate) presupposition (of external reflection) *as* positing (SOI 229) that presupposition.

The basic feature of Hegelian reflection is the inherent necessity of its *re-doubling*. It is not only that the appearance (i.e., the fissure between appearance and essence) is a fissure internal to the essence, a fissure that one experiences as always already necessary for the "mere" appearance characteristic of "*simple*" reflection, it is that the fissure between appearance and essence is internal to the appearance itself. The fissure (i.e., the reflection of essence *itself in appearance* which one experiences as always already necessary for the "mere appearance" characteristic of "*simple*" reflection) is *reflected* in appearance itself. In other words, it is not only that the essence **must** appear (note: according to external reflection, the essence is reflected in appearance, articulates its "hidden" truth, *as* an alien Entity, given in advance, and *excluded* from the movement of reflection), it is that it **must** appear (paradoxically) *as essence in its difference to appearance, as essence itself in the form of a phenomenon that (dis)incarnates the nullity of phenomena as such* (SOI 214–215). Essence appears (paradoxically) as the (dis)incarnation of the fact that there is *nothing beyond* appearance. It appears (paradoxically) as an "image" *without* an original. This reflection of essence *in itself* is an immediacy that is not "mere appearance," but "appearance" *without* an essence, for the essence "is" *itself* (as self-fissured, as reflection) reflected back into "appearance" (FTK 15). Therefore, the "essence" of essence is (paradoxically) "appearance" without an essence. Said otherwise, negation is itself negated; sacrifice is itself sacrificed. Essence "is" *nothing but* redoubled reflection, *nothing but* radical negativity (SOI 206), *nothing but* radical sacrifice that cannot not be (dis)embodied in "appearance."

It is important to note that the relationship **between** "*simple*" (or positing) reflection, in which the appearance reflects the essence, which (as the pure movement of mediation, of self-referential negativity) *presupposes the unmediated world of appearance* in order to *posit*(-mediate-sublate) the appearance as "mere appearance," **and** *redoubled* (or determinate) reflection, is *not* that of a simple succession. The second reflection is the *condition* of the first. It is only the reflection of essence *itself in itself* that opens the space in which the "hidden" essence can reflect itself, i.e., can "appear" (SOI 228; see EYS 184–186). The condition of one's subjective freedom, of one's "positing" (one's "*simple*" reflection) is that it **must** *itself* be *reflected* **in advance** into the substance itself (i.e., into the presupposition of external reflection), as its own "reflexive determination." The substantial-immediate otherness posited/reflected by positing reflection (i.e., the "essence" of positing reflection, the condition of positing reflection, what positing reflection reflects) "is" discovered "after the fact" to be *nothing but* reflection of reflection, sacrifice of sacrifice. Essence (understood *as* reflection) had to come *"before" itself*; that is, there always already had to be a "reflection" (*"before"* . . .) of reflection (. . . *itself*). Paradoxically, there had to be a free act of positing "before" the free act of positing. Said otherwise, essence (understood *as* reflection) presupposes *itself* as positing/reflecting the presupposition (i.e., the substantial-immediate otherness), which is the "essence" of positing reflection, the condition of positing reflection, what positing reflection reflects. The "essence" of free positing is radical sacrifice (radical positing) rather than a substantial-immediate otherness excluded from positing. Therefore, what makes this "essence" *the condition of the possibility* of positing reflection is, at the same time, what makes it *the condition of the impossibility* of positing reflection (insofar as the substantial-immediate otherness is discovered "after the fact" to be *nothing but* the reflection of reflection or the sacrifice of sacrifice). The paradox of this negation of negation is (dis)incarnated in "appearance" as the condition of its (im)possibility. The phrases *"in advance"* and *"before itself"* announce a past that was never present. This calls for a more detailed elaboration.

In the process of knowledge, one does *not* discover some substantial-immediate otherness that is indifferent to one's knowing (i.e., *excluded* from reflection), as appears to be the case with external reflection. One discovers, by means of determinate reflection, that one's act of knowledge is included *in advance* in its substantial-immediate content (FTK 165). As was mentioned earlier, essence (as the pure movement of mediation, of self-referential negativity) *presupposes itself as positing* (SOI 228), *reflects itself* in the (substantial-immediate) presupposition (of external reflection) *as* positing (SOI 229) that presupposition. That is, one *presupposes* one's knowledge (one's knowledge is included *in advance*) in its substantial-immediate otherness. As Hegel puts it (writes Žižek), the path toward truth partakes in truth itself (FTK 165).

Hegel's crucial insight, according to Žižek, is *not* (as is commonly interpreted) that the dialectical movement begins with an initial immediacy, and then moves through the reflective mediation of this immediacy, ending up with the restored mediated immediacy of the result. The initial immediacy is always already "posited" (i.e., accepted as "one's own work") retroactively, so that its emergence *coincides with its loss* (FTK 167).

> Reflection therefore *finds before it* an immediate which it transcends and from which it is to return. But this return is only the presupposing of what reflection finds before it. What is thus found only *comes to be* through being *left behind*; its immediacy is sublated immediacy. (WL vol. 11, 252/SL 402)

The Question of Sacrifice

One recognizes that one's access to the initial immediacy is by means of external reflection. Recall that external reflection exercises its activity of reflection on *what it perceives* as a substantial-immediate otherness, that is, an alien Entity, given in advance, and indifferent to (or excluded from) external's reflection's activity of reflection. The problem is that external reflection's very activity of reflection entails the *loss* of the immediate presence of this alien Entity. External reflection deceives one into thinking that in the process of knowledge, one will discover some substantial-immediate otherness (some alien Entity) that was *once* immediately present, *prior to being lost, prior to being "left behind"* by external reflection's very activity of reflection. This inversion of external into determinate (absolute) reflection occurs when one experiences how the alien Entity in its pre-reflective *givenness* "only *comes to be* through being *left behind*" (WL vol. 11, 252/SL 402); that is, its emergence *coincides with its loss* (FTK 167). Or, said otherwise, the reflective-recuperative return to the immediacy *creates what it returns to* (IR 52), insofar as it is experienced that what is returned to is not some kind of external kernel given in advance (albeit *as lost*) and *excluded* from reflective recuperation, but rather the experience that the *loss* of the *givenness* of the alien Entity "is" the "alien Entity." Therefore, "one's own work" of external reflection is experienced as *creating* what is *returned to*. One experiences that there is no alien Entity excluded from reflection. The alien Entity returned to "is" *nothing but* radical negativity, *nothing but* radical sacrifice.

The inversion of external into determinate (absolute) reflection occurs when one experiences that there was *never* some alien Entity that was *once* immediately present, *prior to being lost, prior to being "left behind"* by external reflection's very activity of reflection since external reflection's very activity of reflection *produces* the retroactive deception that there was some alien Entity given in advance of its loss. Herein consists the Hegelian "negation of the negation," the "sacrifice of the sacrifice," the "loss of the loss": *not* in the reappropriation of the lost Entity in its immediate presence, but in the experience of how one *never* had what one was deceived into thinking one had lost, in the experience that *loss* in a way *precedes* what was perceived to be *lost*. In the inversion of external into determinate (absolute) reflection, *loss* is not abolished in the restored mediated immediacy of the result. It is only the *place* of *loss* that shifts; that is, it is not that the alien Entity is *lost* simply because of one's perspective (i.e., the perspective of external reflection), it is that one experiences the alien "Entity" (from the perspective of determinate reflection) as nothing but *loss* (FTK 168). There is here a simple shift of perspective (FTK 165).

Recall that the relationship **between** *"simple"* (or positing) reflection **and** *redoubled* (or determinate) reflection is *not* that of a simple succession. The second reflection is the *condition* of the first. The condition of one's subjective freedom, of one's "positing" (one's "simple" reflection) is that it **must** *itself* be *reflected* **in advance** into the substance itself (i.e., into the presupposition of external reflection), as its own "reflexive determination." The phrase *"in advance"* (as was mentioned earlier) announces a past that was never present. One recognizes (by means of a dialectical analysis) that *in the midst of one's positing* there was a "*reflection* of reflection" that **must** have taken place "before" one's positing. The subject's positing does not *come after* the substantial-immediate otherness given in advance and *excluded* from reflective recuperation; the subject's positing "*creates*" this otherness and, therefore, comes *in advance* of this otherness. In a first reading, one perceives the Truth as given in advance (*not* as the creation of a free act); in a second reading, one perceives one's free act as included *in advance* in this Truth (which, at the same time, entails the desubstantialization of this "Truth"). Only **on *the way*** to Truth does one discover that one has already arrived at the Truth. Essence (understood *as* reflection) had to come "*before*" *itself*; that is, there always already had to be a "reflection" ("*before*" ...) of reflection (... *itself*). Paradoxically, there had to be a free act of positing "before" the free act of positing, that is, "before" itself. Therefore, the free act occurred in a past that was never present; that is, there was never a time in the past when the "first" free act was perceived *as a free act*. The negation of negation always already had to have taken place, but this is only realized *after the fact*, after a structurally *necessary* delay; that is, one needs the experience of "negation," the experience that the "essence" is *not* available, *followed by* the experience that this "not" is the essence itself. There was never a past present when this took place. According to Žižek, one achieves "determinate reflection" when one recognizes that what appears to "external reflection" as an impediment to one's access to Truth is a condition of one's access to Truth (SOI 214). It is achieved with the vertiginous experience that the Truth is not given in advance (and then appears), rather produced in the advance toward Truth (FTK 171). The Truth is produced through the structurally necessary misrecognition of Truth, that is, through the structurally necessary illusion characteristic of transference (the supposition of Truth behind the appearance). The initial otherness (initially perceived as given in advance) is always already "posited" (i.e., accepted as "one's own work") retroactively, so that its emergence *coincides with its loss*. Although the primordial act of free self-positing (the *negation* of the negation, or *sacrifice* of the sacrifice, characteristic of determinate reflection) never effectively took place within the temporal reality of the positing subject, one has to presuppose it hypothetically in order to account for the consistency of not only the temporal process, but also the consistency of what Lacan refers to as the symbolic order. In both the passage from external to determinate reflection and the Lacanian "forced choice," the subject somehow comes *in advance* of the subject's own existence, and then, by way of a free act, creates (posits) his/her own existence (IR 19).

According to Žižek, there is a connection *between* the passage from external to determinate reflection that is accomplished when the positing subject posits the substantial-immediate "essence" presupposed in external reflection *and* the structure of a "forced choice" (SOI 220). The "forced choice" of Lacanian psychoanalytic theory is an "empty gesture" (SOI 230) of "choosing what is given" (SOI 220). It is an "act before act" (SOI 218) by means of which the subject (through a merely formal conversion) determines as his/her own work the given objectivity presupposed by his/her work. In the "empty gesture" of "choosing what is given" (as well as in the passage from external to determinate reflection), the subject "doesn't really do anything"; that is, the subject accepts as "his/her own work"—through a purely formal act; the truth's content is its *form* (FTK 163)—what was a moment ago perceived as a given substantial-immediate otherness (SOI 218). The "empty gesture," by means of which the given, senseless reality is accepted as "one's own work," *is* the symbolization of the Real, the inscription of the Real into the symbolic order (SOI 230). The significance of this confluence of Hegelian dialectics and Lacanian psychoanalytic theory for a contemporary criticism of ideology becomes apparent when one recognizes this "empty gesture" as the most elementary ideological operation. What a moment ago was perceived as a *given* object (through the activity of external reflection, which deceives one into thinking that in the process of knowledge, one will discover some substantial-immediate otherness that was *once* immediately present, *prior to being lost, prior to being "left behind"* by external reflection's very activity of reflection) is now recognized (through determinate reflection) as *"one's own work"* (i.e., it is recognized that through "one's own work" of external reflection, the object is *"given" as lost*). This "empty gesture" *posits* (*makes exist*) *the big Other*; through this (because of this) "empty gesture" the subject *presupposes the big Other* (SOI 230).

In Hegelian terminology, this structurally necessary illusion that inaugurates the movement of the dialectic is the supposition that the knowledge sought is present in advance in the Other. Because of this presupposition that reality is already in itself "reasonable," the dialectician's role can (as Hegel incessantly reminds the reader) be limited to that of a pure observer who does not apply an external method on the Real, but rather merely discovers the inherent rationality of the Real. But at the end of the dialectical movement, Žižek points out, "this presupposition loses ground: the subject discovers that *from the very beginning there was no support in the Other*, that he was himself producing the 'discovered' meaning" (FTK 171).

The condition of one's subjective freedom, of one's "positing" (one's *"simple"* reflection) is that it **must** *itself* be *reflected* **in advance** into the substance itself (i.e., the presupposition of external reflection), as its own "reflexive determination"; that is, the condition of one's subjective freedom is the "sacrifice of the sacrifice" insofar as the "sacrifice of the sacrifice" is the symbolization of the Real, which is (at the same time) *the condition of the possibility* of the consistency of the symbolic order (which is the condition of one's subjective freedom). It is important to note that *at the moment* one recognizes (through determinate reflection) that the "sacrifice of the sacrifice" is *the condition of the possibility* of the consistency of the symbolic order, one recognizes that it is, *at the same time, the condition of the im*possibility of the consistency of the symbolic order. That is, *at the moment* the subject achieves determinate reflection, the subject is (*if only for a moment*) effaced (FTK 190), the "essence" of the subject is (if only for a moment) desubstantialized. The essence (as the pure movement of mediation, of self-referential negativity) *"comes to be* through being *left behind"* (WL vol. 11, 252/SL 402), its emergence *coincides with its loss* (FTK 167). The psychoanalytic "cure" is the dissolution of transference, the "going through the fantasy" (i.e., the fantasy that is brought about by the activity of external reflection, which deceives one into thinking that in the process of knowledge, one will discover some substantial-immediate otherness that was *once* immediately present, *prior to being lost, prior to being "left behind"* by external reflection's very activity of reflection; see SOI 65, 133), which is equivalent to what is referred to in Lacanian psychoanalysis as "subjective destitution" (SOI 230–231; see IR 94–95, 166–167), that is, being *separated* from, not *alienated* in/by, the symbolic order. Dialectical analysis is nothing but a repeated (at each stage of the dialectic) "going through the fantasy" (FTK 213) insofar as it keeps unconcealed *the condition of the possibility* and *the condition of the impossibility* of the consistency of the symbolic order, that is, *the condition of the possibility* and *the condition of the impossibility* of the subject.

It is not clear whether Lacan (at least from Žižek's perspective) is sufficiently attentive to the *impossibility* of this psychoanalytic "cure." It is clear that there is the recognition of the *necessity* of this "cure," that is, the *necessity* of recognizing that *at the moment* the subject recognizes that it posits the substantial "essence" presupposed in external reflection (SOI 215), *at the moment* that the subject achieves determinate reflection, the subject is (*if only for a moment*) effaced (FTK 190). Lacan (at least from Žižek's perspective) recognizes the *necessity* (insofar as it maintains oneself at a minimal distance from ideology), but perhaps not the *impossibility* of this psychoanalytic "cure." I would argue that there is the *necessity*, yet *impossibility*, of the psychoanalytic "cure." The "cure" can only be accomplished as an incessant task. It is no *way* one can *be*. This is the justification for the qualification *"if only for a moment"* in the sentence *"at the moment* that the subject achieves determinate reflection, the subject is (*if only for a moment*) effaced." The effacement of the subject occurs in the atemporal temporality of the moment.

This consideration of "cure" is to be situated within the context of Lacan's consideration of the ethics of psychoanalysis. With the sacrifice of the sacrifice, the "empty gesture" of the "forced choice," the subject emerges as alienated in/by the symbolic order. With this subordination to the authority of the No/Name of the Father (the Law), the subject contracts a guilt that is constitutive of the subject. Exculpating oneself from this constitutive guilt involves a *repetition* of the "forced choice," a *repetition* of the sacrifice of the sacrifice. This repetition involves not *alienation* in/by, but rather *separation* from, the symbolic order.

Dialectical analysis is a *repetition* of the sacrifice of the sacrifice. It is a *repetition* of the sacrifice of the sacrifice, which is the *production* (i.e., the effectuation of being and the revelation) of what always already had to have happened (the "act before act," the sacrifice of the sacrifice) to account for one's present situation in the symbolic order.

The Question of Sacrifice

The remaining sections of this chapter will consider four paradigmatic moments of this *repetition* of the sacrifice of the sacrifice (i.e., the repetition of the "forced choice"): (1) Antigone's suicidal "No!" to Creon's command to leave the body of her brother Polynices unburied, (2) Abraham's binding (and intention to sacrifice) his son Isaac in unconditional obedience to the command of God, (3) the sacrifice of Jesus Christ, and (4) St. Paul's reading of *agape* as the spontaneous enjoyment of doing one's duty without expectation of a reward.

Antigone

Antigone's act is the Lacanian definition of an authentic ethical act, that is, "an act which reaches the utter limit of the primordial forced choice and repeats it in the reverse sense" (EYS 77). An authentic ethical act in the Lacanian sense is an act of symbolic suicide (which is opposed to suicide "*in* reality," which remains caught within the symbolic order; compare with the consideration of suicide by Levinas and Blanchot), insofar as the act involves the momentary effacement of the subject.

In *The Ethics of Psychoanalysis* (1986; lectures delivered 1959–1960), Lacan chooses the relationship between action and the desire that inhabits it as the standard for a reconsideration of ethics to which psychoanalysis leads one (EdP 361/EoP 313). Antigone's action, her "No!" to Creon, is (according to Lacan) inhabited by the desire of death *as such*. Her action is the sacrifice of the sacrifice characteristic of the symbolic order. Her sacrifice is the sacrifice of the symbolic order itself. I propose to explore how the sacrifice of the sacrifice (which is the [dis]incarnation of the death drive) opens up the space for a reconsideration of ethics, insofar as it describes the *extreme* point of ethics, that is, the moment that is (paradoxically) the suspension of ethical universality.

Having said that the relationship between action and the desire that inhabits it is chosen as the standard for a reconsideration of ethics, Lacan is quick to add that the "ethics of psychoanalysis" is not a speculation about prescriptions for, or the regulation of, what he calls "the service of goods" (EdP 361/EoP 313), which is the position of traditional ethics (EdP 362/EoP 314). After pointing out that the "ethics of psychoanalysis" implies the dimension that is expressed in the "tragic sense [*expérience*] of life," he returns to the relationship between action and desire by way of the space of tragedy.

> Let us say by way of a preliminary sounding that the relationship between action and the desire which inhabits it in the space of tragedy functions in the direction of a triumph of death. And I taught you to rectify the notion as a triumph of being-for-death that is formulated in Oedipus's μὴ φύναι [rather not to be; see EdP 353/EoP 306], a phrase in which one finds that μή, the negation that is identical to the entrance of the subject supported by the signifier. There lies the fundamental character of all tragic action. (EdP 361–362/EoP 313)

114

This "negation" is (according to a Žižekian reading) the negation of the negation, the sacrifice of the sacrifice, characteristic of the "forced choice" that is the emergence of the alienated subject into the symbolic order. It refers, therefore, to the Thing (*das Ding*), the incestuous object of enjoyment, as the "driving force" of desiring (IR 97). This entire passage refers, therefore, to Oedipus's *repetition* of the "forced choice," his *repetition* of the sacrifice of the sacrifice, which involves not *alienation* in/by, but rather *separation* from, the symbolic order.

Returning to the relationship between action and the desire that inhabits it as the standard of the reconsideration of ethics, Lacan says that "it is because we [i.e., psychoanalysts] know better than those who went before how to recognize the nature of desire, which is at the heart of this experience [i.e., the experience of human action], that a reconsideration of ethics is possible, that a form of ethical judgment is possible, of a kind that gives this question the force of a Last Judgment: Have you acted in conformity with the desire that is in you?" (EdP 362/EoP 314). A few moments later, he says, "the only thing of which one can be guilty is of having given ground relative to [i.e., compromising (*cédé sur*)] one's desire" (EdP 368/EoP 319; see EdP 370/EoP 321).

One sees this refusal to compromise desire in Oedipus. The absolute reign of Oedipus's desire is brought out by the fact that "he is shown to be unyielding right to the end, demanding everything, giving up nothing, absolutely unreconciled" (EdP 357–358/EoP 310). Unlike those who die "accidentally," Oedipus "dies from a true death in which he erases his own being. The malediction is freely accepted on the basis of the true subsistence of a human being, the subsistence of the subtraction of himself from the order of the world" (EdP 353/ EoP 306). In sacrificing his own being and thereby separating himself from the symbolic order, Oedipus shows one the *extreme* limit of desire.

The refusal to compromise desire is also characteristic of Antigone. Lacan asks, "Shouldn't it [i.e., Antigone's desire] be the desire of the Other and be linked to the desire of the mother? The text alludes to the fact that the desire of the mother is the origin of everything. The desire of the mother is the founding desire of the whole structure [. . .]; but it is also a *criminal desire*" (EdP 329/ EoP 282–283, emphasis added). It is a "criminal desire" insofar as Antigone's desire is not simply the desire associated with *alienation* in the symbolic order that accompanies the sacrifice of the sacrifice of the mother as incestuous Object, but (more precisely) the *extreme* moment of desire that is an act of *separation* from the symbolic order itself (see EYS 77, 168).

The first mention of "crime" in *The Ethics of Psychoanalysis* occurs in the context of Lacan's reading of Sade. According to Lacan, Sade lays out the theory that "it is through crime that man collaborates in the new creations of nature." The transgressive destructiveness of crime is necessary for creation because "the pure force of nature is obstructed by its own forms" (EdP 248/EoP 210). In the *System of Pope Pius VI* from Volume IV of *The Story of Juliette* (1797), Sade writes:

> [C]rime is necessary in the world. But the most useful crimes are no doubt those that disrupt the most, such as *the refusal of propagation* or *destruction*; all the others are worthless or rather only those two are worthy of the name of crime. [. . .] Nature wants atrocities and magnitude in crimes; the more our destructions are of this type, the more they will be agreeable to it. To be of even greater service to nature, one should seek to prevent the regeneration of the body that we bury. Murder only takes the first life of the individual whom we strike down; we should also seek to take his second life, if we are to be even more useful to nature. For nature wants annihilation; it is beyond our capacity to achieve the scale of destruction it desires. (EdP 249–250/EoP 210–211)

This implies a distinction between two deaths: *biological death* ("Murder only takes the first life of the individual"), which is part of the natural cycle of corruption and generation, and *absolute death*, which is the destruction or annihilation of the natural cycle itself. Insofar as the transgressive destructiveness of the Freudian death drive likewise wipes the slate clean and thereby creates the space for creation from zero, Lacan argues that it is of the same order as the "second death" of Sade's *System of Pope Pius VI*. As in Sade, the death drive "is linked to that structural element which implies that as soon as we have to deal with anything in the world appearing in the form of the signifying chain, there is somewhere — though certainly outside of the natural world — which is the beyond of that chain, the *ex nihilo* on which it is founded and is articulated as such" (EdP 251–252/EoP 212). The "second death" is the *extreme* limit of desire that is the destruction or annihilation of the symbolic order itself. Antigone's "criminal desire" — her refusal to compromise her desire, her pursuit of desire to the limit — is linked, therefore, to the death drive. "[S]he pushes to the limit the realization of something that might be called the pure and simple desire of death as such. She incarnates that desire" (EdP 328–329/EoP 282). She identifies herself with the form in which the Freudian "death drive" is manifested (EdP 327/EoP 281). Her "criminal desire" is linked to the *extreme* moment of desire. Her "criminal desire" is *not* the sacrifice for a cause (and therefore a desire mediated by one's alienation in/by the symbolic order), but rather the sacrifice of the sacrifice, which is a separation from the symbolic order.

Before pursuing Antigone's uncompromising "criminal desire," it is important to situate Creon in Lacan's reading of *Antigone*. Creon has traditionally been read as opposed to Antigone. Lacan, drawing upon Aristotle's *Poetics*, says that Creon has been ἁμαρτών; he has made a mistake (EdP 323/EoP 277; see *Poetics* 53a10). At the end of the tragedy, when Creon returns bearing the body of his son Haemon who has committed suicide, the Chorus says, "If we may say so, it is not a misfortune that is external to him; it is αὐτὸς ἁμαρτών, his own mistake. He's the one who made the mistake of getting himself into the mess" (EdP 323/EoP 277). Creon's ἁμαρτία ("mistake" or "error") is, according to Lacan, wanting to promote the good of all as the law without limits, the sovereign law that goes beyond the limit. Believing that the sovereign law is a law without limits, a law with no remainder, Creon inevitably crosses the limit. What limit? Traditional readings of *Antigone*, including Hegel's, say that it is the laws of the gods defended by Antigone. When one says this, one assumes—wrongly according to Lacan—that enough has been said (EdP 301/EoP 259). Goethe rectifies the Hegelian reading that the opposition of Creon and Antigone is an opposition of human law and divine law. Goethe shows that Creon is driven by his desire and deviates from the straight path. His mistake is wanting to inflict on Polynices the "second death" that he has no right to inflict on him (Lacan admits that although it is not exactly stated in these terms, it is implied, intuited by Goethe, EdP 297/ EoP 254). The limit involved is the limit of the "second death" (EdP 302/EoP 260). In the name of the *universal* validity of the law, Creon desires to obliterate the *singularity* of Polynices, who represents an exception to the universal validity of the law. In wanting to inflict on Polynices a "second death," Creon is wanting to *separate* Polynices from the symbolic order. It is as if his *biological death* was not enough. What Creon wants to inflict is an *absolute death*, a "second death." Every trace of Polynices in the symbolic order is to be obliterated; he is to become a "non-person."

Creon wants the law to have *universal* validity. He wants to promote the good of all as the law *without limits*. This is his mistake. His limitation is that he does not recognize any limits. Creon's language is, according to Lacan, the language of Kantian practical reason. From a Kantian perspective, Creon's refusal to allow the burial of Polynices is "a maxim that can be given as a rule of reason with a *universal* validity" (EdP 301/EoP 259, emphasis added). His refusal is founded on the fact that one cannot *at the same time* honor a traitor to the country and a defender of the country. His misrecognition of the limits of the law means that he "doesn't even notice that he has crossed that famous limit" (EdP 301/EoP 259). He does not recognize any exceptions to the *universal* validity of the law. Tragic consequences follow upon his actions. A remainder or exception to the universal validity of the law emerges, an excess emerges whose fatal consequences are revealed in tragedy (EdP 301/EoP 259).

Antigone is different from Creon. And *not* in the way that the tradition has read the difference. The word that is at the center of Antigone's whole drama is, according the Lacan, ἄτη. According to Lacan's reading of Sophocles' *Antigone*, *Atè* indicates the traumatic limit of the symbolic order; it indicates a remainder or exception that exceeds the symbolic order and around which the symbolic order is structured (TWN 115–116). Antigone desires to go toward *Atè*; she desires to go beyond the limit of *Atè* (ἐκτὸς ἄτας) (EdP 322/EoP 277). "Beyond this *Atè*," Lacan says, "one can only spend a brief period of time, and that's where Antigone wants to go" (EdP 305/EoP 263). This "brief period of time" is, I would argue, the atemporal temporality of the moment.

Antigone is different from Creon. "*Atè* is not ἁμαρτία that is to say a mistake or error; it's got nothing to do with doing something stupid" (EdP 323/EoP 277). When Antigone explains to Creon what she has done, she affirms the autonomy of the absolute individual with the phrase "That's how it is because that's how

117

The Question of Sacrifice

it is" (EdP 323/EoP 278). This phrase, which amounts to a summary interpretation of Antigone's response to Creon, calls for an explanation. Lacan begins by retranslating (and reinterpreting) key phrases in the exchange between Antigone and Creon that Lacan thinks have been mistranslated and thereby misinterpreted. When Antigone says, "For Zeus is by no means the one who proclaimed those things to me," she has traditionally been understood to have said, "It's not Zeus who gives *you* [i.e., Creon] the right to say that." But, according to Lacan, what Antigone denies is that it is Zeus who ordered *her* (Antigone) to bury her brother Polynices. She likewise distinguishes herself from *Δίκη* (justice). Giving an interpretive gloss on Antigone's response to Creon, Lacan says that Antigone, in effect, says, "You have got that all mixed up. [. . .] It may even be that you are wrong in the way you [i.e., Creon] avoid the *Δίκη* [justice]. But I'm not going to get mixed up in it; I'm not concerned with all these gods below who have imposed laws on men" (EdP 323–324/EoP 278).

Heidegger's reading of this dialogue between Creon and Antigone in *Hölderlin's Hymn "The Ister"* (1984; lectures delivered 1942) is instructive. Hölderlin (in his *Remarks on Antigone*) understands this dialogue as undoubtedly the boldest moment of this work of art. Heidegger prefaces his remarks on this dialogue in *Antigone* by writing, "Her suffering the *δεινόν* [uncanny] is her supreme *action*" (HHdI 144/HHtI 115, emphasis added). This raises the question of the proximity of *ἄτη* in Lacan's reading and *δεινόν* in Heidegger's reading, for Heidegger's reading of Antigone's action is in some respects similar to Lacan's reading. Before elaborating on the confluence of these readings of Antigone's action, it is important to point out that there is evidence that both Lacan and Heidegger drew upon Karl Reinhardt's *Sophocles*. Like Reinhardt, Heidegger translates the Creon/Antigone dialogue in a manner that breaks with earlier translations (see Froment-Meurice's "In (the) Place of Being, Antigone (The *Retrait* of the Polis)," 143). At the beginning of his lecture that contains a consideration of the Creon/Antigone dialogue, Lacan mentions the singularity of Reinhardt's work (EdP 316/EoP 271).

Heidegger is concerned with determining why Antigone dared to transgress Creon's law. Preceding his quotation and translation of the Creon/Antigone dialogue, Heidegger sets his translation apart from traditional translations:

> [B]ecause those who seek to explain this tragedy are always eager to find in Antigone's words an explanation for her actions, that is, a statement about whatever it is that causes her deeds, they are concerned only with finding some reference to beings [*Seiendes*], whether the prevailing or ancient cult of the dead, or the familial blood-relatedness. They fail to recognize that in her words, Antigone speaks of neither of these. One is still unable to see that she is not speaking of a being [*von einem Seienden*] at all. This gives rise to the appearance that she speaks indeterminately—whereas she says quite unequivocally the *singular* [*das Einzige*] thing that remains to be said here. (HHdI 144–145/HHtI 115–116, emphasis added)

118

According to Heidegger's reading of the tragedy, *Antigone* is not about the conflict between Creon, representing the "state," and Antigone, representing "religion" (HHdI 147/HHtI 118). Most readers of *Antigone*, Hegel included, understand Antigone to say that her action of burying her brother obeys the unwritten divine edict. But Heidegger argues that Antigone does not comport herself toward anything in particular (*ein Seiendes*) that could be construed as an *explanation* of her action. According to Heidegger, the demonstrative pronoun "this" (τάδε) in Antigone's response to Creon refers *not* to Creon's law forbidding the burial of Polynices, but to Antigone's action of appropriating the unhomely.

> **Creon:** And manifestly you have dared to transgress this <my> law?
> **Antigone:** It was no Zeus that bade me this [τάδε],
> Nor was it Dike [Δίκη], at home amongst the gods below,
> who ordained [ὥρισεν] this law [νόμους] for humans,
> And your command seemed not so powerful to me,
> That it could ever override [ὑπερδραμεῖν] by human wit
> The immutable, unwritten [ἄγραπτα] edict [νόμιμα] divine.
> Not just now, nor since yesterday, but ever steadfast
> this [ταῦτα] prevails. And no one knows from whence it once appeared (HHdI 145/HHtI 116; see Gf 213/Ge 190)

What, therefore, is the "this" (ταῦτα) that comes from neither the present nor the past, is "ever steadfast," and "prevails" *even beyond the gods*? Heidegger writes:

> That which is determinative, that which determines Antigone in her being, is *beyond the upper and the lower gods* [i.e., heavenly Zeus and subterranean Dike]. And yet it is something that pervasively attunes human beings as human beings. Yet it is no mere human ordinance, for such has no power over divine edict and thus falls emphatically below what prevails *even beyond the gods*. At no time can what is determinative here be encountered anywhere as something first posited on a particular occasion, and yet it has already appeared before all else, without anyone being able to name a particular being from which it has sprung forth. It is to that which is unconcealed in this way that the essence of Antigone belongs. To be sheltered within and to become homely in what is thus unconcealed is what she herself names παθεῖν τὸ δεινὸν τοῦτο—passing through this being unhomely amid all beings. In Antigone's taking such being unhomely into her own essence, she is "properly" unhomely. (HHdI 145–146/HHtI 116–117, emphasis added; see HHdI 127/ HHtI 103)

But what does it mean to be " 'properly' unhomely"? What does it mean to "take in" or appropriate the "unhomely"? I would argue that this "taking in" or appropriation of the unhomely echoes the appropriation of death (and all the irreducible aporias pursuant to it) that Heidegger describes in *Being and Time* (1927).

Derrida describes the aporia of death in *Aporias: Dying—Awaiting (One Another at) the "Limits of Truth"* (1994). For Heidegger, death is a paradoxical possibility insofar as it is "the possibility of the absolute impossibility of Dasein" (SZ 250/BT 294). Death is a paradoxical possibility insofar as it is both *possible* (and necessary) for Dasein to appropriate this possibility, and (at the same time) *not possible* for Dasein to appropriate this possibility. Turning what is at the very heart of the possibility of the existential analysis of death (i.e., the appropriation of death) against the very possibility of the existential analysis, Derrida writes, "If death, the most proper possibility of *Dasein*, is the possibility of its impossibility, death becomes the most improper possibility and the most ex-propriating, the most inauthenticating one" (AM 337/AD 77). That is, one sees the ruination of the step that would complete the existential analysis *in the performance of the step itself*. One sees the unworking of the "work" *in* (paradoxically) the "working" of the work. This work of appropriation is the most ex-propriating.

The "logic" of this aporia is echoed, I would argue, in Antigone's appropriation of the uncanny. She says, "You leave this to me, and to that within me that counsels the dangerous and difficult." With what, Heidegger asks, is this counsel concerned? "[T]o take up into my own essence the uncanny that here and now appears [παθεῖν τὸ δεινὸν τοῦτο]" (HHdI 127/HHtI 102–103; see HHdI 146/HHtI 117). Here παθεῖν does not mean, Heidegger argues, the mere "passivity" of accepting and tolerating, but rather the "taking in" or "taking up" of appropriation; that is, it means properly experiencing. "This παθεῖν—experiencing the δεινόν—this enduring and suffering, is the fundamental trait of that doing and action called τὸ δρᾶμα, which constitutes the 'dramatic,' the 'action' in Greek tragedy" (HHdI 128/HHtI 103, emphasis added). This proper experiencing of the δεινόν, which is the "action" in Greek tragedy, means that Antigone is (as was mentioned earlier) " 'properly' unhomely" (HHdI 146/HHtI 117). Echoing Derrida's reading of the existential analysis of death, if the uncanny, the most proper possibility of Antigone (the most proper possibility of her being "homely"), is the possibility of her impossibility (of her being "unhomely"), the uncanny becomes the most improper possibility and the most ex-propriating. This appropriation that is the most ex-propriating is, I would argue, to be " 'properly' unhomely." It is becoming homely in being unhomely (HHdI 143/HHtI 115). This being " 'properly' unhomely" is the *action* in Greek tragedy. Antigone's suffering the δεινόν (uncanny) is her supreme *action* (HHdI 144/HHtI 115), which (as was mentioned earlier) raises the question of the proximity of δεινόν in Heidegger's reading and ἄτη in Lacan's reading.

Antigone's action (as was mentioned earlier) is (according to Lacan) a paradigmatic example of the repetition of the sacrifice of the sacrifice (i.e., the repetition of the "forced choice"). Her act is the Lacanian definition of an authentic ethical act. Antigone's position represents the radical limit that affirms the "unique value" of Polynices' *being* "*without reference to any context*" (EdP 325/EoP 279, emphasis added). The "unique value" or *singularity* involved is essentially that of language, that is, language *as such*. "That purity, that *separation* of being from the characteristics of the historical drama he [i.e., Polynices] has lived through, is precisely the limit or the *ex nihilo* to which Antigone is attached.

It is nothing more than *the break* that the very presence of language inaugurates in the life of man" (EdP 325/EoP 279, emphasis added). Antigone's position—which represents that *separation* of *being* from the characteristics of the historical drama of the symbolic order, which is the "radical limit" or *ex nihilo* to which she is attached—affirms/maintains Polynices' unique value. Her position affirms/maintains the separation of his *being* from the symbolic order. Her position affirms/maintains his singularity; that is, it does *not* compromise his singularity.

> Between the two of them [i.e., Eteocles and Polynices], Antigone chooses to be purely and simply the guardian of the being of the criminal as such. No doubt things could have been resolved if the social body had been willing to pardon, to forget and cover over everything with the same funeral rites. It is because the community refuses this that Antigone is required to *sacrifice* her own being in order to *maintain that essential being* which is the family Atè, and that is the theme or true axis on which the whole tragedy turns. (EdP 329/EoP 283, emphasis added)

Her "criminal desire" is linked to the *extreme* moment of desire. Her "criminal desire" is *not* the sacrifice for a cause (and therefore a desire mediated by one's alienation in/by the symbolic order), but rather the sacrifice of this sacrifice for a cause, which is a separation from the symbolic order. Her position does *not* make sense *in terms of* the universality of ethics, whether it is based on the human law *or* the divine law. If Antigone's position were based on any of the characteristics that Polynices shared with others, it would be comprehensible, and would as such undermine the *unconditional* character of the act. She could explain what she did on the basis of ethics (regardless of whether that ethics was based on human law *or* divine law). Antigone, however, appeals to neither. Her action does *not* make sense; there is no justification for it (*in terms of* the comprehensible signifiers of language). The unique value of Polynices' *being* without reference to any content determines him as absolutely *singular* and her action as absolutely *unconditional*. Her position—which is the "radical limit" or *ex nihilo* to which she is attached—is, I would argue, nothing more than the *repetition of the break* that the very presence of language inaugurates in the life of the human subject. What is this "radical limit" that affirms the "unique value" of Antigone's brother Polynices? What is this "radical limit" that suspends the universality of any contextualization, the universality of any "ethical" justification that Antigone may give for her actions? What is this "radical limit" that is, as I have argued, nothing more than *repetition of the break* that the very presence of language inaugurates in the life of the human subject?

This "radical limit" is associated with the *repetition* of the sacrifice of the sacrifice (i.e., her *repetition* of the "forced choice," by means of which the subject emerges as alienated in/by the symbolic order, i.e., the subject is barred by language). Said otherwise, it is associated with the death drive (EYS 176). At the time of *The Ethics of Psychoanalysis*, the death drive was associated with the possibility of the destruction or annihilation of the symbolic order itself. It was associated with the "second death," which is the *extreme* limit of desire. Antigone's "criminal desire"—her refusal to compromise her desire, her pursuit of desire to the limit—is linked, therefore, to the death drive. If one says that the movement of negation (death) is tied to language, then one can understand Antigone's *action*, her repetition of the sacrifice of the sacrifice as the endeavor to realize the movement of that negation *itself*. "Antigone appears as αὐτόνομος [autonomous], as a pure and simple relationship of the human being to that of which he miraculously happens to be the bearer, namely, the signifying cut that confers on him the indomitable power of being what he is in the face of everything that may oppose him" (EdP 328/EoP 282). Antigone appears as the pure and simple relationship to negation (which is tied to language) *as such* (see EdP 331/EoP 285). "[S]he pushes to the limit the realization of something that might be called the pure and simple desire of death as such. She incarnates that desire" (EdP 328–329/EoP 282). She identifies herself with the form in which the Freudian "death drive" is manifested (EdP 327/EoP 281). This endeavor is, however, tragic because the power of negation (death) is the blind spot of language. It is the condition of the possibility of language's revelatory powers that cannot itself be revealed. Antigone endeavors to reveal what revelation destroys. It is the *singularity* of Antigone's (dis)incarnation of the death drive as such that is the condition of the possibility and the condition of the impossibility of the *universality* of the ethical order. In her *repetition* of the sacrifice of the sacrifice, Antigone's action is the choice of herself as *objet petit a* (EYS 76).

To choose oneself as *objet petit a* is to undergo what Lacan calls radical subjective destitution (SOI 116). A sublime object (*objet petit a*) is an ordinary everyday object "elevated to the level of *das Ding*" (SOI 194). For Lacan, *objet petit a* is that strange object that is radically interior and at the same time radically exterior. It is that strange object in my interior that is "in me more than me" (SOI 76–79, 95); it is in me as that which breaks me up (compare with Levinas's reading of the idea of the infinite), and for which Lacan coined the term "*extime*." This strange object that is "in me more than me" is surplus-enjoyment (SOI 95). It is important to note that there is no "substantial" enjoyment preceding the excess that is surplus-enjoyment (EYS 22). Thought alongside the Hegelian distinction between external and determinate reflection (as Žižek argues), one could say that there is no "substantial" enjoyment (as appears to be the case to external reflection, albeit as a "lost" substance) preceding the excess that is surplus-enjoyment. Enjoyment (*jouissance*) is (from the perspective of determinate reflection) *nothing but* "loss," nothing but surplus-enjoyment, nothing but the negation of negation. Enjoyment *itself* is a kind of surplus produced by the renunciation of renunciation (EYS 22, 170). This is why surplus-enjoyment is not only *produced by* the negation of the negation, but "is" also *nothing but* the negation of the negation, *nothing but* the sacrifice of sacrifice. What is "in the subject more than subject" is constitutive of the subject as originally split, that is, as guilty: $ \mathcal{S} \diamond a $ (SOI 180). This *objet petit a* is a nonsymbolizable surplus produced in the sacrifice of the sacrifice characteristic of the "empty gesture" of the "forced choice," the sacrifice of the sacrifice charac-teristic of the emergence of the subject as alienated in/by the symbolic order. This *objet petit a*, this horrifying *jouissance* as *surplus*-enjoyment—which is pro-duced by/"is" the sacrifice of the sacrifice that constitutes the subject through its own splitting—is the death drive (SOI 181, EYS 176). In her *repetition* of the sacrifice of the sacrifice, Antigone's action is the choice of *herself* as *objet petit a* (EYS 76). At the moment of this choice, if only for a moment, Antigone (dis)incarnates the desire of death as such (EdP 329/EoP 282).

Antigone's *separation* from the universality of the symbolic order is lived as a regret or lamentation for everything in life that she is denied because of her sacrifice (EdP 326/EoP 280). For those inclined to take their cue from those lines of the tragedy that portray Antigone as cold and inflexible, her regret or lamentation over her sacrifice (or more precisely her sacrifice of sacrifice) seems to disturb the unity of the character, leading some readers to cast doubt on this side of the tragedy. Lacan considers this an "absurd misinterpretation" of Antig-one. According to Lacan, "Antigone's point of view can only be approached, can only be lived or thought about, from the place of that limit where her life is already lost, where she is already on the other side. But from that place she can see it and live it in the form of something already lost" (EdP 326/EoP 280). Hers is "a life that is about to turn into certain death, a death lived by anticipation, a death that crosses over into the sphere of life, a life that moves into the realm of death" (EdP 291/EoP 248). She (dis)incarnates the death drive as such, the "second death" that is *nothing but* the interruption of the universality of the symbolic order, *nothing but* "not yet" (biological) death. She finds herself in a limit zone "between-life-and-death" (EdP 317/EoP 272). "Her punishment will consist in her being shut up or suspended in the zone between life and death" (EdP 326/EoP 280).

The *extreme* point of ethics proper ([dis]incarnated in Antigone's pure and simple desire of death as such [EdP 329/EoP 282]) is *improper* (see EYS 177, 82); it is the "place" of the signifier *in its most radical form*, that is, not as part of the signifying chain, but as the pure "essence" of the chain, that *extreme* point that is the condition of the possibility and the condition of the impossibility of the universality of the signifying chain, the universality of the ethical order. An-tigone is the (dis)incarnation of the pure and simple desire of death as such through the *repetition* of the "forced choice," the *repetition* of the sacrifice of the sacrifice. This sacrifice of the sacrifice involves not *alienation* in/by, but rather *separation* from, the symbolic order.

Abraham

Žižek situates two other moments of this *repetition* of the sacrifice of the sacrifice (i.e., this repetition of the "forced choice") within the horizon of the work of Kierkegaard in *Enjoy Your Symptom! Jacques Lacan in Hollywood and out* (1992).

The Question of Sacrifice

According to Kierkegaard in *Fear and Trembling* (1843), in order to be absolutely responsible to God, one must sacrifice ethical duty. In order to be absolutely responsible to God, Abraham must sacrifice his ethical duty to love his son by sacrificing him. But in transgressing the ethical, the ethical must retain all its value. Abraham's love for his son Isaac must remain intact at the same time as the ethical expression for his action is that he hates Isaac.

> In the moment he is about to sacrifice [*offre*] Isaac, the ethical expression for what he is doing is: he hates Isaac. But if he actually hates Isaac, he can rest assured that God does not demand this of him, for Cain and Abraham are not identical. He must love Isaac with his whole soul. Since God claims Isaac, he must, if possible, love him even more, and only then can he *sacrifice* [offre] him, for it is indeed this love for Isaac that makes his act a sacrifice [*Offer*] by its paradoxical contrast to his love for God. But the distress and the anxiety in the paradox is that he, humanly speaking, is thoroughly incapable of making himself understandable. Only in the moment when his act is in absolute contradiction to his feelings, only then does he sacrifice [*offrer*] Isaac, but the reality of his act is that by which he belongs to the universal, and there he is and remains a murderer. (FB 122–123/FT 74)

Every genuine decision demands the sacrifice (and, at the same time, the recognition) of the ethical order, if only for an instant. Quoting Kierkegaard, Derrida writes, "[T]he instant of decision is madness" (DM 66/GD 65). Only in the moment when Abraham's act of raising the knife to sacrifice his son—which is an action of *hatred* (from the perspective of the ethical order)—is in absolute contradiction to his feeling of *love* for his son, only then does Abraham sacrifice his son, but (Kierkegaard reminds the reader) the ethical expression for his action is murder (though the religious expression for his action is sacrifice).

Reading Lacan alongside Kierkegaard, Žižek argues that Abraham's suspension or sacrifice of the ethical (in his unconditional obedience to the command of God to sacrifice his son Isaac) is a *repetition* of the "forced choice," a *repetition* of the sacrifice of the sacrifice. "The fundamental ethical gesture is the subject's alienation in the universality of the symbolic pact, whereas the religious marks the suspension of the ethical, i.e., the moment of the 'mad' decision" (EYS 78) when instead of the universal/general law, the subject chooses him or herself as the singular *objet petit a*.

Jesus Christ

Reading Lacan alongside Kierkegaard, Žižek likewise argues that the Christian of today is called not to remember the scandalous act of Jesus Christ—the scandalous suspension or sacrifice of the Jewish ethical law—but to *repeat* his scandalous act, to repeat his sacrifice of the sacrifice. "Kierkegaard's aim was to reaffirm the Christian attitude in its 'scandalous' reverse, before it settled down into a force of law and order, i.e., to reaffirm it as an *act*, as was the very appearance of Christ in the eyes of the keepers of the old law, before Christ was 'christianized,' made part of the new law of the Christian tradition" (EYS 83). Kierkegaard's point is that the Christian of today is not called to remember the scandalous act of Jesus Christ from the safe and comfortable standpoint of an external, neutral gaze. "[T]he past appears in its 'openness,' in its possibility, only to those whose present situation is threatened by the same abyss, who are caught in the same deadlock" (EYS 79). The Christian of today is called to identify with the humiliated Christ of the Gospels by repeating his scandalous act, his sacrifice of the sacrifice.

St. Paul and *Agape* (Love)

Another paradigmatic moment of this *repetition* of the sacrifice of the sacrifice (i.e., this repetition of the "forced choice") is located in the work of St. Paul. The basic point of Christianity (according to Žižek's reading of St. Paul) is the interruption of the vicious superego cycle of the Law and its transgression by means of *agape*. *Agape* is, I would argue, the *repetition* of the sacrifice of the sacrifice that involves *separation* from the Law of the symbolic order.

St. Paul describes the vicious cycle of the Law and its transgression in his letter to the Romans.

> What then should we say? That the law is sin? By no means! Yet, if it had not been for the law, I would not have known sin. I would not have known what it is to covet if the law had not said, "You shall not covet." But sin, seizing an opportunity in the commandment, produced in me all kinds of covetousness. Apart from the law sin lies dead. I was once alive apart from the law, but when the commandment came, sin revived and I died, and the very commandment that promised life [Lev. 18:5 and Deut. 30:6–20] proved to be death to me. For sin, seizing an opportunity in the commandment, deceived me and through it killed me. So the law is holy, and the commandment is holy and just and good.
>
> Did what is good, then, bring death to me? By no means! It was sin, working death in me through what is good, in order that sin might be shown to be sin, and through the commandment might become sinful beyond measure.
>
> For we know that the law is spiritual; but I am of the flesh, sold into slavery under sin. I do not understand my own actions. For I do not do what I want, but I do the very thing I hate. Now if I do what I do not want, I agree that the law is good. But in fact it is no longer I that do it, but sin that dwells within me. For I know that nothing good dwells within me, that is, in my flesh. I can will what is right, but I cannot do it. (Rom. 7:7–18, NRSV)

For St. Paul, succumbing to the temptations of the flesh — committing sin — does not simply mean (as is commonly thought) indulging in terrestrial pleasures that transgress the prescriptions of the Law (of moral prohibitions). On the contrary, the central point St. Paul is making here is that there is no sin prior to or independent of the Law (what comes before the emergence or intervention of the Law is a simple innocent prelapsarian life inherently lost to mortal human beings). Our way of life—which is the way of the flesh or "death" (it is important to note that when St. Paul opposes spirit/"life" to flesh/"death" this has nothing to do with the biological opposition of life and death as parts of the cycle of generation and corruption, or with the Platonic opposition of soul and body, but two ways to live one's life)—is the life in which sin and Law (desire and its prohibition) are inextricably intertwined: the very act of prohibition gives rise to the desire for its transgression (TS 146–148).

Žižek reads St. Paul's letter to the Romans alongside Freud and Lacan in *The Ticklish Subject: The Absent Centre of Political Ontology* (1999) and *The Fragile Absolute or, Why Is the Christian Legacy Worth Fighting For?* (2000). According to Žižek, the result of the intervention of the Law is that it divides the subject between obedience to the Law and the desire to transgress the Law (generated by the very act of prohibition). Obedience to the Law is a defense against one's sinful desire to transgress the Law; that is, one obeys the Law *by* repressing one's "pathological" sinful desire to transgress the Law. "The superego dialectic of Law and transgression does not lie only in the fact that Law itself invites its own transgression, that it generates the desire for its own violation; our obedience to the Law itself is not 'natural,' spontaneous, but *always-already mediated by the (repression of the) desire to transgress the Law*" (FA 142). But the more one represses his or her sinful desire (in order to obey the Law), the more one bears witness to one's sinful desire, which consequently makes one guiltier (given that, in Christianity, the desire to sin equals the act itself). The superego feeling of guilt: the more one obeys the Law, the more one is guilty. "[T]he direct result of the intervention of the Law is thus that it *divides* the subject and introduces a morbid confusion between life and death: the subject is divided between (conscious) obedience to the Law and (unconscious) desire for its transgression generated by the legal prohibition itself" (TS 149). One's "life" (one's life-impulse, one's "natural" spontaneous *desire*) is perverted, and appears only as a "pathological" sinful *desire* to transgress the Law (which gives rise to guilt). One's "life" appears only as a morbid fascination with "death" that persists independently of one's intention (to obey the Law). The result of the intervention of the Law is the paradox of the superego: one can enjoy only if one feels guilty about it, which means that (in a self-reflexive turn) one can take pleasure in feeling guilty (TS 150).

The emergence or intervention of the Law perverts one's enjoyment of life. This description of the perversion of one's life-impulse (one's desire to *enjoy*) by St. Paul helps to clarify what he means by living one's life according to the way of the flesh or "death." "[T]his perverted universe in which the ascetic who flagellates himself on behalf of the Law enjoys more intensely than the person who takes innocent pleasure in earthly delights—is what St Paul designates as 'the way of the Flesh' as opposed to 'the way of the Spirit': 'Flesh' is not flesh as opposed to the Law, but flesh as an excessive self-torturing, mortifying morbid fascination *begotten by the Law*" (TS 150). It is here, ironically (as both Badiou and Žižek point out), that St. Paul is unexpectedly close to Nietzsche, who is likewise attentive to the question of how to interrupt the vicious cycle of the self-mortifying morbid denial (or sacrifice) of "life" that is nihilism (TS 150).

This perversion of one's enjoyment of life described by St. Paul in his letter to the Romans is likewise considered by Lacan in *The Ethics of Psychoanalysis*. Lacan focuses on Romans 7:7–11 to elaborate on the relationship between the prohibition of the Law and the sinful desire to transgress the Law. He reads sin in this passage from Romans alongside the Thing (understood as the Real Thing/ *jouissance* accessible only by way of the prohibitory Law).

> Is the Law the Thing? Certainly not. Yet I can only know of the Thing by means of the Law. In effect, I would not have had the idea to covet it if the Law hadn't said: "Thou shalt not covet it." But the Thing finds a way by producing in me all kinds of covetousness thanks to the commandment, for without the Law the Thing is dead. But even without the Law, I was once alive. But when the commandment appeared, the Thing flared up, returned once again, I met my death. And for me, the commandment that was supposed to lead to life turned out to lead to death, for the Thing found a way and thanks to the commandment seduced me; through it I came to desire death.
>
> I believe that for a little while now some of you at least have begun to suspect that it is no longer I who have been speaking. In fact, with one small change, namely, "Thing" for "sin," this is the speech of Saint Paul on the subject of the relations between the law and sin in the Epistle to the Romans, Chapter 7, paragraph 7. [. . .]
>
> The relationship between the Thing and the Law could not be better defined than in these terms. [. . .] The dialectical relationship between desire and the Law causes our desire to flare up only in relation to the Law, through which it becomes the desire for death. It is only because of the Law that sin, ἀμαρτία—which in Greek means lack and non-participation in the Thing—takes on an excessive, hyperbolic character. Freud's discovery—the ethics of psychoanalysis—does it leave us clinging to that dialectic? (EdP 101/EoP 83–84)

With the emergence or intervention of the Law, the Thing (*das Ding*) flared up, but in a perverted form: as an excessive, hyperbolic, self-torturing, mortifying morbid fascination with "death" begotten by the Law, that is, as a "pathological" sinful desire to transgress the Law. For Lacan, however, there is "a way of rediscovering the relationship to *das Ding* somewhere beyond the law" (EdP 101/ EoP 84). There is a way of discovering a non-perverted relationship to the Thing. The point of the ethics of psychoanalysis is to formulate the possibility of a relationship to the Thing that avoids the vicious superego cycle of the Law and the sinful desire to transgress the Law (which accounts for the excessive, hyperbolic, self-torturing, mortifying morbid fascination with "death" that is a perversion of the relationship to the Thing), and, at the same time, avoids the claim to a direct insight into the Real Thing. The desire involved in the maxim of the ethics of psychoanalysis ("don't give way on your desire") is *not* the sinful desire to transgress the Law begotten by the prohibitory Law, but rather fidelity to one's desire itself that is elevated to the level of ethical duty (TS 153). Insofar as the

Thing stands for *jouissance*, this maxim (or "Law") of the ethics of psychoanalysis is the injunction of the superego: "Enjoy!" Here the command to *enjoy doing your duty* overlaps with the *duty to enjoy yourself* (FA 135). "[I]t ain't no sin to be glad you're alive" (Bruce Springsteen).

For St. Paul (like Lacan), there is a way of discovering the relationship to the Thing (i.e., for St. Paul, "God" as love, as non-perverted) somewhere beyond the Law. There is a way of discovering a non-perverted relationship to the Thing ("God"). What is this perverted relationship to the Thing ("God")? It is a relationship to the Thing as a perverse substantial alien Entity that brings about the perversion of one's enjoyment of life (insofar as it brings about "pathological" sinful desire). If, as St. Paul points out in his letter to the Romans, our obedience to the Law is always already mediated by the repression of the desire to transgress the Law, then does God's introduction of the Law (that generates its own transgression) make God an omnipotent perverse subject who brings about the perversion of one's enjoyment of life? Does God play obscene games with humanity and his own son by bringing about our Fall so that he may then redeem us through his sacrifice? In his letter to the Romans, St. Paul is concerned with avoiding the perverse conclusion one may reach with the intervention of the Law that generates its own transgression (since it needs this transgression in order to assert itself as Law). St. Paul writes:

> But if our injustice serves to confirm the justice of God, what should we say? That God is unjust to inflict wrath on us? (I speak in a human way.) By no means! For then how could God judge the world? But if through my falsehood God's truthfulness abounds to his glory, why am I still being condemned as a sinner? And why not say (as some people slander us by saying that we say), "Let us do evil so that good may come"? Their condemnation is deserved! (Rom. 3:5–8, NRSV)

This "Let us do evil so that good may come" is an aphorism for a perverse conclusion that one *may* reach with the emergence or intervention of the Law. If God brings about our Fall through the introduction of the Law so that he may then redeem us through his sacrifice, then the answer to the question "Should we continue to sin in order that grace may abound?" (Rom. 6:1, NRSV) is "Yes." It is only our Fall that enables God to redeem us by sacrificing his own son (TS 148–149). But for St. Paul, there is a way of discovering the relationship to the Thing ("God") somewhere beyond the Law. There is a way of discovering a non-perverted relationship to the Thing ("God"): *agape*, the spontaneous enjoyment of doing one's duty without expectation of a reward. St. Paul's problem is not the standard moralistic problem of how to purify oneself of sinful desires, but the problem of how to interrupt the vicious cycle of the Law and its transgression. The basic point of Christianity (according to Žižek's reading of St. Paul) is the interruption of the vicious superego cycle of the Law and its transgression by means of *agape*.

Agape is, I would argue, the repetition of the sacrifice of the sacrifice that involves *separation* from the Law of the symbolic order. This sacrifice of the sacrifice is otherwise than the sacrifice of one's "pathological" sinful desire to transgress the Law characteristic of the vicious superego cycle of the Law and its transgression. Recall that one obeys the Law by sacrificing one's "pathological" sinful desire to transgress the Law. To understand *agape* as the sacrifice of one's "pathological" interests is to *superegotize* Pauline *agape*, to interpret it in an almost Kantian way as a self-sacrificing duty. It is to interpret *agape* as hard *work*, as something to be accomplished. This is love *within the confines of the Law*, love as the struggle to sacrifice the sinful desire to transgress the Law begotten by the prohibitory Law (FA 100). Access to acting *from* duty (i.e., from respect for the law, as opposed to *according to* duty) involves, according to Kant, a sacrifice of the "pathological" interests. The unconditionality of respect for the law involves a sacrifice of everything that links one's sensibility to calculation, that is, the conditionality of hypothetical imperatives. Kant links sacrifice to debt and duty, which are never separable from the guilt from which one can never be acquitted. Here there is an economy of sacrifice from which one can never be redeemed.

This tendency to *superegotize* Pauline *agape* perhaps accounts, I would argue, for Nietzsche's reading of St. Paul as the apostle who advocated the doctrine that the death of Jesus was a sacrificial death for the sins of the guilty. For St. Paul, according to Nietzsche, sacrifice pays insofar as it is performed for the benefit of a state *after* death. One's investment in the suffering and/or death associated with sacrifice is rewarded with a life after death. It is necessary, according to the logic of Nietzsche's work, to sacrifice this economy of sacrifice. However, there is reason to question Nietzsche's reading of St. Paul as an apostle of *ressentiment* who preached the vicious cycle of the self-mortifying morbid denial (or sacrifice) of "life" that is nihilism (TS 150).

Agape is, I would argue, the repetition of the sacrifice of the sacrifice that is otherwise than the sacrifice of one's "pathological" sinful desire to transgress the Law of the symbolic order. *Agape* is the sacrifice *of* the sacrifice of one's "pathological" sinful desire to transgress the Law characteristic of the vicious superego cycle of the Law and its transgression. Sacrifice, by definition (as pointed out by Nancy and Žižek), always has a transcendental intention. As the sacrifice of sacrifice, *agape* unworks the transcendental intention of sacrifice.

> [The] "withdrawal" of the subject from the Other is what Lacan calls "subjective destitution": not an act of sacrifice (which always implies the Other as its addressee) but an act of abandonment which sacrifices the very sacrifice. The freedom thus attained is a point at which we find ourselves not only without the other *qua* our neighbor, but without support in the Other itself— as such, it is unbearably suffocating, the very opposite of relief, of "liberation." (EYS 59)

Agape is the sacrifice of sacrifice. *Agape* is *work*, but it is work that unworks itself *in* the very performance of the work. It is work that interrupts itself *in* the very working of the work. *Agape* unworks the very work of sacrifice. According to this reading (and contrary to Nietzsche's reading), St. Paul does not preach an economy of sacrifice. As the repetition of the sacrifice of the sacrifice, *agape* is not an investment on which one gets a return of life after death.

Agape is the spontaneous enjoyment of doing one's duty without expectation of a reward. *Agape* is *work*, but *for nothing*. Recall that for St. Paul, *agape* is a way of discovering the relationship to the Thing (i.e., for St. Paul, "God") somewhere beyond the Law. For St. Paul, *agape* is a way of discovering a non-perverted relationship to the Thing ("God"). The consequence of this understanding of Pauline *agape* as a non-perverted relationship to the Thing ("God") is that "God" is discovered, "after the fact," to be *nothing but* radical negativity, *nothing but* the sacrifice of the sacrifice. It is discovered "after the fact" that rather than sacrificing for a Cause-Thing in which one believes (e.g., "God"), one sacrifices *for nothing*. This saves God from being a perverse subject, but it comes at the cost of the discovery that "God" is *nothing but* radical sacrifice, *nothing but* radical (dis)incarnation, *nothing but agape*. "God is love [ἀγαπή]" (1 John 4:8, NRSV).

Agape—as the sacrifice *of* the sacrifice of one's "pathological" sinful desire to transgress the Law characteristic of the vicious superego cycle of the Law and its transgression—is what St. Paul calls "dying to the Law."

> [Y]ou have died to the law through the body of Christ, so that you may belong to another, to him who has been raised from the dead in order that we may bear fruit for God. While we were living in the flesh, our sinful passions, aroused by the law, were at work in our members to bear fruit for death. But now we are discharged from the law, dead to that which held us captive, so that we are slaves not under the old written code but in the new life of the Spirit. (Rom. 7:4–6, NRSV)

To become a true Christian and embrace *agape*, one should "die to the Law," one should interrupt the vicious cycle of "our sinful passions, aroused by the law." "Dying to the Law" is what Lacan calls undergoing "subjective destitution" or "symbolic death": the sacrifice of the symbolic order, the sacrifice of the symbolic Law that arouses one's sinful desire (which, in turn, calls for the sacrifice of one's sinful desire to transgress the Law of the symbolic order) (TS 151). This interruption of the vicious cycle of the Law and its transgression that is "symbolic death" involves the terrifying violence of the death drive that wipes the slate clean in preparation for a new beginning (FA 127).

This "symbolic death" or "dying to the Law" that regulates our life opens up a "new creation."

> From now on, therefore, we regard no one from a human point of view; even though we once knew Christ from a human point of view, we know him no longer in that way. So if anyone is in Christ, there is a new creation: everything old has passed away; see, everything has become new! (2 Cor. 5:16–17, NRSV)

The *moment* of "symbolic death" or "dying to the Law" is a revolutionary moment. At this moment, if only for a moment, "everything old has passed away," creating the momentary space for creation from zero (FA 127). Everything is permitted to the Christian believer. That one does not do certain things is based not on prohibitions (which then generate the sinful desire to transgress the Law), but on the affirmative spontaneous overflowing of generosity that is *agape*, which renders meaningless any act that bears witness to the fact that one is not free, but still dominated by the symbolic Law (TS 150): "'All things are lawful for me' [often translated: 'Nothing is prohibited to me'], but not all things are beneficial. 'All things are lawful for me,' but I will not be dominated by anything" (1 Cor. 6:12, 10:23, NRSV). (Compare this moment when "everything is possible" or "everything is permitted" with Blanchot's reading of Hegel [see LDM 309/LRD 318] and Blanchot's reading of Nietzsche [see EI 218–219/IC 145].) The injunction "Love your neighbor" prohibits nothing (as does the even more radical injunction "Love [ἀγαπᾶτε] your enemies" [Matt. 5:44–45, Luke 6:35, NRSV]). This injunction to love one's neighbor enjoins one to work *beyond* the confines of the Law (FA 111). (When St. Paul mentions this injunction, he writes that love is the *fulfilling* of the Law: "The commandments [. . .] are summed up in this word, 'Love [Ἀγαπήσεις] your neighbor as yourself.' Love [ἀγάπη] does no wrong to a neighbor; therefore, love [ἀγάπη] is the fulfilling of the law" [Rom. 13:9–10, NRSV]. How does one "die to the law" and "fulfill the law" at the same time? Drawing on Žižek's reading of the Hegelian triad of positing, external, and determinate reflection, I would suggest the following interpretration: If, in a first reading, one perceives the Law/God as given in advance, in a second reading, one perceives one's free act [love *as* negation of negation] as included *in advance* in the Law/God [which entails the desubstantialization of the Law/God]. Love is the *fulfillment* of the Law, insofar as the substantial alien Entity [the Law/God] "only *comes to be* [is fulfilled] through being *left behind*," i.e., its emergence *coincides with its loss.*) The injunction "Love your neighbor" calls for the incessant work of *agape*, that is, the incessant repetition of the sacrifice of sacrifice. *Agape* is the spontaneous enjoyment of doing one's duty without expectation of a reward. (Žižek argues that it is, perhaps, "only as the result of psychoanalytic treatment that one can acquire the capacity to enjoy *doing* one's duty; perhaps this *is* one of the definitions of the end of psychoanalysis" [FA 141].)

To work at the incessant work of *agape*—that is, the incessant repetition of the sacrifice of the sacrifice of Jesus Christ—is to choose oneself as *objet petit a* (EYS 76). To work at the incessant work of *agape* is to choose oneself (as did Jesus Christ) as the supplement to the symbolic order, the "non-all" (*pas-tout*) that is the condition of the possibility and the condition of the impossibility of the symbolic order. Žižek argues that this paradoxical place of *agape* with regard to a consistent totality is evident in the following passage:

> If I speak in the tongues of mortals and of angels, but do not have love
> [ἀγάπην], I am a noisy gong or a clanging cymbal. And if I have prophetic
> powers, and understand all mysteries and all knowledge, and if I have all faith,
> so as to remove mountains, but do not have love [ἀγάπην], I am nothing. If
> I give away all my possessions, and if I hand over my body so that I may boast,
> but do not have love [ἀγάπην], I gain nothing.
>
> Love [ἀγάπη] is patient; love [ἀγάπην] is kind; love [ἀγάπην] is not en-
> vious or boastful or arrogant or rude. It does not insist on its own way; it is
> not irritable or resentful; it does not rejoice in wrongdoing, but rejoices in the
> truth. It bears all things, believes all things, hopes all things, endures all things.
>
> Love [ἀγάπην] never ends. But as for prophecies, they will come to an
> end; as for tongues, they will cease; as for knowledge, it will come to an end.
> For we know only in part, and we prophesy only in part; but when the com-
> plete comes, the partial will come to an end. When I was a child, I spoke like
> a child, I thought like a child, I reasoned like a child; when I became an
> adult, I put an end to childish ways. For now we see in a mirror, dimly, but
> then we will see face to face. Now I know only in part; then I will know fully,
> even as I have been fully known. And now faith, hope, and love [ἀγάπη] abide,
> these three; and the greatest of these is love [ἀγάπη]. (1 Cor. 13:1–13, NRSV)

What is crucial in this passage, according to Žižek, is the paradoxical place of
agape with regard to All (i.e., to the *completed* series of prophetic powers or
knowledge). Even if I have complete prophetic powers or knowledge, they remain *in a way* non-all, incomplete, because even *as* complete they are, without
love, (paradoxically) incomplete. Therefore, love "adds" "nothing" (love is "nothing"). Therefore, *agape* must be *in a way* the "nothing," the "non-all," the "incomplete," the "gap" (radical negativity) that prevents the completion of the
(supposedly already) complete prophetic powers or knowledge. *Agape* "adds"
(paradoxically) "something" to the complete (i.e., makes of it a consistent totality)
that "subtracts" (paradoxically) from the complete (makes it incomplete). *Agape*
is the condition of the possibility and the condition of the impossibility of the
All of prophetic powers or knowledge. "[T]he point of the claim that even if I
were to possess all knowledge, without love I would be nothing, is not simply
that *with* love, I am 'something' — in love, *I am also nothing* [given that love is
radical negativity, radical sacrifice, the sacrifice of the sacrifice] but, as it were,
a Nothing humbly aware of itself, a Nothing paradoxically made rich through
the very awareness of its lack" (FA 146–147).

According to Žižek's reading of Lacan, the subject emerges as alienated in/by
the symbolic order with the "empty gesture" of the "forced choice" that Žižek
calls the sacrifice of the sacrifice. Exculpating oneself from this constitutive alienation requires a repetition of the sacrifice of sacrifice, which is the production
(i.e., the effectuation of being and the revelation) of the (essenceless) "essence"
of the symbolic order: radical sacrifice. Repetition of the sacrifice of sacrifice is
(in the Lacanian sense) an authentic ethical act. In the Lacanian sense, an
authentic ethical act is an act of symbolic suicide (which is opposed to suicide

"*in* reality," which remains caught within the symbolic order), insofar as the act involves the momentary effacement of the subject. The pure act is "mad" in the sense of radical *unaccountability*. It is an act of sacrificing sacrifice. It is an act of sacrificing the sacrifice that pays, an act of sacrificing the "sacrifice for a cause," insofar as that "cause" is defined by the symbolic order. This act of sacrificing sacrifice is a *separation* from the symbolic order.

8

Derrida

The Double Bind of Sacrifice

Everything on sacrifice in the work of Derrida hinges on that aporetic moment of the double bind of sacrifice: the moment when the sacrifice of (economical) sacrifice turns into the sacrifice of (aneconomical) sacrifice, and vice versa. Here is the sacrifice of sacrifice.

Hegel and the "All (holos) Is Burned (caustos)"

Following his reading of the work of Bataille in "From Restricted to General Economy: A Hegelianism without Reserve" (1967), Derrida's next sustained consideration of sacrifice—Glas (1974)—again occurs within the context of the work of Hegel. The following remarks on Glas are limited to a reading of the Hegel column (i.e., the left-hand column of each page), specifically to a reading of Derrida's reading of the first shape of natural religion in Hegel's *Phenomenology of Spirit* (1807).

Hegel characterizes the first shape of natural religion—essential light or luminous-essence (*Lichtwesen*)—as a shape of shapelessness. "The first figure of natural religion figures the absence of figure, a purely visible, thus invisible sun that allows seeing without showing itself or that shows itself without showing anything, consuming all in its phenomenon: *die Gestalt der Gestaltlosigkeit*" (Gf 265/Ge 238). This absence of shape or representation anticipates the characterization of absolute knowing, which is characterized as free of all *Vorstellung* (Gf 264/Ge 237). As a light that burns everything (including itself), this all-burning is an essenceless play of light that never determines itself as for-(it)self. Hegel writes, "The movements of its own externalization, its creations in the unresisting element of its otherness, are torrents of light; in their simplicity, they are at the same time the genesis of its being-for-self and the return from the existence [of its moments], streams of fire destructive of [all] structured form" (PG 371/PS 419; see Gf 265/Ge 238). If the all-burning burns everything (including itself), leaving no trace of itself (Gf 265/Ge 238), how, Derrida asks, "can it guard the trace of itself and breach/broach a history where it preserves itself in losing itself?" (Gf 267/Ge 240). Or, said otherwise, how is all-burning constricted so as to determine itself as for-(it)self and take on a stable subsistence? Hegel argues that the all-burning *must* pass into its *contrary*.

> However, this reeling, unconstrained Life must [*muβ*] determine itself as being-for-self and endow its vanishing "shapes" with an enduring subsistence. The *immediate being* in which it stands in antithesis to its consciousness is itself the *negative* power which dissolves its distinctions. It is thus in truth the Self; and Spirit therefore passes on to know itself in the form of self. Pure Light disperses its unitary nature into an infinity of forms, and offers up itself as a sacrifice [*gibt sich dem Fürsichsein zum Opfer*] to being-for-self, so that from its substance the individual may take an enduring existence for itself. (PG 371–372/PS 420; see Gf 268/Ge 241)

It is important to note that when Hegel argues that the all-burning *must* "determine itself as being-for-self and endow its vanishing 'shapes' with an enduring subsistence," it is because this demand is an inherent necessity of (as opposed to being externally imposed upon) the all-burning itself. It is an inherent necessity of the all-burning itself that it *both* burns everything, including itself (and, therefore, be what is otherwise than speculative thought), *and* extinguishes itself as all-burning (and, therefore, become a moment of speculative thought).

This all-burning essenceless play of light that never determines itself as for-(it)self, and as such puts the history of Spirit out of order, *can be what it is* (namely, an "all-burning essenceless play of light that never determines itself as for-(it)self, and as such puts the history of Spirit out of order") *only if it turns into its contrary*. Derrida (remaining faithful to the Hegelian text) notes, "In order to be what it is, purity of play, of difference, of consuming destruction, the all-burning *must* pass into its contrary: guard itself, guard its own movement of loss, appear as what it is in its very disappearance" (Gf 267–268/Ge 240, emphasis added). Here one sees the implacable force of the hard-working negative (Gf 267/Ge 240), the constriction of absolute expenditure to an economy that expects a return on its investment. In interpreting negativity as the productivity of labor, Hegel restricts the stakes of his interpretive wager to logic, history, meaning, etc. But Hegel's own interpretation can, by definition, be reinterpreted (EREG 382/RGE 260). This reinterpretation, possible at each stage of the dialectic, is thinkable at this particular stage of the dialectic in the form of the inherent necessity of the all-burning to *both* burn everything, including itself, *and* extinguish itself as all-burning. These two processes are inseparable.

> The difference and the play of the pure light, the panic and pyromaniac dissemination, the all-burning offers itself as a holocaust to the for-(it)self, *gibt*

> *sich dem Fürsichsein zum Opfer.* It sacrifices itself, but only to remain, to
> ensure its guarding, to bind itself to itself, strictly, to become itself, for-(it)self,
> (close)-by-(it)self. In order to sacrifice itself, it burns itself. [. . .] This sacrifice
> belongs, as its negative, to the *logic* of the all-burning, one could say to the
> double register of its accounting, accountable calculus. If you want to burn
> all, you must also consume the blaze, avoid keeping it alive as a precious
> presence. You must therefore extinguish it, keep it in order to lose it (truly),
> or lose it to keep it (truly). Both processes are inseparable; they can be read
> in any sense, any direction whatever, from right to left or left to right; the
> relief of one must value the other. A panic, limitless inversion: the word *ho-*
> *locaust* that happens to translate *Opfer* is more appropriate to the text than the
> word of Hegel himself. In this sacrifice all (*holos*) is burned (*caustos*), and the
> fire can go out only stoked. (Gf 268–269/Ge 241)

Here one can regard the two inseparable processes: the all-burning as burning
everything, including itself (and, therefore, being what is otherwise than speculative thought), and the all-burning as extinguishing itself as all-burning (and,
therefore, becoming a moment of speculative thought). Derrida asks, "What puts
itself in play in this holocaust of play itself?" (Gf 269/Ge 241), and answers,
"This *perhaps*: [. . .] the sacrifice, the putting in play or to fire of all, the holocaust, are under the power of ontology. They carry and de-border it, but they
cannot not give birth to it" (Gf 269/Ge 242, emphasis added). What becomes
thinkable here is sacrifice as absolute expenditure "before" it inevitably (and
according to its own inherent necessity) appears as "appearance," "before" it
inevitably (and according to its own inherent necessity) has become constricted
to an economy of speculative thought that expects a return on its investment.
This reinterpretation remains merely what is *perhaps* at stake, given the irreducibly ambiguous ontological status of what becomes thinkable: sacrifice without
reserve. "[T]he holocaust *is not*. [. . .] But as soon as it burns (the blaze is not
a being), it *must*, burning itself, burn its action of burning and begin to be" (Gf
270/Ge 242, emphasis added to "must"). Sacrifice without reserve is not, but
cannot not be(come).

This all-burning is, therefore, a remainder to the history of Spirit that cannot
be fully appropriated by that history. It is a remainder that suspends itself. It is
what Derrida calls a "suspended remain(s)" (Gf 252/Ge 226). This suspended
remain(s) puts speculative thought or the history of Spirit out of order without
destroying it. This suspended remain(s) is an *interruption* of speculative thought.

But there is an economic restriction of the stake at play, as has already been
pointed out: the all-burning as sacrifice (without reserve) sacrifices itself (Gf 271/
Ge 244). This constriction of the all-burning (into an economy of exchange) can
only be displaced, Derrida writes, by "a displacement that itself escapes the dialectic law and its strict rhythm" (Gf 123/Ge 107). But given that "the counter-
forces of constriction" (Gf 214/Ge 191) can still be interpreted according to the
negativity of speculative thought, another violence (one otherwise than the neg-

ativity of speculative thought) is necessary if what Derrida calls the "strict-ure against strict-ure" (Gf 124/Ge 107) is to succeed. To think this strict-ure against strict-ure is to think the "logic" of (con)striction. The "logic" of constriction (which is otherwise than or "transcends" the transcendental) is the condition of the possibility of the transcendental. The "logic" of (con)striction is always already the transcendental of the transcendental. Derrida writes:

> There is no choosing here: each time a discourse *contra* the transcendental is held, a matrix—the (con)striction itself—constrains the discourse to place the nontranscendental, the outside of the transcendental field, the excluded, in the structuring position. The matrix in question constitutes the excluded as transcendental of the transcendental, as imitation transcendental, transcendental contra-band. The contra-band is *not yet* dialectical contradiction. To be sure, the contra-band necessarily becomes that, but its not-yet is not-yet the teleological anticipation, which results in it never becoming dialectical contradiction. The contra-band *remains* something other than what, necessarily, it is to become.
>
> Such would be the (nondialectical) law of the (dialectical) strict-ure. (Gf 272/Ge 244)

The reference to the transcendental of the transcendental as an "*imitation* transcendental" recalls the minimal distance of the "not yet" that I argue that Bataille calls "fiction." The contra-band is *not yet* dialectical contradiction. The "not yet" of the aporia interrupts the "at the same time" of contradictories. The "not yet" of the aporia interrupts the *presentation* or *recognition* of the identity (the "at the same time") of contradictories insofar as it is discovered that the moments of the aporia are *not* "at the same time"; they can*not* be *presented* or *recognized as* a contradiction. *The aporia of time/death "is" the aporia of dialectic.* To think the "logic" of (con)striction, that is, to think this strict-ure against strict-ure, is to think, I would argue, the sacrifice of (economical) sacrifice. To think the "logic" of constriction is to think, I would argue, the sacrifice *of* (economical) sacrifice that governs the constriction of speculative thought; that is, it is to think the sacrifice *of* the negativity that governs speculative thought. I would argue that such re-(con)striction is the sacrifice of sacrifice. The contra-band is the sacrifice of (economical) sacrifice. Here the sacrifice of sacrifice does *not* refer to the moment when the all-burning as sacrifice (without reserve) sacrifices itself (Gf 271/Ge 244) to become economical sacrifice, *but rather* to the moment when economical sacrifice sacrifices itself to open a space for sacrifice (without reserve). The "logic" of constriction (which is otherwise than or "transcends" the transcendental) is the condition of the possibility of the transcendental. And just as the (con)striction is always already the transcendental of the transcendental, so one could likewise say, I would argue, that the (con)striction is always already the sacrifice of sacrifice. And this sacrifice of (economical) sacrifice inevitably turns into the sacrifice of (aneconomical) sacrifice, and vice versa. Here is the double bind of sacrifice.

Patočka and the Genealogy of Responsibility

Derrida's *The Gift of Death* (1992) is one of Derrida's most sustained considerations of the question of sacrifice. Early in this work, Derrida asks, How does
one give oneself death (*se donner la mort*) in the sense that "putting oneself to
death means dying while assuming responsibility for one's own death, committing suicide but also sacrificing oneself for another, *dying for the other*, thus
perhaps giving one's life by giving oneself death, accepting the gift of death, such
as Socrates, Christ, and others did in so many different ways?" (DM 19/GD 10).
What, Derrida asks, is the relation between suicide and sacrifice?

The *Gift of Death* begins with a reading of "Is Technological Civilization
Decadent, and Why?" one of the *Heretical Essays in the Philosophy of History*
(1990) of the Czech philosopher Jan Patočka. The reading traces a genealogy of
responsibility: demonic or orgiastic mystery, Platonic mystery, Christian mystery.
Each conversion from one mystery to the next conserves something of what is
interrupted. This logic of conservative rupture, Derrida argues, resembles the
economy of a sacrifice and sometimes reminds one of the economy of sublation
(*relève*) or *Aufhebung*.

Plato and μελέτη θανάτου *(Practicing [for] Death)*

What is at stake in the genealogy of the conversion from one secrecy (or mystery)
to another is the gift of death. Derrida indicates that Patočka cautions against an
enthusiasm for fusion with the sacred that has as its effect (and frequently its
intention) absolution from responsibility (DM 11/GD 1). The first awakening to
responsibility in the Platonic turn from this demonic or orgiastic mystery to the
Good corresponds, for Patočka, to a conversion with respect to the apprehension
of death. Philosophy comes into being as such at the moment when the soul
not only assembles itself within itself in "practicing (for) death," but also is ready
to receive death, "giving it to itself even," in a manner that delivers it from the
body as well as from the demonic and the orgiastic (DM 44/GD 40). The famous
passage from Plato's *Phaedo*, to which Patočka only obliquely refers, describes
the practice of philosophy as the soul's attainment of its own freedom and responsibility in its passage to death.

> The truth rather is that the soul which is pure at departing and draws after
> her no bodily taint, having never voluntarily during life had connexion with
> the body [οὐδὲν κοινωνοῦσα αὐτῷ ἐν τῷ βίῳ ἑκοῦσα εἶναι], which she is ever
> avoiding [φεύγουσα], herself gathered in herself [συνηθροισμένη αὐτὴ εἰς
> ἑαυτήν], and making such abstraction her perpetual study [ἅτε μελετῶσα ἀεὶ
> τοῦτο]—all this means that she has been a true disciple of philosophy [ἢ ὀρθῶς
> φιλοσοφοῦσα]; and therefore has in fact been always practising how to die
> without complaint [καὶ τῷ ὄντι τεθνάναι μελετῶσα]. For is not such a life the
> practice of death [ἢ οὐ τοῦτ᾽ ἂν εἴη μελέτη θανάτου]? (*Phaedo* 80e; see Pg 117/
> Pe 133; see DM 21–22/GD 13–14)

In "practicing (for) death" the soul separates from the body to assemble itself within itself (DM 22/GD 14). It is important to point out that the soul does not first exist and *then* become concerned about its death. The soul secrets itself— in the sense of the Latin *secretum* (from *secernere*), separate, distinct—in return- ing to itself (in both senses of assembling itself and waking itself) only in the experience of the μελέτη θανάτου, the care taken with death, the "practicing (for) death" (DM 21–22/GD 13–15).

Christianity and the mysterium tremendum *(Terrifying Mystery)*

The third moment of the genealogy of responsibility, Christian mystery, an- nounces a new apprehension of death, a new gift of death. The conversion from the Platonic mystery to the Christian mystery involves the entrance of the gift upon the scene of Patočka's genealogical drama.

> Responsible life was itself presented as a gift from something which ultimately, though it has the character of the Good, has also the traits of the inaccessible [*nepřistupného*] and forever superior to humans—the traits of the *mysterium* that always has the final word. Christianity, after all, understands the Good differently than Plato—as a self-forgetting goodness and a self-denying (not orgiastic) love. (TCU 115/TCD 106; see DM 36, 45/GD 30, 40–41)

With the conversion, the light or sun of the Platonic Good (as the invisible source of intelligible visibility) becomes in Christianity a personal gaze that sees me without my seeing it (DM 89/GD 93). The gift is received from the other, the transcendent other who sees without being seen, who remains inaccessible. The dissymmetry of this gaze is identified in Christian mystery as the terrifying mystery, the *mysterium tremendum* (DM 34/GD 27). This terror does not play a role in the Platonic moment of the genealogical drama of responsibility. The terror of this secret "exceeds and precedes" the complacent relation of a subject to the Platonic Good (DM 34/GD 28). What is given in this terrifying mystery is a gift of death. The difference between Platonism and Christianity is a new apprehension of death. The difference is "the turn in the face of death and death eternal; which lives in anxiety and hope inextricably intertwined, which trembles in the knowledge of its sin and with its whole being offers itself in the *sacrifice* [*oběť*] of penance" (TCU 116/TCD 108, emphasis added; see DM 37, 90/GD 31, 94). What is this sacrifice of penance? Derrida connects it with the aporetic structure of responsibility. Responsibility requires, Derrida argues, that one re- spond as irreplaceable singularity *and*, paradoxically, that one forget or efface the origin of what one gives (DM 55/GD 51).

What is given in the terrifying mystery—and this represents, as will become apparent in a moment, a new apprehension of death—is a "giving goodness" that forgets itself. Goodness is given in that the inaccessible other calls me to goodness, calls me to be good, that is, to sacrifice myself. "It subjects its receivers, giving itself to them as goodness itself but also as the law" (DM 45/GD 41).

The Question of Sacrifice

With this gift there is the emergence of a new form of responsibility, and, at the same time, a new apprehension of death. The experience of responsibility on the basis of the law that is given, that is, the experience of irreplaceability, is the same as the experience of irreplaceability "given" by the approach of death. "It is the same gift, the same source, one could say the same goodness and the same law" (DM 45/GD 41). It is from the experience of death as the "gift" of irreplaceable singularity that I feel called to responsibility and sacrifice.

Heidegger and Sein zum Tode *(Being-Towards-Death)*

Derrida points out that, up to a certain point, Patočka's analysis is comparable to the existential analysis of Heidegger's *Being and Time* (1927). This reading of the work of Heidegger alongside that moment of Patočka's genealogy of responsibility called "Christianity" focuses, however, only on a reading of death that reads death as possibility, that is, that moment of death that gives irreplaceability. Irreplaceability, according to *Being and Time*, is given by death. "By its very essence, death is in every case mine, in so far as it 'is' at all" (SZ 240/BT 284). This formulation follows a consideration of sacrifice. There is no gift of self, no sacrifice, Derrida writes, apart from the irreplaceability given by the approach of death. Though Heidegger does not formulate it this way, it seems to Derrida that "one does not betray his thinking if one translates it in this way, for it has always, as much as has that of Levinas, paid constant attention to the fundamental and founding possibility of sacrifice" (DM 46/GD 42). In *Being and Time*, Heidegger defines irreplaceability as the condition of the possibility (not the condition of the *im*possibility) of sacrifice. "*No one can take the Other's dying away from him* [Keiner kann dem Anderen sein Sterben abnehmen]. Of course someone can 'go to his death for another'. But that always means to sacrifice [opfern] oneself for the Other '*in some definite affair*'" (SZ 240/BT 284). While I can die for the other (by sacrificing myself for the other "in some definite affair"), I cannot, Heidegger immediately adds, die for the other (by dying in place of the other). "Such 'dying for' can never signify that the Other has thus had his death taken away in even the slightest degree [*daß dem Anderen damit sein Tod im geringsten abgenommen sei*]. Dying is something that every Dasein itself must take upon itself at the time [*Das Sterben muß jedes Dasein jeweilig selbst auf sich nehmen*]" (SZ 240/BT 284). In these sentences Derrida notes a shift from *abnehmen* to *aufnehmen* in the sense of *auf sich nehmen*. The death that cannot be taken away (*abnehmen*) must be taken upon oneself (*auf sich nehmen*). I must appropriate death, I must assume this possibility of impossibility, if I am to have access to what is irreplaceably mine (which is the condition of the possibility of sacrifice). It is not as though there is a self of the *Jemeinigkeit* that *then* comes to be a being-towards-death. It is in the authentic being-towards-death, the appropriation of death, that the self of the *Jemeinigkeit* is constituted, that its irreplaceability is produced. To this extent, Derrida's reading is not unlike his reading of the Platonic moment in Patočka's genealogy of responsibility. In a reading of Plato's

Phaedo, Derrida points out that the soul does not first exist and *then* become concerned about its death. The soul secrets itself in returning to itself (in both senses of assembling itself and waking itself) only in the experience of the μελέτη θανάτου, the care taken with death, the "practicing (for) death" (DM 21–22/GD 13–15). Aware of the essential differences between the two, Derrida seems to make a link between the assembling of oneself in the Platonic sense and the drawing back from inauthenticity effected in authentic being-towards-death. To this extent, the reading of that moment of Patočka's genealogy of responsibility called "Christianity" (at least insofar as it is limited to the link that Derrida makes between the work of Patočka and the work of Heidegger) is not unlike the reading of the "Platonic" moment in the genealogy insofar as it reads death as possibility.

This reading is maintained in Derrida's consideration of the call (*Ruf*). According to *Being and Time,* to the extent that the self of the *Jemeinigkeit* is irreplaceable — which is given by death — it is the place in which the call (*Ruf*) is heard and in which responsibility comes on the scene (DM 49/GD 45–46).

Derrida's reading of the work of Heidegger alongside that moment of Patočka's genealogy of responsibility called "Christianity" is not only limited *to,* but also limited *by,* reading death merely as possibility. This limitation is hinted at in the text with the remark that he will need to come back to the principle involved in Levinas's objection to Heidegger in a rereading of Heidegger's analysis of death as the possibility of the impossibility of Dasein (DM 49–50/GD 46). This rereading, which I would argue is performed in Derrida's *Aporias: Dying — Awaiting (One Another at) the "Limits of Truth"* (1994), corrects the limitation of a particular reading of death in the work of Heidegger (i.e., death as possibility) that prevents a comprehensive reading of it alongside that moment of Patočka's genealogy of responsibility called "Christianity," and raises the question of the proximity of the work of Heidegger and Levinas. This limitation is also hinted at in the text with the remark that the sacrifice made possible by the appropriation of death is *not* a sacrifice without reserve. The death that cannot be taken away (*abnehmen*) must be taken upon oneself (*auf sich nehmen*). I must appropriate death, I must assume this possibility of impossibility, if I am to have access to what is irreplaceably mine (which is the condition of the possibility of sacrifice). But this sacrifice is "a nonexhaustive exchange or sacrifice, an economy of sacrifice" (DM 46/GD 43). Sacrifice without reserve, like responsibility without reserve, requires another reading of Heidegger's existential analysis of death.

It already has been logically and philosophically deduced that the accession to responsibility and sacrifice through the experience of irreplaceability is "given" by the approach of death (DM 54/GD 51). Derrida reads this moment of Patočka's Christianity alongside a reading of death in Heidegger that reads death as possibility. But the mortal thus deduced is one whose responsibility requires that one concern oneself not only with an objective Good that Patočka associates with Platonism, but with a goodness that is forgetful of itself, that is, a goodness that is a gift of infinite love (DM 54/GD 51). Therefore, there is a dissymmetry between the finite and responsible mortal and the goodness of the infinite gift.

One is never responsible enough (and, therefore, guilty before any fault is determined) not only because one is finite, but also because of the aporetic character of responsibility. Recall that it is the knowledge of this originary guilt (this originary sin) that makes one tremble and because of which one offers oneself in the sacrifice of penance (TCU 116/TCD 108; see DM 37, 90/GD 31, 94). Responsibility (like sacrifice) is aporetic insofar as it requires two contradictory movements. "It requires one to respond as oneself and as irreplaceable singularity, to answer for what one does, says, gives; but it also requires that, being good and through goodness, one forget or efface the origin of what one gives" (DM 55/GD 51). It is on this aporetic structure in Patočka's "Christianity," succinctly presented in the last two citations, that I propose to focus. I would argue that it is only Derrida's rereading of Heidegger's analysis of death that is adequate to the aporetic structure of responsibility.

Heidegger says that for Dasein (and for Dasein alone) impossibility as death is possible; that is, it can appear as such and announce itself. Dasein alone is capable of this aporia. "And," Derrida adds in *Aporias*, "it is only in the act of authentic (*eigentlich*), resolute, determinate, and decided assumption by which *Dasein* would take upon itself the possibility of this impossibility that the aporia *as such* would announce itself *as such* and purely to *Dasein* as its most proper possibility, hence as the most proper essence of *Dasein*, its freedom, its ability to question, and its opening to the meaning of being" (AM 336/AD 74–75). Here Derrida asks the possible/impossible question that sets the stage for the ruinous performance of the necessary yet impossible step beyond into authenticity that is at the heart of the possibility of the existential analysis: What difference is there between (1) the possibility of appearing as such of the possibility of an impossibility and (2) the *impossibility* of appearing as such of the possibility of an impossibility? (AM 336/AD 75). Paralleling the first part of this possible/impossible question, Derrida writes, "According to Heidegger, it is therefore the impossibility of the 'as such' that, *as such, would be possible* to *Dasein*" (AM 336/AD 75, emphasis added to "would be possible"), would appear as such to Dasein. It is important to note that this step remains this side of ruination. It remains, as Derrida noted earlier, the act of authentic, resolute, determinate, and decided assumption by which Dasein would take upon itself the possibility of this impossibility. But then a "but" announces a change in nuance. Paralleling the second part of the possible/impossible question, Derrida writes, "But if the impossibility of the 'as such' is indeed the impossibility of the 'as such' [i.e., if the impossibility of the as such is *indeed impossible*], it [i.e., the impossibility of the 'as such'] is *also* what cannot appear as such" (AM 336/AD 75, emphasis added), is *also* what *would not be possible* to Dasein, contrary — and is it contrary? — to what is said in the step performed just prior to the "but." "Indeed," Derrida adds, "this relation to the disappearing as such of the 'as such' — the 'as such' that Heidegger makes the distinctive mark and the specific ability of *Dasein* [i.e., the authentic, resolute, determinate, and decided assumption of the possibility of the impossibility of death]—is also the characteristic common *both* to the inauthentic *and* to the authentic forms of the existence of *Dasein*" (AM 336/AD 75). The fact that the impossibility that *would be possible* to Dasein (in authentic existence) cannot appear as such, that is, *would not be possible* to Dasein (even in authentic existence), erases the distinction between the inauthentic (in which impossibility as death does *not* appear as such, is evaded) and the authentic (in which impossibility as death *supposedly* can appear). Here one sees the ruination of the step that would complete the existential analysis *in the performance of the step itself.* Here one sees the unworking of the work.

With this reading in *Aporias*, Derrida shows how what is at the very heart of the possibility of the existential analysis of death as possibility of the impossibility of Dasein can be turned against the very possibility of the existential analysis, depending on the way one reads the expression "the possibility of impossibility" (AM 336–337/AD 76–77). This is the context of Derrida's remark that "[w]hen Blanchot constantly repeats—and it is a long complaint and not a triumph of life—the impossible dying, the impossibility, alas, of dying, he says at once the same thing and something completely different from Heidegger" (AM 337/AD 77). Turning what is at the very heart of the possibility of the existential analysis of death, that is, the appropriation of death, against the very possibility of the existential analysis, Derrida writes, "If death, the most proper possibility of *Dasein*, is the possibility of its impossibility, death becomes the most improper possibility and the most ex-propriating, the most inauthenticating one" (AM 337/AD 77). This passage, along with the previous passage that raises the question of the proximity of the work of Heidegger and Blanchot, echoes "the radical reversal" referred to by Blanchot in *The Space of Literature* (1955).

> Death, then, would not be "the possibility absolutely proper to man," my own death, that unique event which answers Rilke's prayer: "O Lord, grant to each his own death," but on the contrary, that which never happens to me, so that never do I die, but rather "they die." Men die always other than themselves, at the level of the neutrality and the impersonality of the eternal They.
>
> The characteristics of this reversal can only be recalled briefly here.
>
> *They die:* this is not a reassuring formula designed to put off the fearsome moment. *They die:* he who dies is anonymous, and anonymity is the guise in which the ungraspable, the unlimited, the unsituated is most dangerously affirmed among us. (EL 327/SL 241)

This "radical reversal"—death as possibility turning into death as impossibility—parallels the two contradictory movements of responsibility and sacrifice characteristic, according to Derrida's reading, of Patočka's Christianity. Only it—and not simply death as possibility—is adequate to the aporetic structure of responsibility and sacrifice. Responsibility and sacrifice require, as was mentioned earlier, that one respond as irreplaceable singularity *and*, paradoxically, that one forget or efface the origin of what one gives (DM 55/GD 51). Only the aporia of death—that moment when death as possibility turns into death as impossibility—is adequate to the aporias of responsibility and sacrifice, insofar as death as possibility gives irreplaceable singularity and death as impossibility gives the ex-propriation, the anonymity, that is a forgetting or effacement of oneself.

This reading of death is, I would argue, operative (though not explicitly) in Blanchot's reading of responsibility in the work of Levinas. In *The Writing of the Disaster* (1980), Blanchot shows responsibility's aporetic structure in a fragment that calls for being quoted at length:

> Responsible: this word generally qualifies—in a prosaic, bourgeois manner—a mature, lucid, conscientious man, who acts with circumspection, who takes into account all elements of a given situation, calculates and decides. The word "responsible" qualifies the successful man of action. But now responsi-bility—my responsibility for the other, for everyone, without reciprocity—is displaced. No longer does it belong to consciousness; it is not an activating thought process put into practice, nor is it even a duty that would impose itself from without and from within. My responsibility for the Other [*Autrui*] presupposes an overturning such that it can only be marked by a change in the status of "me," a change in time and perhaps in language. Responsibility, which withdraws me from my order—perhaps from all orders and from order itself—responsibility, which separates me from myself (from the "me" that is mastery and power, from the free, speaking subject) and reveals the other [*autre*] *in place* of me, requires that I answer for absence, for passivity. It requires, that is to say, that I answer for the impossibility of being responsible—to which this responsibility without measure has always already consigned me by holding me accountable and also discounting me altogether. (ED 45–46/ WD 25, translation modified, the phrase "*responsabilité sans mesure*" was omitted)

Responsibility (like sacrifice) requires that I respond as irreplaceable singularity, and it requires that I am exposed to ex-propriation.

Sacrifice without reserve, like responsibility, requires not only death as pos-sibility, but also death as impossibility. Sacrifice without reserve, like responsi-bility, requires irreplaceable singularity and ex-propriation. Recall that the sacrifice made possible by the appropriation of death is *not* a sacrifice without reserve. The sacrifice mentioned by Heidegger in *Being and Time* (SZ 240/BT 284), the sacrifice made possible by the appropriation of death, is "a nonex-haustive exchange or sacrifice, an economy of sacrifice" (DM 46/GD 43). Sac-rifice without reserve (like responsibility without reserve) requires Blanchot's and Derrida's rereadings of Heidegger's analysis of death. In "Postscript to 'What is Metaphysics?'" (1943) from *Pathmarks* (1967), Heidegger refers to a sacrifice without reserve that could be read as Heidegger's own rereading of his existential analysis of death in *Being and Time*. According to *Being and Time*, authentic Being-towards-death is an impassioned *anxious freedom toward death* (Freiheit zum Tode) that is an anticipation that brings Dasein face to face with the pos-sibility of the impossibility of being itself (SZ 266/BT 311). Being-towards-death, as the anticipation of the possibility of impossibility, is what sets possibility *free as* possibility (SZ 262/BT 307), rather than weakening it by *calculating* how we are to have it at our disposal by looking away from the possible to its possible actualization (SZ 261–262/BT 305–306). In "Postscript to 'What is Metaphysics?' " Heidegger writes that the need for the truth of being to be preserved fulfills itself in the freedom of sacrifice (*der Freiheit des Opfers*). This sacrifice is not unlike a rereading of the existential analysis of death that reads death as possibility turning into death as impossibility. This sacrifice is not unlike a rereading of the existential analysis of death that reads death as giving both irreplaceable singularity and ex-propriation.

> The sacrifice [*Opfer*] is that of the human essence expending itself—in a manner removed from all compulsion, because it arises from the abyss of freedom—for the preservation of the truth of being for beings. In sacrifice [*Opfer*] there occurs [*ereignet sich*] the concealed thanks that alone pays homage to the grace that being has bestowed upon the human essence in thinking, so that human beings may, in their relation to being, assume the guardianship of being. Originary thinking [*Das anfängliche Denken*] is the echo of being's favor, of a favor in which a singular event is cleared and lets come to pass [*sich ereignen*]: that beings are. (NWM 310/PWM 236)

This is *not* "a nonexhaustive exchange or sacrifice, an economy of sacrifice" (DM 46/GD 43). This is sacrifice without reserve. This sacrifice is not a *calculated* action that is obsessed with ends.

> Sacrifice [*Opfer*] is at home in the essence of the event whereby being lays claim upon the human being for the truth of being. For this reason, sacrifice [*Opfer*] tolerates no calculation, which can only ever miscalculate it in terms of utility or uselessness, whether the ends are placed low or set high. Such miscalculation distorts the essence of sacrifice [*das Wesen des Opfers*]. The obsession with ends confuses the clarity of the awe, ready for anxiety, that belongs to the courage of sacrifice [*Opfermutes*] which has taken upon itself the neighborhood of the indestructible. (NWM 311/PWM 237)

This is not a calculated sacrifice, an economical sacrifice, but the essence of sacrifice. This is an essential sacrifice. This echoes Heidegger's remark in "The Origin of the Work of Art" (1935–1936) from *Holzwege* (1950). The essential sacrifice (*das wesentliche Opfer*) is one of five ways mentioned by Heidegger of "an original happening of truth [*ursprüngliches Geschehen der Wahrheit*]."

> One essential way in which truth establishes itself in the beings it has opened up is truth setting itself into work. Another way in which truth occurs is the act that founds a political state [on the inevitable sacrifice of the founders, see Heidegger's *Hölderlins Hymnen »Germanien« und »Der Rhein«*]. Still another way in which truth comes to shine forth is the nearness of that which is not simply a being, but the being that is most of all. Still another way in which truth grounds itself is the essential sacrifice [*das wesentliche Opfer*]. Still another way in which truth becomes is the thinker's questioning, which, as the

> thinking of Being, names Being in its question-worthiness. (UK 49/OWA
> 61–62)

This essence of sacrifice — which is essential sacrifice — is, I would argue, a sacrifice of sacrifice. It is not a calculated sacrifice made possible by the appropriation of death (an economy of sacrifice), but a sacrifice without reserve that requires death as possibility turning into death as impossibility (an economy of sacrifice turning into a sacrifice of economy).

A Heretical and Hyperbolic Form of Christianity

Returning to Derrida's consideration of sacrifice in the work of Patočka, Derrida writes that Patočka's work is a "heretical and hyperbolic form" of Christianity (if, in fact, it does involve Christianity). Derrida points out that "Patočka speaks and thinks in the places where Christianity has not yet thought or spoken of what it should have been and is not yet" (DM 52/GD 49). What produces the Christian themes considered by Patočka is, according to Derrida, a logic that ultimately has no need of the event of a revelation or the revelation of an event. This logic needs to think the *possibility* of the event of a revelation or the revelation of an event, but not the event itself (DM 52/GD 49). The possibility of the Christian event — that is, the gift of infinite love (the Good as goodness that forgets itself) linked to death — can be logically deduced through the aporias of death, responsibility, and sacrifice. Derrida suggests a list of philosophers, which includes Heidegger and Levinas, that belong to a tradition "that consists of proposing a non-dogmatic doublet of dogma, a philosophical and metaphysical doublet, in any case a *thinking* that 'repeats' [«*répète*»] the possibility of religion without religion" (DM 53/GD 49). But this repetition contaminates the purity of the non-dogmatic doublet of dogma. In the wake of his rereading of Heidegger's analysis of death as possibility of the impossibility of Dasein, Derrida writes in *Aporias* that since the contaminating contraband of Christian ontotheology remains irreducible, it already insinuates itself through the very idiom of the existential analysis of death (AM 338/AD 79). Therefore, he continues, "[d]espite all the distance taken from anthropo-theology, indeed, from Christian onto-theology, the analysis of death in *Being and Time* nonetheless repeats [*répète*] all the essential motifs of such onto-theology, a repetition [*répétition*] that bores into its originarity right down to its ontological foundation" (AM 338/AD 80). This passage shows that the repetition does not leave the originarity of the Heideggerian analysis unsullied. This passage marks an interruption effected in Derrida's rereading of Heidegger's analysis of death. The interruption of the boundary between the authentic and the inauthentic effected in Derrida's rereading effects an interruption of the originarity of the Heideggerian analysis. The fact that this repetition contaminates the purity of the non-dogmatic doublet of dogma, the philosophical and metaphysical doublet, is likewise evident in *The Gift of Death*. Immediately after writing that "[e]verything *comes to pass* as though only the analysis of the concept of responsibility [i.e., as it is given by death] were ultimately capable of producing Christianity, or more precisely the possibility of Christianity," Derrida adds, "One might as well conclude, conversely, that this concept of responsibility is Christian through and through and is produced by the event of Christianity" (DM 53/GD 50). There is, in a sense, a double origin at work here. There is no choice to be made here between a logical and philosophical deduction of religious themes, that is, one that is not related to a revelatory event, and the reference to a revelatory event. "One implies the other" (DM 53/GD 50). In *Aporias*, Derrida writes, "Considering what we just have seen considering borders, demarcations, and limits, the only characteristic that we can stress here is that of an irreducibly double inclusion: the including and the included [i.e., the existential analysis of death and the Judeo-Christiano-Islamic experience of death, though not necessarily respectively] regularly exchange places in this strange topography of edges" (AM 338/AD 80).

Not only is one pole of this double origin—the "nondogmatic doublet of dogma," that is, the logical deduction of responsibility and sacrifice given by the approach of death—contaminated by the reference to a revelatory event, but it likewise contaminates the purity of the dogma associated with the revelatory event, calling for a rereading of Christianity and opening a space for Patočka's "heretical and hyperbolic form" of Christianity (if, in fact, it does involve Christianity). In the conversion from Platonism to Christianity the Good is no longer a transcendental objective, but the relation to the other. It is "an experience of personal goodness and a movement of intention" (DM 54/GD 50). This goodness is a goodness that forgets itself, and this movement is a movement of the gift that renounces itself, that is, a movement of infinite love. "Only infinite love," Derrida writes, "can renounce itself and, in order to *become finite*, become incarnated in order to love the other, to love the other as a finite other" (DM 54/GD 51). Patočka's reading of Christianity involves, therefore, a double effacement or renunciation. It has already been noted that goodness is given in that the inaccessible other calls me to goodness, calls me to be good, that is, forget myself. "It subjects its receivers, giving itself to them as goodness itself but also as the law" (DM 45/GD 41). Here it must be noted also that in the incarnation of goodness as law, the infinite being effaces itself. Thus when one reads that responsibility requires both that one respond as irreplaceable singularity and that one efface the origin of what one gives, one can read this effacement as encompassing both the infinite and the finite being. There is an effacing of the infinite being in its becoming finite/incarnate and an effacing of the finite/incarnated being. There is a sacrifice of the transcendent God with the attending sacrifice of the subject. The reading of death—death as possibility turning into death as impossibility—that I argued earlier should be read alongside responsibility in that moment of Patočka's genealogy called "Christianity" effects a transformation of the reading of revelation by drawing God out of objectivity, thereby keeping Patočka's reference to a supreme being distinct from all ontotheological meaning in the sense that Heidegger gave to it (DM 39/GD 33).

Derrida's reading of Patočka's genealogy of responsibility—which finds its fulfillment in the God of Christianity whose gift of goodness calls one to goodness—raises the question of the role of the demonic in Patočka's Christianity. Recall that according to Patočka's genealogy of responsibility—demonic or orgiastic mystery, Platonic mystery, Christian mystery—each conversion from one mystery to the next conserves something of what is interrupted. This logic of conservative rupture, Derrida argues, resembles the economy of a sacrifice and sometimes reminds one of the economy of sublation (relève) or Aufhebung. Patočka employs the terms incorporation (přivtělení) and repression (potlačení) to describe this double conversion: Platonic mystery incorporates demonic or orgiastic mystery and Christian mystery represses Platonic mystery. This vocabulary indicates—if these words were meant to be given the meanings that they possess in psychoanalytic discourse—that in the conversion from one mystery to another the first is not destroyed, but kept inside unconsciously, after effecting a topical displacement and a hierarchical subordination (DM 18/GD 9). This language also suggests—again, if these words were meant to be given the meanings that they possess in psychoanalytic discourse—that conversion amounts to a process of mourning, to keeping within oneself that whose death must be endured (DM 18/GD 9). Even if these words were not meant to have these meanings, nothing prevents one, Derrida argues, from experimenting with a psychoanalytic reading, or at least a hermeneutics that takes psychoanalytic concepts corresponding to these words into account. This is especially true given that Derrida's reading concentrates on "secrecy" (or mystery), which cannot remain immune to the psychoanalytic ideas of incorporation and repression. Derrida points out that in the conversion from demonic or orgiastic mystery to Platonic mystery, the mystery of the demonic is kept within oneself and endured (which, Derrida argues, amounts to a process of mourning). "The secret of responsibility would consist of keeping secret, or 'incorporated,' the secret of the demonic and thus of preserving within itself a nucleus of irresponsibility or of absolute unconsciousness, something Patočka will later call 'orgiastic irresponsibility'" (DM 27/GD 20). Derrida is referring specifically to the conversion from demonic or orgiastic mystery to Platonic mystery, but there is no reason that the demonic does not recur in the Christian mystery. "Orgiastic mystery recurs indefinitely, it is always at work: not only in Platonism, [...] but also in Christianity and even in the space of the Aufklärung and of secularization in general" (DM 28/GD 21). This preservation of the demonic in the Christian mystery contaminates the Christian mystery. The Christian mystery "will never become" (quoting Derrida, though with respect to the Platonic mystery and its incorporation of the demonic) "pure and authentic, or absolutely new" (DM 27/GD 20). Derrida's choice of words here echoes the aporetic character of Heidegger's existential analysis of death—death, the most proper possibility of Dasein, becomes the most improper pos-

sibility and the most ex-propriating, the most inauthenticating possibility (AM
337/AD 77). The aporias of death, responsibility, and sacrifice characteristic of
that moment of Patočka's genealogy of responsibility called "Christianity" attest, I would argue, to the contamination of the God of infinite love by the demonic. They attest to the ruination of the conversion to Christianity (insofar as
Christianity is understood as characterized *merely* by a God whose gift of goodness calls one to goodness) because the sacrifice and responsibility demanded
of me hold me accountable and discount me. Sacrifice and responsibility require—using words of Blanchot that echo Heidegger's analysis of death as the
possibility of the impossibility of Dasein—that I answer for the impossibility of
sacrifice, for the impossibility of being responsible, which makes me always already guilty or irresponsible. The God of Christianity calls one to goodness
and badness, to responsibility and irresponsibility.

Kierkegaard and the *Akedah* (Binding)

In *The Gift of Death*, Derrida next extends his consideration of the aporias of
death, responsibility, and sacrifice to a reading of Genesis 22. The *Akedah* "belongs to what one might just dare to call the common treasure, the terrifying
secret of the *mysterium tremendum* that is a property of all three so-called religions
of the Book [that is, Judaism, Christianity, and Islam], the religions of the races
of Abraham" (DM 65/GD 64). Up to this point the couple responsibility/irre-
sponsibility has been considered only with respect to the asymmetrical relationship of the self and the other. It has not played a role in the relationship of the
self with the other other. Derrida's reading of Genesis 22 considers the role of
the couple responsibility/irresponsibility in the relationship of the self with the
other other.

   What makes one tremble in the *mysterium tremendum* of Patočka's Christian
responsibility is the gift of infinite love, the dissymmetry between the divine gaze
that sees me, and myself, who does not see the hidden, silent, and secret God,
all of which is logically deduced from the disproportion between the experience
of responsibility and sacrifice as irreplaceability (which is given in death read as
possibility) and the experience of responsibility and sacrifice that is the forgetting
or effacement of oneself (which is given, I have argued, in death read as impossibility) (DM 58/GD 55–56).

   Derrida uses this consideration of trembling to segue to Kierkegaard's *Fear
and Trembling* (1843). The *mysterium tremendum*, like the title of Kierkegaard's
work, includes "at least an implicit and indirect reference" (DM 58/GD 56) to
a passage in Philippians: "Therefore, my beloved, just as you have always obeyed
me, not only in my presence, but much more now in my absence, work out
your own salvation with fear and trembling" (Phil. 2:12, NRSV). The disciples
are asked to work out their own salvation in the absence of the master. Derrida
argues that if Paul says "adieu" as he asks the community to obey, in fact ordering
them to obey, "it is because God is himself absent, hidden and silent, separate,

secret, at the moment he has to be obeyed" (DM 59/GD 57). God does not give reasons; otherwise God would not be God as wholly other. Paul continues: "[F]or it is God who is at work in you, enabling you both to will and to work for his good pleasure" (Phil. 2:13, NRSV). In a footnote to this passage Derrida notes that "his good pleasure" does not refer to God's pleasure but to God's sovereign will "that is not required to consult, just as the king acts as he intends without revealing his secret reasons, without having to account for his actions or explain them" (DM 107n5/GD 57n3).

In *Fear and Trembling*, Kierkegaard considers a double secret in God's commanding Abraham to sacrifice his son Isaac (Genesis 22): the secret between God and Abraham and the secret between Abraham and his family. When Isaac asks where the sacrificial lamb is to be found, Abraham responds while keeping the secret: "God himself will provide the lamb for a burnt offering, my son" (Gen. 22:8, NRSV). This double secret also involves the double necessity of keeping the secret—Abraham must keep the secret because it is his duty, and he must keep the secret because, as Derrida notes, he can do nothing but keep it (DM 60/GD 59) insofar as he does not know it.

Derrida writes, within the context of his consideration of Genesis 22, that responsibility demands absolute singularity and substitution (DM 62/GD 61). But these two demands are contradictory, for the general answering-for-oneself in the medium of language and the concept before the generality of others, the translation of absolute singularity into universal principles, suspends my absolute responsibility to God. By translating the decision from the "solitary, secret, and silent" into the general by answering for myself in the public arena, that is, by suspending my absolute irreplaceable singularity, I renounce my freedom and absolute responsibility. This translation into what Kierkegaard calls the "ethical" is always a temptation (DM 62/GD 61). In the "instant of decision" one is absolutely singular. One is a singular person that has an absolute responsibility to a singular other. Falling back on precedents or universal principles serves only to *generalize* the situation, which makes one irresponsible (but it is important to keep in mind that not generalizing the situation, that is, not responding to the other other, also makes one irresponsible). As soon as one succumbs to the temptation of the ethical, one loses that irreplaceable singularity given by death (one also loses, it is important to note, the ex-propriation, the substitution likewise given by death and likewise required by absolute responsibility). It is as if absolute responsibility must be irresponsible to be absolutely responsible. It must transgress the ethical order, which for Kierkegaard stands for Hegelian *Sittlichkeit* (but also arguably includes Kantian *Moralität* and Habermasian *Diskursethik*). It must be irresponsible insofar as it must not answer for itself (that is, before the law of some universal tribunal); it must resist translation into the general; it must remain un*concept*ualizable (DM 62/GD 61); it must remain un*present*able. Abraham presents himself before God, the one to whom he says, "Here I am," at the same time as he refuses to present himself before the community (DM 63/GD 62).

The necessity yet impossibility of thinking the two moments of the paradox together "remains irreducible to presence or to presentation, it demands a temporality of the instant without ever constituting a present" (DM 66/GD 65). It demands the "atemporal temporality" (DM 66/GD 65) of the instant, a duration that cannot be stabilized; it cannot be grasped or comprehended. With every genuine decision, there is, if only for an instant, a suspension of comprehension. There is, if only for an instant, a suspension of the work of negation and the work itself. The work of absolute responsibility is inevitably irresponsible. To put one's faith in God to work, that is, to assume one's absolute responsibility, one must be guilty or irresponsible, one must transgress ethical duty. But in transgressing it one belongs to it and at the same time recognizes it. "Abraham must assume absolute responsibility for sacrificing his son by sacrificing ethics, but in order for there to be a sacrifice, the ethical must retain all its value" (DM 66/GD 66). Here one sees the ruination of the step that is the work of absolute responsibility *in the performance of the step itself.* Here one sees the unworking of the work of absolute responsibility. Every genuine decision demands the sacrifice (and, at the same time, the recognition) of the ethical order, if only for an instant. The necessary yet impossible paradox "must be endured *in the instant itself*" (DM 66/GD 66). The aporia must be endured. But what does this mean? One cannot underestimate the profound unworking at the heart of this work of enduring the aporia. In *Aporias*, following his rereading of Heidegger's existential analysis of death considered earlier, Derrida writes, "[I]f one must endure the aporia, if such is the law of all decisions, of all responsibilities, of all duties without duty, and of all the border problems that ever can arise, *the aporia can never simply be endured as such.* The ultimate aporia is the impossibility of aporia *as such*" (AM 337/AD 78). A name for this aporia is *sacrifice:* "Paradox, scandal, and aporia are themselves nothing other than *sacrifice*, the revelation of conceptual thinking at its limit, at its death and finitude" (DM 68/GD 68, emphasis added). Quoting Kierkegaard, Derrida writes, "[T]he instant of decision is madness" (DM 66/GD 65). It is important to note that madness does not arise because one has a choice between two different but equally plausible choices. It is rather the case that choosing one is choosing the other, being responsible is transgressing responsibility, being responsible is being irresponsible, if only for an instant. If a decision did not involve a sacrifice of ethics, that is, if a decision were merely between two extant choices, no "call to action" or "call of conscience" would be unconditional. The decision would be generalized. It would be comfortably situated within past or present contexts of origination or within future horizons of expectation. For example, "I made that decision because, given the circumstances, it was the best decision" or "I made that decision because it will further my (future) salvation." With this stabilization of the aporia, an ethics of good conscience reinstalls itself. One is obliged to behave not only in a responsible manner, but also in an irresponsible manner, and one is obliged to do that *in the name of* absolute duty (DM 67/GD 67). And this name which must always be singular is, as Derrida points out, the name of God as absolutely other to which I am bound by an absolute obligation (DM 67/GD 67). "God is the name of the absolute other as other and as unique (the God of Abraham defined as the one and unique)" (DM 68/GD 68).

The aporia of responsibility is complicated by the formula *tout autre est tout autre*, every other (one) is every (bit) other, which disturbs Kierkegaard's discourse on the absolute uniqueness of Jahweh (DM 77/GD 79) while at the same time reinforcing its most extreme ramifications, because it implies that the wholly other God is everywhere one finds the wholly other. "And since each of us, everyone else, each other is infinitely other in its absolute singularity, inaccessible, solitary, transcendent, nonmanifest, originarily nonpresent to my *ego* [. . .], then what can be said about Abraham's relation to God can be said about my relation without relation [*rapport sans rapport*] to *every other* (one) *as every* (bit) *other* [tout autre comme tout autre], in particular my relation to my neighbor or my loved ones who are as inaccessible to me, as secret and transcendent as Jahweh" (DM 76–77/GD 78). "God"—serving as the index not only of the *wholly other* (tout autre) but also of *every* (other) *other* (tout autre)—is other than himself; God is his "own" other (and given that this perhaps calls into question God's gender and personhood, perhaps it would be more appropriate to write that God is other than him/her/itself, God is his/her/its own other). But is not God, as Levinas maintains in "God and Philosophy" (1975) from *Of God Who Comes to Mind* (1986), "not simply the 'first other,' or the 'other *par excellence,*' or the 'absolutely other,' but other than the other, other otherwise, and other with an alterity prior to the alterity of the other, prior to the ethical obligation to the other and different from every neighbor" (DP 115/GP 69)? Perhaps. But is it not this uncertainty that constitutes the other as wholly other? Otherwise would not the wholly other be an apodictic notion, something clear and distinct, rather than something to be believed?

The border between the religious and the ethical—a border that both Kierkegaard and Levinas want to maintain—becomes, therefore, questionable. If every other (one) is every (bit) other (*tout autre est tout autre*), then Kierkegaard can no longer distinguish between a generality of ethics (that would need to be sacrificed) and the faith that turns toward God alone (and away from human duty), since what Kierkegaard calls "ethics" is also (as Levinas reminds him) the order of and respect for absolute singularity (that is, ethics is not only the order of generality). Therefore, Kierkegaard cannot distinguish between the ethical order and the religious order. But in taking into account the absolute alterity in relations between one human being and another, Levinas likewise can no longer distinguish between the alterity of God and the "same" alterity of every human being (which he wants to do). He likewise can no longer determine the limit between the ethical order and the religious order. "His ethics is already a religious one" (DM 81/GD 84). Levinas, therefore, cannot say something completely different from Kierkegaard, and vice versa (Derrida refers the reader to DM 108n8/ GD 78n6, and to VeM 143, 162ff./VaM 96, 110ff.).

The trembling of the formula *tout autre est tout autre* circles back upon the earlier reading of Patočka's Christianity. Recall that in the conversion from Platonism to Christianity the Good is no longer a transcendental objective, but the relation to the other. It is "an experience of personal goodness and a movement of intention" (DM 54/GD 50). This goodness is a goodness that forgets itself, and this movement is a movement of the gift that renounces itself, that is, a movement of infinite love. "Only infinite love," Derrida writes, "can renounce itself and, in order to *become finite*, become incarnated in order to love the other, to love the other as a finite other" (DM 54/GD 51). Could one, perhaps, read the phrase *tout autre est tout autre* as an articulation of the infinite *becoming* finite, because as radically other, God is other than him/her/itself?

The trembling of the formula *tout autre est tout autre* also calls for a re-reading of the relationship between Levinas's reading of the alterity of the infinite in Descartes's *Meditations on First Philosophy* (1641) and Levinas's reading of the alterity of the other person. This relationship is ambiguous. Is Levinas's reading of Descartes's *Meditations* in *Totality and Infinity* (1961) merely a formal reading of the idea of infinity that then needs to be deformalized or concretized in the face (TeI 21/TaI 50)? Is the subject's relationship with the infinite as it is articulated in Descartes's *Meditations* maintained at a distance from the subject's relationship with the other person? With the formula *tout autre est tout autre*, the relationship with God serves as an index of not only the *wholly other* (*tout autre*) but also of *every* (other) *other* (*tout autre*). This formula helps to articulate better the relationship between Levinas's reading of the alterity of the infinite in Descartes's *Meditations* and Levinas's reading of the alterity of the other person, but it comes at the expense, as was mentioned earlier, of the distinction Levinas attempts to maintain between the alterity of God and the alterity of every human being (DM 81/GD 84).

The ambiguity of the word *à-Dieu* serves to gather together many of the ideas considered up to this moment. Recall that only the aporia of death—that moment when death as possibility turns into death as impossibility—is adequate to the aporias of responsibility and sacrifice, insofar as death as possibility gives irreplaceable singularity and death as impossibility gives the ex-propriation, the anonymity, that is a forgetting or effacement of oneself. The aporias of responsibility and sacrifice call for being read alongside the aporia of death. The more I am responsible or the more I sacrifice, the more I am irresponsible, guilty, because (on the one hand) responsibility and sacrifice hold me accountable, and (on the other hand) responsibility and sacrifice discount me (insofar as they require that I be selfless, that I be nothing but "for the other"). This irresponsibility at the heart of responsibility and sacrifice is compounded in the reading of Genesis 22. It is as though in the singular relationship with the singular other (God), which already involves irresponsibility, one is inevitably implicated in *another* form of irresponsibility—the sacrifice of the other other, the other others. Therefore, in absolute responsibility and sacrifice a going *to God* and a *good-bye* coincide: *à-Dieu*. The *à-Dieu* serves to gather together several movements. This "good-bye" of/to God has several different (are they different?) trajectories: (1) good-bye of/to God as palpably present insofar as God is absent, hidden and silent, separate, secret, at the moment that God has to be obeyed (DM 59/GD 57), (2) good-bye of/to God as transcendent insofar as God becomes its own other, becomes finite, becomes incarnated as command (DM 45, 54/GD 41, 51), with the self thereby becoming its own other, and (3) good-bye of/to God as transcendent guarantee of the Good, of responsibility, insofar as God becomes its own other, that is, the demonic. The à-Dieu marks the aporia that responsibility and sacrifice *have* to be transgressed *in the name of* an absolute obligation to God, which merely serves as an index of not only the *wholly other* (*tout autre*) but also of *every* (other) *other* (*tout autre*). The à-Dieu marks the moment when a linear movement oriented in the direction of a goal, a production, a work, finds itself at a distance from itself, is interrupted.

But the dissymmetry between the divine gaze that sees me, and myself, who does not see the hidden, silent, and secret God—that is, the dissymmetry that is the essence of responsibility in *both* the singular relationship with the singular other *and* the relationship with the other other—simultaneously sets up the search for salvation through sacrifice (DM 89/GD 94). For example, in the moment of responsibility without reserve (that is, in the moment of the renunciation of hope), Abraham receives from God the very thing that Abraham had already (in the same moment) decided to sacrifice. Derrida writes, "Demystifiers of this superior or sovereign calculation that consists in no more calculating might say that he played his cards well" (DM 91/GD 97). They might say Abraham played his cards well because the return of his son cannot not resemble a reward for his sacrifice (DM 91/GD 95–96). The *an*economy of sacrifice without reserve cannot not be reappropriated by the economy of sacrifice (concerning this economy of sacrifice, Derrida refers the reader to *Glas*, notably Gf 40, 51ff. [on Hegel, Abraham, the "sacrifice" of Isaac and the "economic simulacrum"], 80ff., 111, 124, 136, 141, 158, 160, 175ff., 233, 262, 268ff., 271, 281ff., 288ff./Ge 32–33, 41ff. [on Hegel, Abraham, the "sacrifice" of Isaac and the "economic simulacrum"], 68ff., 96, 108, 119, 123, 139–141, 155ff., 207–208, 235, 240–243, 253ff., 259ff., and to "Economimesis").

The Gospel of Matthew and the God Who Sees in Secret

Derrida considers this sacrifice of (aneconomical) sacrifice within the context of a series of passages from the Gospel of Matthew to which Kierkegaard alludes in *Fear and Trembling*. Kierkegaard writes:

> But there was no one who could understand Abraham. And yet what did he achieve? He remained true to his love. But anyone who loves God needs no tears, no admiration; he forgets the suffering in the love. Indeed, so completely has he forgotten it that there would not be the slightest trace of his suffering left if God himself did not remember it, *for he sees in secret* and recognizes distress and counts the tears and forgets nothing.
>
> Thus, either there is a paradox, that the single individual as the single individual stands in an absolute relation to the absolute, or Abraham is lost. (FB 165/FT 120, emphasis added; see DM 79, 90/GD 81, 95)

The phrase "your Father *who sees in secret* will reward you" appears on three occasions in chapter 6 of the Gospel of Matthew:

- But when you give alms, do not let your left hand know what your right hand is doing, so that your alms may be done in secret; and your Father who sees in secret will reward you. (Matt. 6:3, NRSV)
- But whenever you pray, go into your room and shut the door and pray to your Father who is in secret; and your Father who sees in secret will reward you. (Matt. 6:6, NRSV)
- But when you fast, put oil on your head and wash your face, so that your fasting may be seen not by others but by your Father who is in secret; and your Father who sees in secret will reward you. (Matt. 6:17, NRSV)

Said otherwise, you can count on the celestial economy if you sacrifice the terrestrial economy. The reward of the celestial economy is invisible to the "unhealthy" eye of the corrupted and corruptible body. It is invisible to the "unhealthy" eye of the terrestrial economy. There is the good and simple eye, and the bad and corrupt eye:

> The eye is the lamp of the body. So, if your eye is healthy, your whole body will be full of light; but if your eye is unhealthy, your whole body will be full of darkness. If then the light in you is darkness, how great is the darkness! (Matt. 6:22–23, NRSV)

The eye, as a lamp, does not receive light. It does not regard or receive the Good as the external solar source of visibility. It gives light, from the "inside." Alluding to the conversion from the Platonic mystery to the Christian mystery in his reading of Patočka's genealogy of responsibility, Derrida writes, "It is therefore the Good become goodness, the becoming-good of the Good, since it lights from the interior, from the inside of the body, namely, the soul" (DM 93/GD 99). Although internal in its source, this light is also "outside." Derrida writes, "However, although it is internal in its source, this light doesn't belong to this world or this earth" (DM 93/GD 99). This light belongs to an absolutely heterogeneous interiority, an inside without an outside. If there were no heterogeneous interiority, no inside that could not be objectified, then there could be no absolute invisibility/secrecy. "It can seem obscure, somber, nocturnal, secret, invisible to eyes of flesh, to corrupted eyes, and that is why 'seeing in secret' becomes necessary. In this way God the Father reestablishes an economy that was interrupted by the dividing of earth and heaven" (DM 93/GD 99). An absolute secret is secret even from me. It is invisible "to eyes of flesh, to corrupted eyes." That is why the God "who is in secret," "sees in secret."

The interiorization of the source of light simultaneously marks the end of secrecy (insofar as there is no longer any secret hidden from God) and the beginning of secrecy (insofar as secrecy is, paradoxically, irreducible in its interiority, i.e., it is an inside without any outside, it is secret to me).

> [A]s *soon as* there is no longer any secret hidden from God or from the spiritual light that passes through every space, then a recess of spiritual subjectivity and of absolute interiority is constituted allowing secrecy to be formed within it. Subtracted from space, this incommensurable inside of the soul or the conscience, this inside without any outside carries with it both the end and the origin of the secret. *Plus de secret* [no more secrecy/more secrecy]. For if there were no absolutely heterogeneous interiority separate from objectivity, if there were no inside that could not be objectified, there would be no secrecy either. (DM 95/GD 101)

Citing the traditional Judeo-Christiano-Islamic prohibition of idolatry, and at the acknowledged risk of turning that prohibition against that tradition, Derrida argues that it is perhaps necessary to stop thinking about God as a transcendent supreme being capable of seeing into the most secret of the most interior places, and to start thinking about "God" as the name for the structure of invisible interiority (in Kierkegaard's sense, subjectivity), that is, an incommensurable inside, an inside without any outside, an inside invisible both to others and to me. This structure of consciousness is a "witness" that is not only (1) *in* me, but is more intimate with me than myself (a secret even to me), and as such, (2) *external* to me, other than me (DM 101–102/GD 108–109). This structure of consciousness (1) is the "internal" light, that (2) is "external," insofar as it is subtracted from space, an incommensurable inside, an inside without any outside (compare with Levinas's description of the idea of infinity in his reading of Descartes's *Meditations* in *Totality and Infinity*, where according to the chronological order the other is *in* me, and according to the "logical" order the other is *outside* me). God manifests his/her/its non-manifestation when there appears the possibility of secrecy, that is, "when there appears the desire and power to render absolutely invisible and to constitute within oneself a witness of that invisibility" (DM 102/GD 109).

This structure of consciousness—which is named "God," understood in a non-idolatrous manner—both founds and destroys the Christian concepts of responsibility and justice (DM 105/GD 112). The Christian concepts of responsibility and justice, which are a sacrificing or giving without reserve, call for the double "suppression of the object" (compare with "double repression" [DM 35/GD 29]):

> [A]s soon as it is calculated (starting from the simple intention of giving *as such*, starting from sense, knowledge, and whatever takes recognition into account), the gift suppresses the object (of the gift). It denies it as such. In order to avoid this negation or destruction at all costs, one must proceed to *another* suppression of the object: that of keeping in the gift only the giving, the act of giving and intention to give, not the given which in the end doesn't count. One must give without knowing, without knowledge or recognition, without *thanks*: without anything, or at least without any object. (DM 104/GD 112, emphasis added to "intention"; see Derrida's *Given Time: I. Counterfeit Money*)

It is important to note that in this passage the phrase "that of keeping in the gift only the giving, the act of giving and the intention to give, not the given which in the end doesn't count" elaborates the calculated "simple intention of giving *as such.*" The object (of the gift) is giving *as such.* Giving *as such* is suppressed (denied, negated, destroyed) when there is calculation. One must suppress this suppression (i.e., the suppression that results from calculating); that is, in order to avoid the suppression (of giving *as such*) one must suppress this suppression (of giving *as such*). Said otherwise, calculated sacrifice (i.e., economical sacrifice) sacrifices (i.e., suppresses) sacrificing *as such.* One must sacrifice (i.e., suppress) calculated sacrifice (which, as was evident in the previous sentence, is the sacrifice [i.e., suppression] of sacrificing *as such*) to preserve sacrificing *as such.* One must sacrifice (calculated) sacrifice in order to preserve sacrificing *as such,* that is, in order not to have a "sacrifice of sacrifice" (as this phrase is understood in DM 106/GD 114, that is, as a sacrifice of sacrifice *as such*).

Nietzsche and Irigaray on the Risk of Belief

Believing that God *knows* (or witnesses) this secreted secret founds and destroys the Christian concepts of responsibility and justice. It founds the Christian concepts of responsibility and justice insofar as one has faith that there is a *celestial* witness to one's giving without reserve *within the terrestrial economy,* and it destroys the Christian concepts of responsibility and justice because the giving without reserve is integrated into the *celestial economy* (DM 105/GD 112).

According to the stroke of genius on the part of Christianity, God sacrifices himself for the guilt of humankind. Christians have to believe that God's crediting is suspended between knowing and not knowing, which means that their faith (which seems to be understood here as a form of knowledge) is suspended between knowing and not knowing. God can only credit the account of the debtor by sacrificing without knowing (which makes the crediting impossible) and the believer can only have faith without knowing (which makes confidence in an assured redemption impossible). Both the credit of the creditor and the faith (i.e., knowledge) of the believer unwork themselves. Believing is suspended in the "not yet" of credit and the "not yet" of faith.

The irreducible experience of belief is, I would argue, the aporia of the believing suspended *between* the sacrifice of the (economical) sacrifice — which requires not knowing — and the sacrifice of the (aneconomical) sacrifice — which comes with knowing.

This risk of belief characteristic of sacrificing sacrificing is not unlike what Irigaray calls "belief *itself,*" rather than *safe* belief. Belief is safe when it succeeds in making the other the other *of the same,* rather than giving up narcissistic self-sufficiency and being open to the other. Belief *itself* is the "true meaning" (or essence) of belief that undermines the language of safe belief. There is no project here because Irigaray's new sacrifice, which I argue is the sacrifice of sacrifice, is both *necessary* and *useless.* With this new sacrifice the truth is "still to come"

(CM 65/BI 53). The credit of the creditor and the faith of the debtor are "not yet."

The Religious Bond as a Double Bind

In "Faith and Knowledge: The Two Sources of 'Religion' at the Limits of Reason Alone" (1996), Derrida again refers to a sacrifice of sacrifice. Derrida writes, "[L]ife has absolute value only if it is worth *more than* life" (FS 68/FK 50). The respect of life in religious discourse bears witness to the *infinite* transcendence of what is worth more than life (and not to the *illusory* transcendence of the theological machine, which is, according to Bergson, the "machine for making gods"). Bearing witness to the infinite transcendence of what is worth more than life requires, therefore, not only a sacrifice in the name of transcendence, but also a sacrificing of transcendence. Life "is sacred, holy, infinitely respectable only in the name of what is worth more than it and what is not restricted to the naturalness of the bio-zoological (sacrificable)—although true sacrifice ought to sacrifice not only 'natural' life, called 'animal' or 'biological', but also that which is worth more than so-called natural life" (FS 68/FK 50–51). A sacrificing of transcendence is a sacrificing of that in the name of which one sacrifices, which is a sacrificing of the very reason of sacrifice, insofar as sacrifice involves a transcendental intention. A sacrificing of transcendence is, therefore, a sacrificing of sacrifice. To sacrifice transcendence is to sacrifice economical sacrifice. It is here that the *possibility* of religion (the "not yet" of religion) persists. It persists in the religious bond *between* (1) the absolute dignity of life (which requires transcendence, an excess above and beyond the living) *and* (2) the theological machine (the "machine for making gods"), which is an illusory transcendence that it is necessary to exclude. Therefore, the religious bond, I would argue, both *requires and excludes* transcendence. The possibility of religion persists in the religious bond in which one is called—in the wake of the death of God—to dwell in the "not yet" that is suspended between the immanent and the transcendent. Therefore, the religious bond turns out to be a *"double bind,"* insofar as it *"both requires and excludes* sacrifice" (FS 69/FK 52), insofar as it involves a sacrifice of sacrifice. Bearing witness to the infinite transcendence of that which is sacrosanct (the holy, the sacred, the absolute other, the future, death, freedom, etc.) and *not* the illusory transcendence of the theological machine requires a "self-contesting attestation," a "self-sacrificial supplementarity" (FS 69/FK 51) that, I would argue, is a sacrifice of sacrifice. Said otherwise, it *"both requires and excludes* sacrifice," which involves a sacrifice of sacrifice. The sacrifice of sacrifice both requires and excludes sacrifice insofar as the first "sacrifice" is an ethical action that one is obliged to do, but that interrupts itself *in the very "doing" of the action.* The sacrifice of sacrifice is the price to pay for doing no violence to the sacrosanct. "**Violence** of sacrifice in the name of non-violence" (FS 69/FK 52).

In "The Onto-theo-logical Constitution of Metaphysics," from *Identity and*

Difference (1957), Heidegger defines the god of the philosophers, the *causa sui* of ontotheology, as a god to whom one does not offer sacrifices. "Man can neither pray nor sacrifice [*opfern*] to this god. Before the *causa sui*, man can neither fall to his knees in awe nor can he play music and dance before his god" (OVM 70/ OCM 72). The implication is that the form of address to the god who is "not yet" *is* sacrifice (P 306–307). Religion is not imaginable without sacrifice. But religion (as a response that is both ambiguous and ambivalent) is, according to Derrida, "the ellipsis of **sacrifice**" (FS 69/FK 51–52), that is, the sacrifice of sacrifice. What is called for is not the single focus of the circle, but rather the double foci of the ellipsis. The *possibility* of religion (the "not yet" of religion) persists in the sacrifice of sacrifice, which is the form of address to the god that is coming—*not* a god that already "is" and that will come at some undetermined time in the future, but a god that "is" *nothing but* "coming," *nothing but* "not yet," *nothing but* approach.

Everything on sacrifice in the work of Derrida hinges on the ellipsis of sacrifice. It hinges on that aporetic moment when the sacrifice of (economical) sacrifice turns into the sacrifice of (aneconomical) sacrifice, and vice versa. Here is the sacrifice of sacrifice. Here is the double bind of sacrifice.

9

Hegel at the Chiasm of Derrida and Lacan/Žižek

My God, my God, why have you forsaken me?
—Psalm 22:1, Matthew 27:46, Mark 15:34 (NRSV)

God Himself is dead.
—Hegel, Phenomenology of Spirit

Despite protestations to the contrary (on the part of Žižek), I would argue that the work of Derrida and Lacan/Žižek forms an equivocal chiasm: an atemporal non-spatial momentary point of intersection. This point of intersection is the sacrifice of sacrifice: the sacrifice of sacrifice understood as both the sacrifice of (economical) sacrifice and the sacrifice of (aneconomical) sacrifice, neither merely sacrifice without reserve nor economical sacrifice. The work of Hegel plays a pivotal role at this sacrificial intersection.

Contemporary Continental philosophy stands in the wake of the work of G. W. F. Hegel (1770–1831). In "Hegel's Existentialism" from Sense and Non-sense (1948), Merleau-Ponty writes, "All the great philosophical ideas of the past century—the philosophies of Marx and Nietzsche, phenomenology, German existentialism, and psychoanalysis—had their beginnings in Hegel" (EH 125/HE 63). In Positions (1972), Derrida mentions that différance is "at a point of almost absolute proximity to Hegel" (POf 60/POe 44). He says that "[w]e will never be finished with the reading or rereading of Hegel, and, in a certain way, I do nothing other than attempt to explain myself on this point" (POf 103/POe 77).

One of the aims of Žižek's *The Sublime Object of Ideology* (1989) is "to accomplish a kind of 'return to Hegel'—to reactualize Hegelian dialectics by giving it a new reading on the basis of Lacanian psychoanalysis" (SOI 7).

The Revealed Religion

The starting point of this consideration of the chiasm of the work of Derrida and Lacan/Žižek (though it is as arbitrary as any starting point) will be "The Revealed Religion" (*Die offenbare Religion*) from the *Phenomenology of Spirit* (1807), specifically the appropriation of the sacrifice of Jesus Christ (the mediator between the divine and the human) by the religious community. The Christian doctrine of the incarnation presents the divine initiative as passing through three stages. First, God (the divine substance) empties itself (kenosis). This "externalization [*Entäußerung*] of substance" is "its growth into self-consciousness." And this "externalization [*Entäußerung*] of self-consciousness" expresses that it is "*in itself* the universal essence" (PG 403/PS 457). Spirit, in the form of the self-consciousness of Jesus Christ, comes into existence as the unity of this reciprocal externalization.

> This incarnation of the divine Being, or the fact that it essentially and directly has the shape of self-consciousness, is the simple content of the absolute religion [i.e., Christianity]. In this religion the divine Being is known as Spirit, or this religion is the consciousness of the divine Being that it is Spirit. For Spirit is the knowledge of oneself in the externalization [*Entäußerung*] of oneself; the being that is the movement of retaining its self-identity in its otherness. (PG 405/PS 459)

As the unity of the reciprocal externalizations, the self-consciousness of Jesus Christ is the self-consciousness of God. In Jesus Christ, Spirit is "*immediately present* as a self-conscious Being" (PG 404/PS 458), immediately present as an individual finite self-consciousness situated in a particular time and space. Second, this individual finite self-consciousness dies. This sacrifice is confirmation of the finitude of the incarnate one. Third, the *particular* self-consciousness of this individual is resurrected as the *universal* self-consciousness of the religious community.

> In the vanishing of the immediate existence known to be absolute Being the immediacy receives its negative moment; Spirit remains the immediate Self of actuality, but as the *universal self-consciousness* of the community [*Gemeine*], a self-consciousness which reposes in its own substance, just as in it this Substance is a universal Subject: not the individual by himself, but together with the consciousness of the community and what he is for this community, is the complete whole of the individual as Spirit. (PG 408/PS 462)

God, in the form of the resurrected Jesus Christ, is present in the work and worship of the community as the Holy Spirit.

This Christian doctrine of the incarnation is not, however, appropriated in an appropriate way. The *appropriation* of divine reality is accomplished by way of a dynamic involving the Christian community, specifically, a dynamic that requires the representation of the history of salvation as its necessary condition. This happens in three stages: (1) the creation and the fall, (2) the divine initiative to become incarnated as a human being and sacrifice itself in order to reconcile humankind and its evil with God, and (3) the acknowledgment by the religious consciousness that the dynamic of the reconciling events is accomplished in the living consciousness of the religious community.

According to the picture-thinking [*Vorstellung*] characteristic of the Christian doctrine, God created the universe from nothing and he created human beings on the earth in his own image. "[T]he merely eternal or abstract Spirit becomes an 'other' to itself, or enters into existence, and directly into *immediate* existence. Accordingly, it *creates* a world. This 'creating' is picture-thinking's word for the Notion itself in its absolute movement" (PG 412/PS 467). Spirit becomes self in the creation of the world, but insofar as the world expresses this movement itself, it becomes a finite self dwelling in the world. And just as the eternal or abstract Spirit exhibits itself as the movement of being self-identical in being "other" to itself, so the movement of the withdrawal into itself (i.e., being self-identical) is the "othering" of the finite self. "Since this Spirit is determined as at first an *immediate* existence, or as dispersed into the multifariousness of its consciousness, its othering of itself is the withdrawal *into itself*, or self-centeredness, of knowing as such" (PG 412/PS 468). When human beings sought to become independent as God is thought to be, they introduce discordance into the universe. They lost the form of being at one with themselves by plucking the fruit of the tree of the knowledge of good and evil. "Since this withdrawal into itself or self-centeredness of the existent consciousness immediately makes it self-discordant, Evil appears as the primary existence of the inwardly turned consciousness; and because the thoughts of Good and Evil are utterly opposed and this antithesis is not yet resolved, this consciousness is essentially only evil" (PG 412–413/PS 468). Human beings (as self-contained finitude) are essentially evil. At this stage of salvation history, death is the evidence of the "wages of sin," of the finitude of human beings.

According to picture-thinking, the creation and the fall were followed by the divine initiative to become incarnated as a human being and sacrifice itself in order to reconcile humankind and its evil with itself. "The picture-thought is in this way still *immediate*, and therefore not spiritual, i.e. it knows the human form of the divine Being at first only as a particular, not yet as a universal, form; it becomes spiritual for this consciousness in the movement whereby this divine Being in human shape sacrifices [*aufzuopfern*] his immediate existence again and returns to the divine Being: only when essence is reflected into itself is it Spirit" (PG 415/PS 472). At this stage of salvation history, death is the negation of the immediately present individual self-consciousness so that the *particular* self-consciousness of the incarnate one is resurrected as the *universal* self-consciousness of the religious community. "The *death* of the divine Man, *as death*, is *abstract* negativity, the immediate result of the movement which ends only in *natural* universality. Death loses this natural meaning in spiritual self-consciousness [. . .]; death becomes transfigured from its immediate meaning, viz. the non-being of this *particular* individual, into the *universality* of the Spirit who dwells in His community, dies in it every day, and is daily resurrected" (PG 418/PS 475). The incarnate one dies and is raised again daily in the work and worship of the religious community.

Finally, religious consciousness acknowledges that the dynamic of these reconciling events—the negation of evil's limitation or negation (i.e., its withdrawal into itself, or self-centeredness) into the positive community—is accomplished *in* the living universal self-consciousness of the religious community. That is, according to Hyppolite, "[t]he movement that took place in Christ *must now be executed in the midst of the community* and must become *its own* movement instead of being alien to it." The religious community must "reconcile finite existence with divine essence, by internalizing the death and resurrection of Christ" (GSP 546/GSH 567). This requires that the sacrifice of Jesus Christ be grasped or appropriated by the believing self. "The death of the Mediator as grasped by the Self is the supersession [*Aufheben*] of his objective existence or his particular being-for-self: this *particular* being-for-self has become a universal self-consciousness" (PG 419/PS 476). The believing self grasps or appropriates the sacrifice of Jesus Christ *as* the *Aufheben* of the objective existence or particular being-for-self of, I would argue, *both* Jesus Christ *and* the believing self. This *particular* self-consciousness becomes the *universal* self-consciousness of the religious community. "On the other side, the *universal* has become self-consciousness, just because of this, and the pure or non-actual Spirit of mere thinking has become *actual*" (PG 419/PS 476). Through this universal self-consciousness, the non-actual abstract spirit of the religious community leaves the world of thought and becomes actual.

> The death of the Mediator is the death not only of his *natural* aspect or of his particular being-for-self, not only of the already dead husk stripped of its essential Being, but also of the *abstraction* of the divine Being. For the Mediator, in so far as his death has not yet completed the reconciliation, is the one-sidedness which takes as *essential Being* the simple element of thought in contrast to actuality: this one-sided extreme of the Self does not as yet have equal worth with essential Being; this it first has as Spirit. The death of this picture-thought contains, therefore, at the same time the death of the *abstraction of the divine Being* which is not posited as Self. That death is the painful feeling of the Unhappy Consciousness that *God Himself is dead* [Gott selbst gestorben ist]. This hard saying is the expression of innermost simple self-knowledge, the return of consciousness into the depths of the night in which "I"="I", a night which no longer distinguishes or knows anything outside of it. This feeling is, in fact, the loss of substance and of its appearance over against consciousness; but it is at the same time the pure *subjectivity* of substance, or the pure certainty of itself which it lacked when it was object, or the immediate, or pure essence. This Knowing is the inbreathing of the Spirit,

> whereby Substance becomes Subject, by which its abstraction and lifelessness
> have died, and Substance therefore has become *actual* and simple and universal
> Self-consciousness. (PG 419/PS 476)

The sacrifice of Jesus Christ is not only the sacrifice of this particular self-consciousness, but also the sacrifice of God understood as a particular being, above and beyond human existence. It is the sacrifice of the abstraction of the divine being. It is the painful feeling of the death of God. It is the dark night of the soul, a "night which no longer distinguishes or knows anything outside of it." It is the death of particularity into the abyss of radical negativity.

This dynamic—which *both* reaches out to, and appropriates, what is independent, *and* ex-propriates one's own independence—has become *identical* in finite human beings and God. At this stage of salvation history, death is neither merely evidence of the "wages of sin," of the finitude of human beings (as is the case in the first stage), nor merely the negation of the immediately present individual self-consciousness (as is the case in the second stage), but reveals the *identity* of finite human beings and God. As Burbidge writes, "Both become actual by negatively dissolving the negativity through which their negatively determined isolation (whether abstract beyond or self-contained evil) is cancelled" (MGD 194). Both become actual in the form of the concrete universal, the Holy Spirit. The Holy Spirit is the universal self-consciousness of the religious community. "The difficulty that is found in these Notions stems solely from clinging to the 'is' and forgetting the thinking of the Notions in which the moments just as much *are* as they *are not*—are only the movement which is Spirit" (PG 416–417/PS 473). "When its *moments* are grasped in their purity, they are the restless Notions which only *are*, in being in themselves their own opposite, and in finding their rest in the whole" (PG 410/PS 465). Spirit is the movement by which contradictory things (finite human beings and God) are recognized as moments of one and the same process (i.e., the process of radical negativity).

Everything turns on the reading of this *identity* of finite human beings and God. This identity—effected by negatively dissolving the negativity by means of which their negatively determined isolation (whether self-contained evil or abstract beyond) is negated—will be the starting point of the following consideration of the chiasm of the work of Derrida and Lacan/Žižek.

Derrida and the *Identity* of Finite Human Beings and God

This identity, according to a Derridean reading, is subject to two readings (it is important to point out that Derrida himself does not offer a reading of this particular part of Hegel's *Phenomenology of Spirit*). *According to one reading*, this identity is the positive identity of the religious community, that is, a community of human beings who have appropriately appropriated the sacrifice of Jesus Christ. Recall that for Hegel, death is productive insofar as one appropriates it. This appropriation of death, according to the Hegelian interpretation of *Aufhebung*, effects the *presentation* or *recognition* of the identity (the "at the same time") of contradictories (in this particular case, the human and the divine). The contradictories are identified only *as* a contradiction. This recognition effects the step into the next shape of the dialectical progression. Here one sees the implacable force of the hard-working negative (Gf 267/Ge 240), the constriction of the absolute expenditure of death to an economy that expects a return on its investment. While *seeming* to put everything at stake at the moment of death, Hegel in fact restricts the stakes of the wager to the appropriation of death. And given that the Hegelian interpretation of *Aufhebung* is an interpretation that restricts the stakes of Hegel's interpretive wager to logic, history, meaning, etc., it can be reinterpreted (EREG 382/RGE 260). Therefore, *according to another reading*, the identity of the religious community, effected by the appropriation of death, can be reinterpreted in a way that does *not* guarantee a return on one's investment. If the sacrifice of Jesus Christ is "permitted to take off," then the appropriate appropriation of this death effects *not* the positive identity of the religious community, but an identity defined (paradoxically) by ex-propriation. Recall that the appropriation of death, according to the Hegelian interpretation of *Aufhebung*, effects the *presentation* or *recognition* of the identity (the "at the same time") of contradictories (in this particular case, the human and the divine). But the "not yet" of the aporias of time and death interrupts the "at the same time" of contradictories (see AE 9/OB 7, and EL 22–23/SL 30–31). The "not yet" of the aporia interrupts the *presentation* or *recognition* of the identity (the "at the same time") of contradictories insofar as it is discovered that the moments of the aporia are *not* "at the same time"; they can*not* be *presented* or *recognized as* a contradiction. The truth of contradiction (to speak Hegelese) is aporia. *The aporia of time/death "is" the aporia of dialectic.* What becomes thinkable here is the "not yet" of (productive) sacrifice. What becomes thinkable here is sacrifice as absolute expenditure "before" it inevitably (and according to its own inherent necessity) has become constricted to an economy of speculative thought that expects a return on its investment. What becomes thinkable here is the religious community understood as the (dis)incarnation of *nothing but* radical negativity, *nothing but* radical sacrifice, *nothing but* the sacrifice of sacrifice.

This understanding of the religious community echoes the work of Blanchot and Bataille. In "The Negative Community" from *The Unavowable Community* (1983), Blanchot quotes the following passage from Bataille's *Theory of Religion* (1973): "To sacrifice is not to kill but to relinquish and to give" (TdR 310/ToR 48–49; see CI 30/UC 15). A reading of Bataille's reading of sacrifice must be attentive to the sacrifice of sacrifice characteristic of the aporia of death, that is, the irreducible undecidability of the double meaning of death articulated by that moment when death as possibility turns into death as impossibility. To sacrifice, according to Blanchot's reading of the passage from Bataille's *Theory of Religion*, is "*to give oneself wholly to limitless abandonment*" (CI 30/UC 15). Blanchot continues: "That is the sacrifice that founds the community by undoing it" (CI 30/UC 15). The sacrifice of sacrifice founds the community insofar as it is shared by all members of the community, and insofar as it opens sacrifice to others, it is a giving of oneself wholly to limitless abandonment, it is (in the words of Levinas) to be *nothing but* "for the other." But this sacrifice of sacrifice undoes the community

> by handing it over to time the dispenser, time that does not allow the community nor those who give themselves to it, any form of presence, thereby sending them back to a solitude which, far from protecting them, disperses them or dissipates itself without their finding themselves again or together. The gift or the abandonment is such that, ultimately, there is nothing to give or to give up and that time itself is only one of the ways in which this nothing to give offers and withdraws itself like the whim of the absolute which goes out of itself by giving rise to something other than itself, in the shape of an absence. An absence which, in a limited way, applies to the community whose only clearly ungraspable secret it would be. The absence of community is not the failure of community: absence belongs to community as its extreme moment or as the ordeal that exposes it to its necessary disappearance. (CI 30–31/UC 15)

This absence of community "puts an end to the hopes of the groups" (CI 38/UC 20). In contrast to Girard's economic reading of sacrifice (in which guilt is projected upon a scapegoat who dies for the community), Blanchot writes, "Each person should have to die for all, and it is in the death of all that each person would determine the community's destiny" (CI 32n1/UC 58n7). The community's destiny is to be founded *in* the death of *all* members of the community, which is accomplished by *each* (and every) person (*not* merely the scapegoats) dying *for all* (i.e., dying *for* the founding of the community). Here (paradoxically) is a community founded on radical anonymity and passivity (i.e., on being nothing but "for the other"). The community's destiny is the impossibility of community. The possibility of the community is *at the same time* its impossibility. As radical anonymity and passivity, being nothing but "for the other" is *not* a project. If it were, it would break the law of the group: "But to give oneself, as a project, the execution of a sacrificial death means to break the law of the group [i.e., the group that defines itself as *nothing but* the (dis)incarnation of the sacrifice of sacrifice] whose first requirement is to renounce creating a *work* (even though it be the work of death) and whose essential project excludes all projects" (CI 32n1/UC 58n7). From this, Blanchot concludes, follows a completely different kind of sacrifice: an obsessive sacrifice of sacrifice that opens sacrifice to others and separates it violently from itself. This sacrifice of sacrifice founds the community by undoing it insofar as it is founded upon the death of particularity into the abyss of radical anonymity and passivity.

Each particular self-consciousness (in the universal self-consciousness of the religious community) recognizes itself as *nothing but* the (dis)incarnation of the sacrifice of sacrifice. It recognizes itself as identified with others in this particular way. That everyone is *nothing but* the (dis)incarnation of the sacrifice of sacrifice is the condition of the possibility of the identity of the universal self-consciousness of the religious community. But, that everyone is *nothing but* the (dis)incarnation of the sacrifice of sacrifice is, at the same time, the condition of the impossibility not only of each particular self-consciousness, but also the universal self-consciousness of the religious community insofar as it is the death of particularity into the abyss of radical anonymity and passivity. The sacrifice of Jesus Christ is not only the sacrifice of this particular self-consciousness, but also the sacrifice of God understood as a particular being, above and beyond human existence. It is the sacrifice of the abstraction of the divine being. It is the painful feeling of the death of God. It is the dark night of the soul. The death of God is the death of particularity into the abyss of radical anonymity and passivity.

Lacan/Žižek and the *Identity* of Finite Human Beings and God

Recall that everything turns on the reading of the *identity* of finite human beings and God, which is effected by negatively dissolving the negativity by means of which their negatively determined isolation (whether self-contained evil or abstract beyond) is negated. This identity, according to Žižek (and his "new reading" of Hegelian dialectics on the basis of Lacanian psychoanalysis) is the (dis)incarnation of radical sacrifice, the (dis)incarnation of the sacrifice of sacrifice. Said otherwise, the identity of the universal self-consciousness of the religious community is brought about by the (dis)incarnation of the Holy Spirit understood as *nothing but* the negation of the negation, *nothing but* the sacrifice of sacrifice. In Lacanian terminology, each particular self-consciousness (in the universal self-consciousness of the religious community) chooses itself, I would argue, as *objet petit a*. To choose oneself as *objet petit a* is to undergo what Lacan calls radical subjective destitution (SOI 116). For Lacan, *objet petit a* is that strange object that is "in me more than me"; it is in me as that which breaks me up. This strange object that is "in me more than me" is surplus-enjoyment. At the moment of choosing itself as *objet petit a* (of repeating the sacrifice of sacrifice), if only for a moment, each particular self-consciousness (dis)incarnates the desire of death as such (EdP 329/EoP 282). It is (in this particular case) the (dis)incarnation of the Holy Spirit in an ordinary everyday self-consciousness (of the universal self-consciousness of the religious community). Each particular self-consciousness (of the universal self-consciousness of the religious community) recognizes itself as *nothing but* the (dis)incarnation of the sacrifice of sacrifice. It recognizes itself as identified with others in this particular way. That everyone is *nothing but* the (dis)incarnation of the sacrifice of sacrifice is the condition of the possibility of the identity of the universal self-consciousness of the religious community. But, that everyone is *nothing but* the (dis)incarnation of the sacrifice of sacrifice is, at the same time, the condition of the impossibility not only of each particular self-consciousness, but also the universal self-consciousness of the religious community.

The identity of finite human beings and God is the positive identity of the religious community, that is, a community of human beings who have appropriately appropriated the sacrifice of Jesus Christ. What the believing self grasps or appropriates is the death of the Mediator, the sacrifice of Jesus Christ. "The picture-thought is in this way still *immediate*, and therefore not spiritual, i.e. it knows the human form of the divine Being at first only as a particular, not yet as a universal, form; it becomes spiritual for this consciousness in the movement whereby this divine Being in human shape sacrifices [*aufzuopfern*] his immediate existence again and returns to the divine Being: only when essence [as the pure movement of mediation, of self-referential negativity] is *reflected into itself* is it Spirit [*das Wesen als in sich reflectirtes ist erst der Geist*]" (PG 415/PS 472, emphasis added). Essence is here revealed as *nothing but* redoubled reflection. In *Science of Logic* (1812–1816; 2nd ed. 1832), Hegel thematizes this redoubled reflection (this reflection of essence into itself) as determinate reflection. Though not thematized as such in *Phenomenology of Spirit*, it can (with certain reservations) be instructive to a reading of this part of *Phenomenology of Spirit*.

According to Žižek, one passes from external to determinate (or *redoubled*) reflection when one experiences the *image* of the substantial-immediate otherness as *nothing but* the inverse-alienated reflection of essence *as* the pure movement of mediation, of self-referential negativity. This *image* is the way self-referential negativity appears. This is the *form* of its appearance.

This is akin to Derrida's reading of radical sacrifice in Hegel's *Phenomenology of Spirit*. Hegel characterizes the first shape of natural religion—essential light or luminous-essence *(Lichtwesen)*—as a shape of shapelessness. This all-burning essenceless play of light that never determines itself as for-(it)self, and as such puts the history of Spirit out of order, *can be what it is* (namely, an "all-burning essenceless play of light that never determines itself as for-(it)self, and as such puts the history of Spirit out of order") *only if it turns into its contrary*. What becomes thinkable here is sacrifice as absolute expenditure "before" it inevitably (and according to its own inherent necessity) sacrifices itself and appears *as* "appearance," "before" it inevitably (and according to its own inherent necessity) appears (paradoxically) in the form of an "image" *without* an original. This reinterpretation of Hegel's interpretive wager remains merely what is *perhaps* at stake, given the irreducibly ambiguous ontological status of what becomes thinkable: sacrifice without reserve, which is not, but cannot not be(come).

Returning to Žižek's "new reading" of Hegelian dialectics on the basis of Lacanian psychoanalysis (specifically, Žižek's reading of redoubled reflection), one could state that reflection is *redoubled* insofar as it not only reflects *itself in appearance* (in the person of Jesus Christ, as described in the *Phenomenology of Spirit*) *as* an alien Entity (God, as described in the *Phenomenology*), given in advance, and *excluded* from the movement of reflection, but it also reflects *itself into itself*, that is, reflects *itself as reflecting* (this is the *redoubled* reflection characteristic of determinate reflection). This reflection of *itself in itself* (as is the case with the sacrifice of Jesus described in the *Phenomenology*) is an immediacy that is not "mere appearance," but rather *essence itself* (as the pure movement of mediation, of self-referential negativity) *in the form of its otherness, in the form of a phenomenon that* (paradoxically) *(dis)embodies the fact that there is nothing beyond phenomena* (*nothing beyond* the universal self-consciousness of the religious community, as described in the *Phenomenology*). Essence appears (para-doxically) as the (dis)incarnation of the fact that there is *nothing beyond* appear-ance. It appears (paradoxically) as an "image" *without* an original. It appears with the "death of God" in the sacrifice of Jesus Christ. This reflection of essence *into itself* (as is the case with the sacrifice of Jesus described in the *Phenomenology*) is an immediacy that is not "mere appearance," but "appearance" *without* an es-sence, for the essence "is" *itself* (as self-fissured, as reflection) reflected back into "appearance." Therefore, the "essence" of essence is (paradoxically) "appearance" without an essence. Said otherwise, negation is itself negated; sacrifice is itself sacrificed. Essence "is" *nothing but* redoubled reflection, *nothing but* radical sac-rifice that cannot not be (dis)embodied in "appearance," that cannot not be (dis)embodied in the universal self-consciousness of the religious community.

The negation of the negation (i.e., the negation of Jesus as the negation of the abstract Beyond/God *and* the negation of the believing self as the negation of God or as self-contained evil) is not (merely) an appropriation of negation (i.e., the annulment, canceling, or negation of loss/negation), the (re)-appropriation of the "lost" object (i.e., God) in its full presence (i.e., in the universal self-consciousness of the religious community). It is the experience that (at the same time) one is the *reflection of essence into itself*. It is the experience that the "essence" of oneself is (not the "lost" object God, but) *nothing but* the (dis)incarnation of self-referential negativity, of the negation of the negation, of radical sacrifice, of the sacrifice of the sacrifice, which is the recognition of oneself as *nothing but* the (dis)incarnation of the condition of the possibility and the condition of the impossibility of the identity of the universal self-consciousness of the religious community. It is the recognition of oneself as *nothing but* the (dis)incarnation of the Holy Spirit, that is, the community of believers *separated* from, not *alienated* in/by, the symbolic order (FA 157–158). The appropriation of the sacrifice of Jesus Christ (i.e., the appropriation of the death of God on the cross) can no longer simply appear as a liberating experi-ence, as the negation of the abstract transcendent Beyond that dominates the lives of human beings. It can no longer simply appear as a liberating experience opening up to human beings the domain of immanent terrestrial reality as the site in which they affirm their autonomous creative subjectivity.

> [T]he "death of God" involves the loss of the consistent "terrestrial" reality itself. [. . .] [T]he "death of God" is more akin to what the great texts of mysticism usually designate as the "night of the world": the dissolution of (symbolically constituted) reality.
>
> In Lacanian terms, we are dealing with the suspension of the big Other, which guarantees the subject's access to reality: in the experience of the death of God, we stumble upon the fact that "the big Other doesn't exist [*l'Autre n'existe pas*]" (Lacan). (ME 42)

The appropriation of the death of God is at the same time an ex-propriation. It is the recognition that each believer in the community of believers is *separated* from, not *alienated* in/by, the symbolic order.

The Question of Sacrifice

The psychoanalytic "cure" is the dissolution of transference, the "going through the fantasy," which is equivalent to what is referred to in Lacanian psychoanalysis as "subjective destitution," that is, being *separated* from, not *alienated* in/by, the symbolic order. Dialectical analysis is nothing but a repeated (at each stage of the dialectic) "going through the fantasy" insofar as it keeps unconcealed *the condition of the possibility* and *the condition of the impossibility* of the consistency of the symbolic order, that is, *the condition of the possibility* and *the condition of the impossibility* of the subject. The perspicacity of the dialectical analysis is, according to Žižek, the recognition that what makes identity possible (the negation of negation) is what (at the same time) makes it impossible. "[E]very positively given object is possible, it emerges only against the background of its impossibility, it can never fully 'become itself', realize all its potential, achieve full identity with itself. [. . .] *This discord is a positive condition of the object's ontological consistency*" (FTK 68). The possibility of every positively given object is its impossibility. "[A]n entity 'becomes what it is' by realizing its *inherent* negativity—in other words, by taking cognizance of its own death" (FTK 67, emphasis added). Every partial moment (every "identity") of the Hegelian system is "truncated *from within*," it can never fully become "itself," it is marked with an *inherent* impediment, and it is this *inherent* impediment that "sets in motion" the dialectical development (FTK 68–69).

> Hegel knows very well that every attempt at rational totalization ultimately fails, this failure is the very impetus of the "dialectical progress"; his "wager" [. . .] concerns [. . .] the possibility of "making a system" out of the very series of *failed* totalizations, to enchain them in a rational way, to discern the strange "logic" that regulates the process by means of which the breakdown of a totalization itself begets another totalization. What is *Phenomenology of Spirit* ultimately if not the presentation of a series of aborted attempts by the subject to define the Absolute and thus arrive at the longed-for synchronism of subject and object? This is why its final outcome ("absolute knowledge") does not bring about a finally found harmony but rather entails a kind of reflective inversion: it confronts the subject with the fact that *the true Absolute is nothing but the logical disposition of its previous failed attempts to conceive the Absolute*—that is, with the vertiginous experience that Truth itself coincides with the path towards Truth. (FTK 99–100; see Žižek's remarks on Kafka's "Before the Law," SOI 65–66, and FTK 90–91, 106, 108–109; see Derrida's "Before the Law")

Absolute knowing is, according to Žižek, the name for the final moment of dialectical process when "consciousness" purifies itself of every presupposition of a positive being. This moment coincides with radical negativity, with the negation of the negation, with the sacrifice of the sacrifice. It coincides with pure nothingness. "This 'nothingness' reached at the very end of the *Phenomenology of Spirit* is just another name for the fact that 'Notion doesn't exist'—or, to use Lacan's terms, that 'the big Other doesn't exist,' that it is a 'dead,' purely formal structure without any substantial content" (FTK 67). The possibility of " 'absolute knowledge' implies the recognition of an absolute, insurmountable *impossibility*" (FTK 68). Dialectical analysis (according to Žižek's "new reading" of Hegelian dialectics on the basis of Lacanian psychoanalysis) reveals, I would argue, that the condition of identity is (*aporetically*) what makes it impossible. This aporia raises the question of the proximity of the work of Žižek and Derrida.

The Chiasm of Derrida and Lacan/Žižek

Žižek insists that what eludes Derrida is that this "condition of (im)possibility" is inherent within Hegelian dialectics.

> Derrida incessantly varies the motif of how full identity-with-itself is impossible; how it is always, constitutively, deferred, split; how the condition of its possibility is the condition of its impossibility; how there is no identity without reference to an outside which always-already truncates it, and so on, and so on. Yet what eludes him is the Hegelian inversion of *identity qua impossible* into *identity itself as a name for a certain radical impossibility*. The impossibility unearthed by Derrida through the hard work of deconstructive reading supposed to subvert identity constitutes the very definition of identity. (FTK 37)

According to Žižek's "new reading" of Hegelian dialectics on the basis of Lacanian psychoanalysis, Hegel defines identity as "reflective determination," as a result of the self-referential movement of negativity (FTK 40). Identity is the *form* of appearance of radical negativity. The "truth" or "essence" (the "*content*") of identity itself "is" radical negativity, that is, pure lack of any determinate content. Identity "is" nothing (or, to be more precise, radical negativity, the excessive sacrifice of sacrifice) in the *form* of something. It "is" "Nothing counted as Something" (FTK 52–53, 47).

> Derrida remains prisoner of the [...] conception which aims at freeing heterogeneity from the constraints of identity; of a conception which is obliged to presuppose a constituted field of identity (the "metaphysics of presence") in order to be able to set to the unending work of its subversion. The Hegelian answer to this would be: we "deconstruct" identity by retroactively ascertaining how identity itself is a "reflexive determination," a *form* of appearance of its opposite—identity as such is the highest affirmation of difference; it is the very way differentiality, the space of differences "as such," inscribes–reflects itself within the field of differences (of the series of different determinations). (FTK 88, emphasis added)

According to Žižek's "new reading" of Hegelian dialectics, identity "is" nothing but the inverted representative of the space of its own condition of (im)possibility (FTK 88). Identity "is," for Hegel, nothing but the *form* of appearance of radical negativity, nothing but the *form* of appearance of "death" (understood as the condition of the possibility and condition of the impossibility of identity).

The Question of Sacrifice

> One of the great motifs of the Derridean deconstruction is [. . .] the reversal
> or complement of the Kantian transcendental formula of the "conditions of
> possibility." The "infrastructural" condition of possibility of an entity is at the
> same time the condition of its impossibility, its identity-with-itself is possible
> only against the background of its self-relationship—of a minimal self-
> differentiation and self-deferment which opens up a gap forever hindering its
> full identity-with-itself. . . . It should also be clear [. . .] how the same paradox
> is inscribed in the very heart of Hegelian dialectics. The key "reversal" of the
> dialectical process takes place when we recognize in what at first appeared as
> a "condition of impossibility"—as a hindrance to our full identity, to the re-
> alization of our potential—the *condition of the possibility* of our ontological
> consistency. (FTK 70)

It seems as though Žižek, like Derrida, is attentive to the fact that everything
turns on how one reads the appropriation of death (radical negativity, the sacrifice
of sacrifice). It is a matter of emphasis. It turns on which moment of this pos-
sibility/impossibility the reader emphasizes (though this possibility/impossibility
is ultimately aporetic, ultimately undecidable). Žižek calls "deconstruction" to
recognize in identity the name for the impossibility that hinders the constitution
of a full identity-with-itself (FTK 37). Žižek is calling Derrida to be as attentive
to this aporia of death in the work of Hegel as Derrida was to the aporia of death
in his reading of Heidegger's existential analysis of death. Just as the appropriation
of death is the condition of the (im)possibility of authentic Dasein, dialectical
analysis shows (according to Žižek's "new reading" of Hegelian dialectics) that
the appropriation of death is the condition of (im)possibility of what Hegel calls
identity. Derrida seems to acknowledge as much when, in an interview, he says:

> We will never be finished with the reading or rereading of Hegel, and, in a
> certain way, I do nothing other than attempt to explain myself on this point.
> In effect I believe that Hegel's text is necessarily fissured; that it is something
> more and other than the circular closure of its representation. It is not reduced
> to a content of philosophemes, it also necessarily produces a powerful writing
> operation, a remainder of writing, whose strange relationship to the philo-
> sophical content of Hegel's text must be reexamined, that is, the movement
> by means of which his text exceeds its meaning, permits itself to be turned
> away from, to return to, and to repeat itself outside its self-identity. (POf 103–
> 104/POe 77–78)

Derrida's reading of the work of Hegel, Žižek's reading of the work of Hegel,
and Žižek's (mis)reading of the work of Derrida all seem to turn on how one
reads (or misreads) the other's reading of the aporia of death, the aporia of the
sacrifice of sacrifice. (*For They Know Not What They Do* situates Derrida's reading of Hegel with respect to Žižek's reading of Hegel primarily by way of Gasché's
The Tain of the Mirror: Derrida and the Philosophy of Reflection. Gasché responds
to Žižek in "Yes Absolutely" from *Inventions of Difference: On Jacques Derrida*,
see 278n14. For Žižek's rejoinder to Gasché, see IR 180n45.)
    The work of Derrida and Lacan/Žižek forms an equivocal chiasm: an atem-

172

poral non-spatial momentary point of intersection. This point of intersection is the sacrifice of sacrifice, radical negativity, death. Everything turns on the reading of the possibility/impossibility of the sacrifice of sacrifice. The sacrifice of sacrifice is both the sacrifice of (economical) sacrifice and the sacrifice of (aneconomical) sacrifice, neither merely sacrifice without reserve nor economical sacrifice. This possibility/impossibility is irreducibly aporetic. It is irreducibly undecidable.

10
The Sacrifice *of* the Eucharist

> You shall not make for yourself an idol, whether in the form of anything that is in heaven above, or that is on the earth beneath, or that is in the water under the earth.
>
> —Exodus 20:4 (New Revised Standard Version)

> Perhaps there is no sublimer passage in the Jewish law than the command, "Thou shalt not make to thyself any graven image, nor the likeness of anything which is in heaven or in the earth or under the earth," etc.
>
> —Kant, Critique of Judgement

> While they were eating, he took a loaf of bread, and after blessing it he broke it, gave it to them, and said, "Take; this is my body." Then he took a cup, and after giving thanks he gave it to them, and all of them drank from it. He said to them, "This is my blood of the covenant, which is poured out for many."
>
> —Mark 14:22–24 (New Revised Standard Version)

> [W]hat you receive is the mystery that means you. It is to what you are that you reply Amen, and by so replying you express your assent. [. . .] [R]eceive what you are.
>
> —Augustine, "Sermon 272"

Sacrifice sacrifice. Ours is the moment in history that calls for this strange imperative. This moment in the genealogy of sacrifice is (in the words of Derrida) a dissident and inventive rupture with respect to tradition. It is a moment in history that calls for the sacrifice of sacrifice. It is a strange moment and a strange imperative insofar as it calls into question (or sacrifices) the work of *both* sacrifice *and* the imperative itself. The first "sacrifice" is an ethical action that one is obliged to do, but that interrupts itself *in the very "doing" of the action*. The interruption of the "work" of sacrifice is an interruption of the transcendental intention of sacrifice. I argue that "The Revealed Religion" from Hegel's *Phenomenology of Spirit* is a work on the incessant dying of God. One is called to dwell—in the wake of the incessant dying of God—in the "not yet" that is suspended between the immanent and the transcendent. I will argue that a ritualized way of dwelling in this "not yet" is the liturgy of the sacrifice of the Eucharist (according to both senses of the genitive): the (economical) sacrifice that is a constitutive element of the liturgy of the Eucharist, and the sacrifice *of* this (economical) sacrifice, which interrupts sacrifice *in the very "doing" of the action*. I am arguing not for a change in the liturgy of the sacrifice of the Eucharist, but rather for a radical change in perspective on the sacrifice *of* the Eucharist as it is currently performed. This will disturb this sacrifice on one level while at the same time reinforcing its most extreme ramifications.

In the wake of (1) the cosmological decentering of the human being inaugurated by the Copernican revolution, (2) the critiques of the existence of God by Marx, Nietzsche, and Freud, (3) the naturalistic mechanisms of evolution proposed by Darwin, and (4) the staggering amount of evil in the world, the death of a representable all-good God (let alone a personal God) is, I would argue, a reality with which all thinkers are called to respond. It is of course still possible for one to maintain a belief in such a representable all-good God even in this wake. For example, one can continue to believe in divine providence despite the sheer insignificance of the place of human beings in the incomprehensibly vast universe, or one can insist that the critiques of Marx, Nietzsche, and Freud apply merely to inauthentic ideas of God that need to be stripped away to reveal a more authentic idea of God, or one can appeal to a God who providentially directs evolution, or one can construct a variety of theodicies. But ultimately, such attempts smack of desperation in the face of overwhelming evidence (even an appeal to a direct experience of the divine is greeted, especially in the wake of the work of Freud, with skepticism). A responsible attentiveness to this evidence inevitably involves what Derrida calls a "dissident and inventive rupture" with respect to tradition (DM 33–34/GD 27). Perhaps there is, as Kant argues, no more sublime passage in the Jewish law than the prohibition of idolatry insofar as one is called, in the name of the tradition, to inventively rupture that tradition.

Kant and the Sublime Commandment against Idolatry

The sublimity of the traditional commandment of the Hebrew Scriptures against idolatry must be understood initially within the context of Kant's *Critique of Judgement* (1790), and then within the context of Žižek's Hegelian reading of the Kantian sublime in *The Sublime Object of Ideology* (1989). According to

Kant, the gap separating the phenomenal object of experience from the noumenal Thing-in-itself (the supersensible idea) is unbridgeable. This is why the object that evokes a feeling of the sublime gives one pleasure and pain at the same time. It gives one pain because it is a representation that cannot adequately present the Thing-in-itself, and pleasure because this inadequacy itself indicates the incomprehensible greatness of the Thing-in-itself that overflows every phenomenal object of experience.

> The feeling of the sublime is therefore a feeling of pain arising from the want of accordance between the aesthetical estimation of magnitude formed by the imagination and the estimation of the same formed by reason. There is at the same time a pleasure thus excited, arising from the correspondence with rational ideas of this very judgment of the inadequacy of our greatest faculty of sense, in so far as it is a law for us to strive after these ideas. (KU 257/CJ 96)

Kant stresses that the feeling of pleasure and the feeling of pain are interrelated moments: the feeling of pleasure in correspondence is aroused by the feeling of pain in the want of accordance.

> Therefore the inner perception of the inadequacy of all sensible standards for rational estimation of magnitude indicates a correspondence with rational laws; it involves a pain, which arouses in us the feeling of our supersensible destination, according to which it is purposive and therefore pleasurable to find every standard of sensibility inadequate to the ideas of understanding. (KU 258/CJ 97)

The feeling of pleasure that attests to a correspondence, a purposiveness, is *not* a purposiveness that dissolves the want of accordance, but is rather a purposiveness *of* that want of correspondence. The want of correspondence between imagination and reason is precisely what corresponds with reason. What is sublime (what is purposive) is the complex feeling to which is disclosed *both* the difference between imagination (the sensible) and reason (the supersensible) *and* (in and through that disclosure) one's essential orientation to the supersensible as one's genuine destination (T 116–117, 120–121, 126–127). This disclosure prohibits images in favor of a "merely negative presentation" (T 121, SOI 205) of the supersensible. Referring to the Jewish law of prohibition against idolatry (Exod. 20:4), Kant writes, "Perhaps there is no sublimer passage in the Jewish law than the command, 'Thou shalt not make to thyself any graven image, nor the likeness of anything which is in heaven or in the earth or under the earth,' etc." (KU 274/CJ 115). What is sublime (what is purposive) is the complex feeling that moves the mind.

> This movement may (especially in its beginnings) be compared to a vibration, i.e. to a quickly alternating attraction toward, and repulsion from, the same object. The transcendent (toward which the imagination is impelled in its apprehension of intuition) is for the imagination like an abyss in which it fears

to lose itself; but for the rational idea of the supersensible it is not transcendent, but in conformity with law to bring about such an effort of the imagination, and consequently here there is the same amount of attraction as there was of repulsion for the mere sensibility. (KU 258/CJ 97)

This movement is a rapid alternation between being attracted to and repulsed by the same object. The object is the object (customarily, though improperly, called sublime) that imagination strives (unsuccessfully) to comprehend. The recoil of imagination from what exceeds comprehension discloses (as was mentioned earlier) *both* the difference between imagination and reason *and* (in and through that disclosure) one's essential orientation to the supersensible as one's genuine destination. What produces the vibration is the difference between the appearances that this object can assume for imagination and for reason. For imagination, the object appears as an abyss in which it fears to lose itself. The subject is repulsed by it. For reason, the striving of imagination for comprehension is not an excessive impulse toward an abyss, but rather appears in conformity with the law of reason itself. The disclosure of the *difference* between imagination and reason (characteristic of the first appearance) is in *conformity* with reason (according to the second appearance), and discloses one's essential orientation to the supersensible as one's genuine destination (T 126–127). This vibration echoes, I would argue, the trembling of Derrida's reading of Kierkegaard's *Fear and Trembling* (1843) in *The Gift of Death* (1992), for (according to Derrida) what makes one tremble is what interrupts or sacrifices (while, at the same time, recognizing) comprehension. Recall that the disclosure — of *both* the difference between imagination and reason *and* (in and through that disclosure) one's essential orientation to the supersensible as one's genuine destination — prohibits images in favor of a "merely negative presentation" of the supersensible. The imagination "thus acquires an extension and a might greater than it sacrifices [*aufopfert*] — the ground of which, however, is concealed from itself — while yet it *feels* the sacrifice [*Aufopferung*] or the deprivation and, at the same time, the cause to which it is subjected" (KU 269/CJ 109). It feels the sacrifice as a merely negative presentation of the concealed ground (the noumenal Thing-in-itself, the supersensible idea) to which it is purposively subjected.

Žižek's Hegelian reading of the Kantian sublime in *The Sublime Object of Ideology* adds nothing to the Kantian notion; it merely takes the Kantian notion of the sublime "more *literally* than Kant himself" (SOI 205). This also applies, in turn (as will become apparent in a moment), to the Kantian reading of the sublime Jewish law of prohibition against idolatry. What Kant takes for the negative presentation of the noumenal Thing-in-itself (the supersensible idea) is for Hegel the Thing-in-itself as *nothing but* radical negativity. "The experience of the Sublime thus remains the same: all we have to do," Žižek writes, "is to subtract its transcendent presupposition — the presupposition that this experience indicates, in a negative way, some transcendent Thing-in-itself persisting in its positivity beyond it" (SOI 206). Recall that the imagination feels the sacrifice as a merely negative presentation of the concealed ground (the noumenal Thing-in-itself, the supersensible idea) to which it is purposively subjected. The Hegelian speculative twist pointed out by Žižek is, I would argue, a sacrifice of *this* sacrifice (which has a transcendental intention). The sacrifice of *this* sacrifice means that one *feels* the sacrifice, the negativity, *as itself* the cause to which it is subjected, *as itself* the ground to which it is purposively subjected. Said otherwise, the cause to which it is subjected, the ground to which it is purposively subjected, is *nothing but* radical negativity, *nothing but* the sacrifice of sacrifice. Here the vibration/trembling, as well as the sublime prohibition of idolatry, is taken to the extreme point, insofar as even the presupposition of a positive entity (albeit concealed) behind the negative presentation of the noumenal Thing-in-itself is considered idolatrous. Žižek's Hegelian reading of the Kantian sublime disturbs the traditional commandment of the Hebrew Scriptures against idolatry on one level while at the same time reinforcing its most extreme ramifications. In the name of the tradition, one is called to inventively rupture that tradition. The exercise of this traditional commandment must always run the risk of conversion and apostasy (DM 33/GD 27).

Eucharistic Sacrifice as Incessant *Repetition* of the *Singular* Sacrifice of Jesus Christ

This dissident and inventive rupture is, I would argue, ritualized in (among other events) the sacrifice *of* the Eucharist. A genealogy of the metaphor of sacrifice in eucharistic theology can (with some justification) be constructed around the distinction between eucharistic sacrifice understood as a *repetition* of the sacrifice of Jesus Christ and eucharistic sacrifice understood as a memorial (*anamnesis*) of the *singular* sacrifice of Jesus Christ. In contrast to this distinction, I would argue that what is called for is (paradoxically) an incessant *repetition* of the *singular* sacrifice of Jesus Christ (whether it be in a good work or in liturgy). In *The Gift of Death*, Derrida writes:

> The concept of responsibility is one of those strange concepts that give food for thought without giving themselves over to thematization. It presents itself neither as a theme nor as a thesis, it gives without being seen, without presenting itself in person by means of a "fact of being seen" that can be phenomenologically intuited. This paradoxical concept also has the structure of a type of secret—what is called, in the code of certain religious practices, mystery. The exercise of responsibility seems to leave no choice but this one, however uncomfortable it may be, of paradox, heresy, and secrecy. More serious still, it must always run the risk of conversion and apostasy: there is no responsibility without a dissident and inventive rupture with respect to tradition, authority, orthodoxy, rule, or doctrine. (DM 33–34/GD 27)

I would also argue that the interiorization of the body and blood of Jesus performed in the eucharistic sacrifice gives (like responsibility) "food for thought" (without giving itself over to thematization) insofar as it is a ritualized mourning

of the incessant dying of God and an unconditional call to sacrifice and responsibility.

This reading of eucharistic sacrifice as a dissident and inventive rupture of
tradition "consists," according to Derrida in *The Gift of Death*, "of proposing a
nondogmatic doublet of dogma, a philosophical and metaphysical doublet, in
any case a *thinking* that 'repeats' the possibility of religion without religion" (DM
53/GD 49), that is, a thinking that repeats the possibility of religion without the
event itself of sacrifice or responsibility (as inscribed within traditional religious
dogma). It is a thinking that repeats the possibility of religion without the special
moral *experience* of sacrifice or responsibility. This nondogmatic doublet of
dogma is, I would argue, the excessive sacrifice of sacrifice that interrupts sacrifice
in the very "doing" of the action. This "other" sacrifice, this sacrifice of sacrifice
(which is an interruption of the "work" of sacrifice), is an interruption of the
transcendental intention of sacrifice. This "other" sacrifice must always run the
risk of conversion and apostasy. This "other" sacrifice is to be read alongside the
overwhelmingly predominant economical reading of sacrifice inscribed within
traditional religious dogma. As such, the purity of this "repetition" (this nondogmatic doublet of dogma) that has no need of a revelatory event is always already
contaminated, for Derrida is quick to add that "[t]here is no choice to be made
here between a logical deduction, or one that is not related to the event, and
the reference to a revelatory event. *One implies the other*" (DM 53/GD 50,
emphasis added). It is within the horizon of this irreducible ambiguity of a logically deduced nondogmatic doublet of dogma that both *produces* (the possibility
of) Christianity and is *produced by* Christianity that I propose to trace a genealogy
of the metaphor of sacrifice in eucharistic theology. This genealogy is traced not
with an eye toward a change in the liturgy of the sacrifice of the Eucharist, but
rather a radical change in perspective on the sacrifice *of* the Eucharist as it is
currently performed, a radical change in perspective akin to Žižek's Hegelian
reading of the Kantian sublime. Like Žižek's Hegelian reading of the Kantian
sublime, the ritual appropriation of the sacrifice of Jesus Christ (whose death is
the death of God himself) is the ritual appropriation of the sacrifice of sacrifice
(the sublime) that is a mourning of the incessant dying of God and an unconditional call to responsibility.

Augustine and the Church as the Mystical Body of Christ

It was the understanding of eucharistic sacrifice as a *repetition* of the sacrifice of
Jesus Christ—which received validation with the *Dialogues* of Pope Gregory the
Great and achieved prominence in the Middle Ages—that prompted the critiques of the reformers. Various thinkers of the Reformation regarded the sacrifice
of the mass as a propitiatory sacrifice. Sacrifice, they contended, was understood
as a good work performed as expiation for sins. The implication is that this
understanding undermines the ἐφάπαξ of the letter to the Hebrews: "Unlike the
other high priests, he has no need to offer sacrifices [θυσίας] day after day, first

for his own sins, and then for those of the people; this he did *once for all* [ἐφάπαξ] when he offered himself" (Heb. 7:27, NRSV, emphasis added). Sacrifice understood as a good work performed as expiation for sins undermines, they contended, the all-sufficiency of the sacrifice of Jesus Christ, which in turn removes the ground of the doctrine of Christian assurance. It also calls into question Jesus Christ as agent in the Eucharist and provides the ideological grounding for a hierarchical understanding of the church. In *A Treatise on the New Testament, that is, the Holy Mass* (1520) and *The Babylonian Captivity of the Church* (1520), Martin Luther, while criticizing an understanding of the sacrifice of the mass as a good work we offer to God, allows for an understanding of the Eucharist as a sacrifice that echoes Augustine's understanding of the Eucharist as a sacrifice.

> [W]e do not offer Christ as a sacrifice [*opffert*], but [...] Christ offers us. And in this way it is permissible, yes, profitable, to call the mass a sacrifice [*opffer*]; not on its own account, but because we offer ourselves as a sacrifice [*opffern*] along with Christ. That is, we lay ourselves on Christ by a firm faith in his testament and do not otherwise appear before God with our prayer, praise, and sacrifice [*opffer*] except through Christ and his mediation. (SNT 369/TNT 99)

Augustine of Hippo understands the Eucharist as a memorial (*anamnesis*) of the *singular* sacrifice of Jesus Christ. The logic of Augustine's idea of sacrifice in *The City of God* relies on the concept of the church as the mystical body of Christ. The sacrificial gift of bread and wine, which represent the sufferings of the faithful, is joined to the Christ-victim. Since the church is the body of Christ, the sufferings of the faithful are Christ's suffering and are offered to God. The representation on the altar of Christ's self-sacrifice includes the sacrifice of those who make up the mystical body of Christ.

> [T]he whole redeemed city, that is to say, the congregation or community of the saints, is offered to God as our sacrifice [*universale sacrificium*] through the great High Priest, who offered Himself to God in His passion for us, that we might be members of this glorious head, according to the form of a servant. [...] This is the sacrifice [*sacrificium*] of Christians: we, being many, are one body in Christ. And this also is the sacrifice which the Church continually celebrates in the sacrament of the altar, known to the faithful, in which she teaches that she herself is offered in the offering she makes to God. (CD 34: 446, 448/CG 310)

Augustine's work can likewise be situated within a line of the tradition that witnessed the progressive interiorization and spiritualization of sacrifice. In accordance with the interpretation of sacrifice that places utmost importance on one's interior disposition, Israelite sacrificial practice was subjected to critique (as well as a progressive interiorization and spiritualization) by the prophets (Isaiah 1:11–17, Jeremiah 7:21–23, Hosea 6:6, Amos 5:21–24, Micah 6:6–8), in the psalms (Psalms 40:6–8, 50:7–15, 51:16–19), and in the later wisdom literature. This development reflects the transformation of Jewish sacrificial practice by the Yahwist faith, which understood Yahweh as sovereign over all creation, and therefore in need of nothing. Things offered to God are not needed by God (CD 34: 438, 440, 442, 444/CG 307–309). The progressive interiorization and spiritualization of sacrifice did not, however, represent a repudiation of sacrifice, but rather the necessity of the proper interior disposition accompanying the outward act.

> A sacrifice [*Sacrificium*], therefore, is the visible sacrament or sacred sign of an invisible sacrifice [*invisibilis sacrificii*]. Hence that penitent in the psalm, or it may be the Psalmist himself, entreating God to be merciful to his sins, says, "If Thou desiredst sacrifice [*sacrificium*], I would give it: Thou delightest not in whole burnt-offerings. The sacrifice [*Sacrificium*] of God is a broken heart: a heart contrite and humble God will not despise" [Ps. 51:16–17]. Observe how, in the very words in which he is expressing God's refusal of sacrifice [*sacrificium*], he shows that God requires sacrifice [*sacrificium*]. He does not desire the sacrifice [*sacrificium*] of a slaughtered beast, but He desires the sacrifice [*sacrificium*] of a contrite heart. (CD 34: 440/CG 308)

Sacrifice becomes an ethical, as well as a cultic, category. The true sacrifice is an invisible sacrifice that is visible to God and that reflects the proper interior disposition of the ethical agent. The true sacrifice is mercy.

> In the epistle entitled "To the Hebrews" it is said, "To do good and to communicate, forget not: for with such sacrifices [*sacrificiis*] God is well pleased" [Heb. 13:16]. And so, when it is written, "I desire mercy rather than sacrifice [*sacrificium*]" [Hos. 6:6, Matt. 9:13, 12:7], nothing else is meant than that one sacrifice [*sacrificium*] is preferred to another [*sacrificio*]; for that which in common speech is called sacrifice [*sacrificium*] is only the symbol of the true sacrifice [*veri sacrificii*]. Now mercy is the true sacrifice [*verum sacrificium*], and therefore it is said, as I have just quoted, "with such sacrifices [*sacrificiis*] God is well pleased" [Heb. 13:16]. (CD 34: 442, 444/CG 309)

For Augustine, therefore, the true sacrifice is an invisible sacrifice that is visible to God, and that reflects the proper interior disposition of the ethical agent. The true sacrifice is the sacrifice of a contrite heart. The true sacrifice is mercy.

A true sacrifice, according to Augustine, is not done to overcome alienation or expiate sins. "[A] true sacrifice [*verum sacrificium*] is every work which is done that we may be united to God in holy fellowship, and which has a reference to that supreme good and end in which alone we can be truly blessed" (CD 34: 444/CG 309). Such "work" (*opus*) constitutes fellowship itself and is not done to overcome alienation or expiate sins (SG 262).

There are those who argue that the implication of the Augustinian point of view on sacrifice is that those Christians who sacrifice themselves to God must not expect (even secretly) a divine gift in return (SG 280). The expectation of a divine gift is a characteristic of eucharistic sacrifice understood as a *repetition* of the sacrifice of Jesus Christ. Those who argue that the implication of the Augustinian point of view prohibits this expectation must agree with Jung, who argues in "Transformation Symbolism of the Mass" (1954) that a gift "only becomes a sacrifice [*geopfert*] if I give up the implied intention of receiving something in return. If it is to be a true sacrifice [*Opfer*], the gift must be given as if it were being destroyed" (WM 293–294/TSM 256). But sacrifice, by definition (as pointed out by Nancy and Žižek), always has a transcendental intention. Sacrifice without reserve is not truly sacrifice without reserve if there is faith in a witness, as is the case in the work of Augustine. Sacrifice without reserve is only truly at "work" if one understands sacrifice as the sacrifice of sacrifice.

Sacrifice without reserve is, for Augustine, predicated upon faith in a witness. For Augustine, as was pointed out earlier, the true sacrifice is an invisible sacrifice that is visible to God, and that reflects the proper interior disposition of the ethical agent. The true sacrifice is the sacrifice of a contrite heart. The true sacrifice is mercy. But believing that God *knows* (or witnesses) the secreted secret founds (insofar as one has faith that there is a *celestial* witness to one's giving without reserve *within the terrestrial economy*) and destroys (because the giving without reserve is integrated into the *celestial economy*) the Christian concepts of responsibility and justice (DM 105/GD 112). Even though there are those who argue that the implication of the Augustinian point of view is that sacrifice is a sacrifice without reserve (given that those Christians who sacrifice themselves to God must not expect—even secretly—a divine gift in return), sacrifice without reserve is not truly sacrifice without reserve if there is faith in a witness. Sacrifice without reserve is the sacrifice of sacrifice, which has profound consequences not only for the subject, but also for God. The sacrifice of sacrifice involves (paradoxically) the sacrifice of the transcendent presupposition of sacrifice. It is the recognition of the fact that the subject "is" *nothing but* radical sacrifice. It is the recognition of the fact that God "is" *nothing but* radical sacrifice, *nothing but* radical (dis)incarnation.

Derrida and God as Nothing But Agape (Love)

This understanding of God as *nothing but* radical sacrifice, *nothing but* radical (dis)incarnation, is addressed by Derrida in *The Gift of Death*. Derrida points out that "Patočka speaks and thinks in the places where Christianity has not yet thought or spoken of what it should have been and is not yet" (DM 52/GD 49). Patočka's work is, according to Derrida, a "heretical and hyperbolic form" of Christianity (if, in fact, it does involve Christianity). Patočka traces a genealogy of responsibility: (1) demonic or orgiastic mystery, (2) Platonic mystery, (3) Christian mystery. In the conversion from Platonism to Christianity the Good is no longer a transcendental objective, but the relation to the other. It is "an experience of personal goodness and a movement of intention" (DM 54/GD 50). This goodness is a goodness that forgets itself, and this movement is a movement of the gift that renounces itself, that is, a movement of infinite love. "Only infinite love," Derrida writes, "can renounce itself and, in order to *become finite*, become incarnated in order to love the other, to love the other as a finite other" (DM

54/GD 51). Earlier in *The Gift of Death*, Derrida pointed out that goodness is given in that the inaccessible other calls me to goodness, calls me to be good, that is, forget myself. "It subjects its receivers, giving itself to them as goodness itself but also as the law" (DM 45/GD 41). This (dis)incarnation of goodness as law *is*, I would argue, the effacement of the infinite being in its becoming finite/incarnate and the effacement of the finite/incarnated being in its being nothing but "for the other." There is a sacrifice of the transcendent God with the attending sacrifice of the subject. The (dis)incarnation of goodness as law *is* the sacrifice or effacement of God with the attending sacrifice or effacement of the incarnated subject.

Derrida connects this understanding of God as *nothing but* radical sacrifice, as *nothing but* radical (dis)incarnation, with the movement of infinite love. This suggests that the sacrifice of sacrifice — which involves (paradoxically) the sacrifice of the transcendent presupposition of sacrifice — is the recognition not only of the fact that God "is" *nothing but* radical sacrifice, *nothing but* radical (dis)incarnation, but also that God "is" *nothing but agape*. "God is love [ἀγάπη]" (1 John 4:8, NRSV). (Paradoxically, one of the consequences of God being *nothing but agape* is that this God of infinite love is contaminated by the demonic. That this God of infinite love is contaminated by the demonic is attested to by the aporias of death, responsibility, and sacrifice. As was pointed out earlier, they attest to the contamination of Christianity — insofar as "Christianity" is understood as characterized *merely* by a God whose gift of goodness calls one to goodness — because the sacrifice and responsibility demanded of me hold *me* accountable and *discount* me. Sacrifice and responsibility require — using words of Blanchot that echo Heidegger's analysis of death as the possibility of the impossibility of Dasein — that I answer for the impossibility of sacrifice, for the impossibility of being responsible, which makes me always already guilty or irresponsible. Given this understanding of God, sacrifice, and responsibility, there is no way to secure oneself against the conclusion that the God of Christianity calls one to goodness *and* badness, to responsibility *and* irresponsibility. "I make weal and create woe; I the LORD do all these things" [Isa. 45:7, NRSV].)

Žižek and God as Nothing But Agape (Love)

According to St. Paul, the Law arouses one's sinful desire to transgress the Law. Obeying the Law seems to call for the sacrifice of one's sinful desire, which bears witness to one's sinful desire to transgress the Law, which consequently makes one guiltier. The basic point of Christianity (according to Žižek's reading of St. Paul) is the interruption of this vicious superego cycle of the Law and its transgression by means of *agape*. *Agape* is the sacrifice *of* the sacrifice of one's "pathological" sinful desire to transgress the Law characteristic of the vicious superego cycle of the Law and its transgression. It is the sacrifice of sacrifice. It is work that interrupts itself *in* the very working of the work. *Agape* unworks the very work of sacrifice. *Agape* is *work*, but *for nothing*.

It is discovered "after the fact" that rather than sacrificing for a Cause-Thing in which one believes (e.g., "God"), one sacrifices *for nothing*. As was pointed out earlier, this saves God from being a perverse subject (who brings about our Fall so that he can then redeem us through his sacrifice), but it comes at the cost of the discovery that "God" is *nothing but* radical sacrifice, *nothing but* radical (dis)incarnation, *nothing but agape*. "God is love [ἀγάπη]" (1 John 4:8, NRSV). (To become a true Christian and embrace *agape*, one should "die to the Law." Paradoxically, "dying to the Law" is what Lacan calls undergoing "subjective destitution" or "symbolic death," which involves the terrifying violence of the death drive that wipes the slate clean in preparation for a new beginning. "I make weal and create woe; I the LORD do all these things" [Isa. 45:7, NRSV].)

Returning to the distinction between eucharistic sacrifice understood as a *repetition* of the sacrifice of Jesus Christ and eucharistic sacrifice understood as a memorial (*anamnesis*) of the *singular* sacrifice of Jesus Christ (i.e., one sacrifices only insofar as one is incorporated into the mystical body of Christ, only insofar as one participates in the singular sacrifice of the Christ-victim), I would argue that what is called for is (paradoxically) an incessant *repetition* of the *singular* sacrifice of Jesus Christ (whether it be in a good work or in liturgy). What is called for (paradoxically) is a sharing (i.e., repetition) of what cannot be shared (insofar as it is absolutely singular). This, I would argue, is what the Augustinian theology of eucharistic sacrifice as a memorial (*anamnesis*) of the *singular* sacrifice of Jesus Christ is trying to say in a tortured way by means of the concept of the church as the mystical body of Christ. In the epilogue of *Fear and Trembling*, Kierkegaard repeatedly states that the "highest passion" that is faith must be started over by each generation. In *The Gift of Death*, Derrida writes regarding this "highest passion": "Each generation must begin again to involve itself in it without counting on the generation before. It thus describes the nonhistory of absolute beginnings which are repeated, and the very historicity that presupposes a tradition to be reinvented each step of the way, in this incessant repetition of the absolute beginning" (DM 78/GD 80). We share with Jesus Christ (i.e., we repeat) a secret that cannot be shared (i.e., what is absolutely singular for each generation, for each person, i.e., the singularization/ex-propriation characteristic of sacrifice without reserve). This singular sacrifice without reserve that must be incessantly repeated is appropriated by an economy of sacrifice in which sacrifice pays, either (1) in terms of eucharistic sacrifice understood as a repetition of the sacrifice of Jesus Christ, or (2) in terms of eucharistic sacrifice understood as a memorial (*anamnesis*) of the *singular* sacrifice of Jesus Christ, which is in turn understood as a sacrifice performed in order to overcome alienation or expiate sins.

The gaze of God that is Jesus Christ's singularization/ex-propriation is simultaneously *singular* and *universal*; that is, the person of faith must *repeat* the *singular* sacrifice of Jesus Christ (whether it be in a good work or in liturgy). It must be repeated in the non-history of an absolute beginning. It is important to note that the sacrifice of Jesus Christ is singular only for the believer situated within a particular sociocultural context. There is no reason why this sacrifice cannot be "modeled" by others (e.g., Abraham or Antigone), and therefore not be absolutely singular with respect to the model. Faith in a particular model is culturally determined. There is no singularity to the model, insofar as *any* model chosen can (must) be repeated. The (paradoxical) incessant repetition of the singular sacrifice of Jesus Christ disturbs the orthodoxy of the traditional understanding of eucharistic sacrifice while at the same time reinforcing its most extreme ramifications.

The irreducible ambiguity of the necessary, yet impossible, call for an incessant *repetition* of the *singular* sacrifice of Jesus Christ (whether it be in a good work or in liturgy) explains, I would argue, the ever-potential sliding into either (1) eucharistic sacrifice understood as a *repetition* of the sacrifice of Jesus Christ, or (2) eucharistic sacrifice understood as a memorial (*anamnesis*) of the *singular* sacrifice of Jesus Christ, which is in turn understood as a sacrifice performed in order to overcome alienation or expiate sins.

Eucharist as Mourning the Incessant Dying of God and Call to Responsibility

The ambiguity of the word *à-Dieu* serves to gather together many of the ideas considered up to this moment. In absolute sacrifice and responsibility a going *to* God and a *good-bye* coincide: *à-Dieu*. This "good-bye" of/to God has several different (are they different?) trajectories: (1) good-bye of/to God as palpably present, (2) good-bye of/to God as transcendent insofar as God becomes its own other, becomes finite, becomes (dis)incarnated as the command of *agape*, with the self thereby becoming its own other, becoming the (dis)incarnation of *agape*, and (3) good-bye of/to God as transcendent guarantee of the Good, of responsibility, insofar as God becomes its own other, that is, the demonic. God makes weal and woe; God establishes peace and is the author of evil.

This *à-Dieu*, which marks an unconditional call to sacrifice and responsibility, likewise marks, I would argue, a mourning of the incessant dying of God. Since Freud (and Abraham and Torok), the normal work of mourning is described as an interiorization of the other, an attempt to keep the other in me, in memory. But faithful interiorization is unfaithful in that it effaces the radical otherness of the other, and unfaithful interiorization is faithful in that it respects the radical otherness of the other. This is what Derrida calls "ex-appropriation" (P 321). In mourning one is "obliged to harbor something that is greater and other" than oneself (Mf 54/Me 34). Here one sees an ex-appropriation that is not unlike Lacan's description of *objet petit a* and Levinas's description of the idea of the infinite. This describes an appropriation that both singularizes (insofar as the self is appropriated) and ex-propriates the self. It describes the singularity/ ex-propriation given by death and required by sacrifice and responsibility characteristic of the relation to the other. "If *Jemeinigkeit*, that of *Dasein* or that of

185

the ego (in the common sense, the psychoanalytic sense, or Levinas's sense) is constituted in its ipseity in terms of an originary mourning, then this self-relation welcomes or supposes the other within its being-itself as different from itself. And reciprocally: the relation to the other (in itself outside myself, outside myself in myself) will never be distinguishable from a bereaved apprehension" (AM 331/ AD 61). If the *relation to the other* is indistinguishable from a bereaved apprehension, then according to the "logic" of the formula *tout autre est tout autre*, does this include God? That is, is the *relation to God* indistinguishable from a bereaved apprehension? I would argue that there is a mourning of the incessant dying of God that is articulated by *à-Dieu*.

This *à-Dieu* that marks this mourning of the incessant dying of God and an unconditional call to sacrifice and responsibility involves, I would argue, what Irigaray calls a "*new* sacrifice." Irigaray argues that under eucharistic sacrifice is hidden another sacrifice: the sacrifice of woman. What is called for is a new sacrifice, which is the sacrifice *of* the revealed sacrifice of man that hides the sacrifice of woman. This new sacrifice, this sacrifice of sacrifice, is an interruption of the (patriarchal) fantasy of God and woman, both understood as substantial alien Entities. Rather than the safe belief that succeeds in making the other the other *of the same* and displaces the work of mourning, belief *itself* is a mourning of the primordial "loss" of woman and God. What it means to mourn the primordial "loss" of woman and God is the sacrifice of sacrifice. It is woman and God "in me more than me." It is the (momentary) ex-appropriation of woman and God.

This mourning of a primordial "loss" is, I would argue, ritualized in liturgy. In "Meaning and Sense" from *Humanisme de l'autre homme* (1972), Levinas writes that liturgy designates (in its primary meaning) "the exercise of a function which is not only totally gratuitous, but requires on the part of him who exercises it a putting out of funds at a loss" (SS 45/MS 92–93). It designates, I would argue, the (im)possible exercise of responsibility without reserve, of the sacrifice of sacrifice. In "Revelation in the Jewish Tradition" (1977) from *Beyond the Verse: Talmudic Readings and Lectures* (1982), Levinas writes, "In ritual a distance is taken up *within* nature *in respect of* nature [dans *la nature* à l'égard *de la nature*], and perhaps therefore it is precisely the waiting for the Most-High which is a relation to Him — or, if one prefers, a deference, a deference to the beyond which creates here the very concept of a beyond or a towards-God [*à-Dieu*]" (RTJ 173/ RJT 143). The work of ritual is commonly seen as a moment in nature when nature is revealed in its truth, specifically, a moment in nature when the Most-High who transcends nature is revealed. This reading of ritual is not unlike the reading of the transformative power of death that effects a step beyond. But, for Levinas, the work of ritual is arguably read alongside the aporia of death — death as possibility turning into death as impossibility. Ritual is a movement in nature in which "a distance is taken up *within* nature *in respect of* nature." Ritual is the performance of what Levinas calls the "not yet" of dead time.

This *à-Dieu* that marks this mourning of the incessant dying of God and an unconditional call to sacrifice and responsibility is, I would argue, ritualized in the liturgy of the sacrifice *of* the Eucharist. If the interiorization of the body and blood of Jesus performed in the liturgy of the Eucharist were no more than an interiorization, then what would be ritualized is not the constitutive failure that is mourning as described by Derrida, but merely a loss of respect for the radical otherness or exteriority of the other. The interiorization of the body and blood of Jesus performed in the liturgy of the Eucharist is, however, to be understood by the communicant as the interiorization of the wholly other (God, or Jesus as indistinguishable from the wholly other) that is greater and other than oneself (which describes the constitutive failure that is mourning, and which is in turn indistinguishable from the relation to the other). As such, it is the interiorization of the wholly other (God, or Jesus as indistinguishable from the wholly other) that, insofar as it is greater and other than oneself, singularizes and ex-propriates the self, making it nothing but (in Levinas's words) "for the other." The interiorization of broken bread and poured wine is an interiorization of the call to singularity and ex-propriation characteristic of the aporias of sacrifice, responsibility, and death. It is an interiorization of the singularizing call to be nothing but "for the other."

This interiorization of the singularizing call to be nothing but "for the other" means, I would argue, that the communicant is ritually acknowledging that he or she is to become what he or she already is: the Messiah. By eating the body and blood of the Messiah, I become what I already am: the Messiah. Augustine says as much in "Sermon 272": "[W]hat you receive is the mystery that means you. It is to what you are that you reply *Amen,* and by so replying you express your assent. [. . .] [R]eceive what you are [*accipite quod estis*]" (Sl 1247–1248/ Se 300–301). In "Messianic Texts" from *Difficult Freedom: Essays on Judaism* (1963), Levinas writes,

> The Messiah is Myself; to be Myself is to be the Messiah.
> We have just seen that the Messiah is the just man who suffers, who has taken on the suffering of others. Who finally takes on the suffering of others, if not the being who says 'Me'?
> The fact of not evading the burden imposed by the suffering of others defines ipseity itself. All persons are the Messiah. (TM 120/MT 89)

This passage echoes themes in the fourth of the so-called "Servant Songs" found in the book of Isaiah (Isa. 52:13–53:12): "Surely he has borne our infirmities and carried our diseases" (Isa. 53:4, NRSV). Early Christian interpretation applied this passage to Jesus (Matt. 8:17).

The liturgy of the sacrifice *of* the Eucharist, which ritualizes the mourning of the incessant dying of God and an unconditional call to sacrifice and responsibility, ritualizes the irreducible ambiguity of the necessary, yet impossible, call for the person of faith to incessantly *repeat* the *singular* sacrifice of Jesus Christ.

This (im)possible "work" of liturgy is ritualized in (among other things) the taking leave of the ritual to do the "work" of responsibility (in this way, both the self and the ritual itself are sacrificed). The concluding rite of the liturgy of the Eucharist consists of a dismissal that sends each member of the worshiping community to do good works, praising and blessing the Lord (see *The Roman Missal: The Sacramentary*). The (im)possible "work" of liturgy also reveals, I would argue, the necessity that the Roman Rite is not the sole appropriate form of liturgy. If it is structured by the "logic" of the "not yet" of dead time, then it necessarily has to be open to the possibility of its being called into question, of its becoming its "own" other, that is, of its being sacrificed. This is in consonance with the earlier argument that the "model" for the singular sacrifice to be re-peated *cannot* be absolutely singular, i.e., it can be "modeled" by others (e.g., Abraham or Antigone).

The sacrifice *of* the Eucharist is a sacrifice that founds a community by undoing it. It is a ritualized going *to* God that is a *good-bye* insofar as God sacrifices itself, becomes (dis)incarnated (in Jesus or myself) *as* the command of *agape,* with the self (Jesus or myself) thereby sacrificing itself insofar as it becomes the (dis)incarnation of *agape: à-Dieu.*

This "work" — *of* sacrificing sacrifice, *on* sacrificing sacrifice — has accomplished very little, almost nothing. And that has made all the difference.

BIBLIOGRAPHY

Abraham, Nicolas, and Maria Torok. *The Shell and the Kernel*, vol. I. Edited and translated by Nicholas T. Rand. Chicago: University of Chicago Press, 1994.

———. *The Wolf Man's Magic Word: A Cryptonymy*. Translated by Nicholas Rand. Minneapolis: University of Minnesota Press, 1986.

Anselm. *Why God Became a Man*. In *Anselm of Canterbury*, vol. 3, 39–137. Edited and translated by Jasper Hopkins and Herbert Richardson. Toronto: Edwin Mellen Press, 1976.

Aquinas, Thomas. *Summa Theologiæ*. Blackfriars, in conjunction with New York: McGraw-Hill Company, 1964–1981.

Armour, Ellen. "Beyond Belief? Sexual Difference and Religion After Ontotheology." In *The Religious*, edited by John D. Caputo, 212–226. Oxford: Blackwell Publishers, 2001.

Arnould, Elisabeth. "The Impossible Sacrifice of Poetry: Bataille and the Nancian Critique of Sacrifice." In *Diacritics* 26.2 (Summer 1996): 86–96.

Attali, Jacques. "Sacrificing." In *Noise: The Political Economy of Music*, translated by Brian Massumi, 21–45. Minneapolis: University of Minnesota Press, 1985.

Auerbach, Erich. "Odysseus' Scar." In *Mimesis: The Representation of Reality in Western Literature*, translated by Willard R. Trask, 3–23. Princeton, N.J.: Princeton University Press, 1953.

Augustine. *The City of God*. Translated by Marcus Dods. New York: Random House, 1950.

———. "Sermon 272." In *The Works of Saint Augustine*, part III, vol. 7, 300–301. Translated by Edmund Hill. Edited by John E. Rotelle. New Rochelle, N.Y.: New City Press, 1993.

Bakan, David. *Disease, Pain and Sacrifice: Toward a Psychology of Suffering*. Chicago: University of Chicago Press, 1968.

Bataille, Georges. *The Accursed Share: An Essay on General Economy*. Translated by Robert Hurley. New York: Zone Books, 1991–1993.

———. "L'art, exercice de cruauté." In *Œuvres complètes*, vol. XI, 480–486. Paris: Éditions Gallimard, 1988.

———. "Hegel, Death and Sacrifice." Translated by Jonathan Strauss. In *Yale French Studies* 78 (1990): 9–28.

———. *Inner Experience*. Translated by Leslie Anne Boldt. Albany: State University of New York Press, 1988.

———. "The Notion of Expenditure." In *Visions of Excess: Selected Writings, 1927–1939*, translated by Allan Stoekl, with Carl R. Lovitt and Donald M. Leslie, Jr., 116–129. Minneapolis: University of Minnesota Press, 1985.

———. "Sacrifices." In *Visions of Excess: Selected Writings, 1927–1939*, translated by Allan Stoekl, with Carl R. Lovitt and Donald M. Leslie, Jr., 130–136. Minneapolis: University of Minnesota Press, 1985.

Bibliography

————. "Sacrificial Mutilation and the Severed Ear of Vincent Van Gogh." In *Visions of Excess: Selected Writings, 1927–1939*, translated by Allan Stoekl, with Carl R. Lovitt and Donald M. Leslie, Jr., 61–72. Minneapolis: University of Minnesota Press, 1985.

————. *Theory of Religion*. Translated by Robert Hurley. New York: Zone Books, 1989.

Beckwith, Roger T., and Martin J. Selman, eds. *Sacrifice in the Bible*. Grand Rapids, Mich.: Baker Book House, 1995.

Bergmann, Martin S. *In the Shadow of Moloch: The Sacrifice of Children and Its Impact on Western Religions*. New York: Columbia University Press, 1992.

Berman, Louis A. *The Akedah: The Binding of Isaac*. Northvale, N.J.: Jason Aronson, 1997.

Blanchot, Maurice. *The Infinite Conversation*. Translated by Susan Hanson. Minneapolis: University of Minnesota Press, 1993.

————. "Literature and the Right to Death." Translated by Lydia Davis. In *The Work of Fire*, translated by Charlotte Mandell, 300–344. Stanford, Calif.: Stanford University Press, 1995.

————. *The Space of Literature*. Translated by Ann Smock. Lincoln: University of Nebraska Press, 1982.

————. *The Unavowable Community*. Translated by Pierre Joris. Barrytown, N.Y.: Station Hill Press, 1988.

————. *The Writing of the Disaster*. Translated by Ann Smock. Lincoln: University of Nebraska Press, 1986.

Bloch, Maurice. *Prey into Hunter: The Politics of Religious Experience*. Cambridge: Cambridge University Press, 1992.

Boothby, Richard. "Altar-Egos: Psychoanalysis and the Theory of Sacrifice." In *Journal for the Psychoanalysis of Culture and Society* 1.2 (Fall 1996): 47–61.

Bourdieu, Pierre. *The Logic of Practice*. Translated by Richard Nice. Stanford, Calif.: Stanford University Press, 1992.

Bourdillon, M. F. C., and Meyer Fortes, eds. *Sacrifice*. London: Academic Press, 1980.

Bracken, Christopher. *The Potlatch Papers: A Colonial Case History*. Chicago: University of Chicago Press, 1997.

Brown, Shelby. *Late Carthaginian Child Sacrifice and Sacrificial Monuments in Their Mediterranean Context*. Sheffield, England: Sheffield Academic Press, 1991.

Burbidge, John. "Man, God, and Death in Hegel's *Phenomenology*." In *Philosophy and Phenomenological Research* 42.2 (1981): 183–196.

Burke, Kenneth. *The Rhetoric of Religion: Studies in Logology*. Boston: Beacon Press, 1961.

Burkert, Walter. *Creation of the Sacred: Tracks of Biology in Early Religions*. Cambridge, Mass.: Harvard University Press, 1996.

————. *Homo Necans: The Anthropology of Ancient Greek Sacrificial Ritual and Myth*. Translated by Peter Bing. Berkeley: University of California Press, 1983.

Caldwell, Anne. "Transforming Sacrifice: Irigaray and the Politics of Sexual Difference." In *Hypatia: A Journal of Feminist Philosophy* 17.4 (Fall 2002): 16–38.

Carlson, Thomas A. "Possibility and Passivity in Kierkegaard: The Anxieties of Don Giovanni and Abraham." In *Journal of the American Academy of Religion* 62.2 (Summer 1994): 461–481.

Carrasco, Davíd. *City of Sacrifice: The Aztec Empire and the Role of Violence in Civilization*. Boston: Beacon Press, 1999.

Cassirer, Ernst. *The Philosophy of Symbolic Forms*. Translated by Ralph Manheim. New Haven, Conn.: Yale University Press, 1955.

Chauvet, Louis-Marie. *Symbol and Sacrament: A Sacramental Reinterpretation of Christian Existence*. Translated by Patrick Madigan and Madeleine Beaumont. Collegeville, Minn.: Liturgical Press, 1995.

Combs-Schilling, M. E. *Sacred Performances: Islam, Sexuality, and Sacrifice*. New York: Columbia University Press, 1989.

Copjec, Joan. *Read My Desire: Lacan Against the Historicists*. Cambridge, Mass.: MIT Press, 1994.

Crenshaw, James L. "A Monstrous Test: Genesis 22." In *A Whirlpool of Torment*, 9–29. Philadelphia: Fortress Press, 1984.

Crockett, William R. *Eucharist: Symbol of Transformation*. New York: Pueblo Publishing Company, 1989.

Cyprian. "Letter 63." *The Letters of St. Cyprian of Carthage*, vol. III (Letters 55–66). Translated by G. W. Clarke. In *Ancient Christian Writers: The Works of the Fathers in Translation*, no. 46, edited by Johannes Quasten, Walter J. Burghardt, and Thomas Comerford Lawler, 98–109. New York: Newman Press, 1986.

Daly, Robert J. *Christian Sacrifice: The Judaeo-Christian Background Before Origen*. Washington, D.C.: Catholic University of America Press, 1978.

———. *The Origins of the Christian Doctrine of Sacrifice*. Philadelphia: Fortress Press, 1978.

Davies, Paul. "On Resorting to an Ethical Language." In *Ethics as First Philosophy: The Significance of Emmanuel Levinas for Philosophy, Literature and Religion*, edited by Adriaan T. Peperzak, 95–104. London: Routledge, 1995.

de Beistegui, Miguel. "Sacrifice Revisited." Translated by Simon Sparks. In *On Jean-Luc Nancy: The Sense of Philosophy*, edited by Darren Sheppard, Simon Sparks, and Colin Thomas, 157–173. London: Routledge, 1997.

de Heusch, Luc. *Sacrifice in Africa: A Structuralist Approach*. Translated by Linda O'Brien and Alice Morton. Bloomington: Indiana University Press, 1985.

de Vries, Hent. "Adieu, à dieu, a-Dieu." In *Ethics as First Philosophy: The Significance of Emmanuel Levinas for Philosophy, Literature and Religion*, edited by Adriaan T. Peperzak, 211–220. London: Routledge, 1995.

———. *Philosophy and the Turn to Religion*. Baltimore, Md.: Johns Hopkins University Press, 1999.

———. "Violence and Testimony: On Sacrificing Sacrifice." In *Violence, Identity, and Self-Determination*, edited by Hent de Vries and Samuel Weber, 15–43. Stanford, Calif.: Stanford University Press, 1997.

Derrida, Jacques. *Aporias: Dying—Awaiting (One Another at) the "Limits of Truth."* Translated by Thomas Dutoit. Stanford, Calif.: Stanford University Press, 1993.

———. "Before the Law." Translated by Avital Ronell. In *Kafka and the Contemporary Critical Performance: Centenary Readings*, edited by Alan Udoff, 128–149. Bloomington: Indiana University Press, 1987.

———. "Désistance." Translated by Christopher Fynsk. In *Typography: Mimesis, Philosophy, Politics*, translated by Christopher Fynsk, 1–42. Stanford, Calif.: Stanford University Press, 1998.

———. "Economimesis." Translated by R. Klein. In *Diacritics* 11 (June 1981): 3–25.

———. "Faith and Knowledge: The Two Sources of 'Religion' at the Limits of Reason

Alone." In *Religion*, edited by Jacques Derrida and Gianni Vattimo, 1–78. Stanford, Calif.: Stanford University Press, 1998.

———. "Force of Law: The 'Mystical Foundation of Authority.'" Translated by Mary Quaintance. In *Deconstruction and the Possibility of Justice*, edited by Drucilla Cornell, Michel Rosenfeld, and David Gray Carlson, 3–67. London: Routledge, 1992.

———. "*Fors*: The Anglish Words of Nicolas Abraham and Maria Torok." Translated by Barbara Johnson. In *The Wolf Man's Magic Word: A Cryptonymy*, translated by Nicholas Rand, xi–xlviii. Minneapolis: University of Minnesota Press, 1986.

———. "From Restricted to General Economy: A Hegelianism without Reserve." In *Writing and Difference*, translated by Alan Bass, 251–277. Chicago: University of Chicago Press, 1978.

———. *The Gift of Death*. Translated by David Wills. Chicago: University of Chicago Press, 1995.

———. *Given Time: I. Counterfeit Money*. Translated by Peggy Kamuf. Chicago: University of Chicago Press, 1992.

———. *Glas*. Translated by John P. Leavey, Jr., and Richard Rand. Lincoln: University of Nebraska Press, 1986.

———. "Mnemosyne." Translated by Cecile Lindsay. In *Memoires for Paul de Man*, 1–43, rev. ed. New York: Columbia University Press, 1989.

———. "*Ousia* and *Grammē*: Note on a Note from *Being and Time*." In *Margins of Philosophy*, translated by Alan Bass, 29–67. Chicago: University of Chicago Press, 1982.

———. *Points . . . : Interviews, 1974–1994*. Translated by Peggy Kamuf & others. Edited by Elisabeth Weber. Stanford, Calif.: Stanford University Press, 1995.

———. *Positions*. Translated by Alan Bass. Chicago: University of Chicago Press, 1981.

———. *The Post Card: From Socrates to Freud and beyond*. Translated by Alan Bass. Chicago: University of Chicago Press, 1987.

———. *Specters of Marx: The State of the Debt, the Work of Mourning, and the New International*. Translated by Peggy Kamuf. London: Routledge, 1994.

———. "Violence and Metaphysics: An Essay on the Thought of Emmanuel Levinas." In *Writing and Difference*, translated by Alan Bass, 79–153. Chicago: University of Chicago Press, 1978.

Desmonde, William H. *Magic, Myth, and Money: The Origin of Money in Religious Ritual*. New York: Free Press of Glencoe, 1962.

Detienne, Marcel. "Culinary Practices and the Spirit of Sacrifice." In *The Cuisine of Sacrifice among the Greeks*, Marcel Detienne and Jean-Pierre Vernant, translated by Paula Wissing, 1–20. Chicago: University of Chicago Press, 1989.

The Didache, or Teaching of the Twelve Apostles. In *The Apostolic Fathers*, translated by Kirsopp Lake, vol. I, 303–333. Cambridge, Mass.: Harvard University Press, 1952.

Durkheim, Émile. *The Elementary Forms of Religious Life*. Translated by Karen E. Fields. New York: Free Press, 1995.

Eilberg-Schwartz, H. *The Savage in Judaism: An Anthropology of Israelite Religion and Ancient Judaism*. Bloomington: Indiana University Press, 1990.

Evans-Pritchard, E. E. *Nuer Religion*. Oxford: Oxford University Press, 1956.

———. *Theories of Primitive Religion*. Oxford: Oxford University Press, 1965.

Firestone, Reuven. "Merit, Mimesis, and Martyrdom: Aspects of Shi'ite Meta-historical Exegesis on Abraham's Sacrifice in Light of Jewish, Christian, and Sunni Muslim

Tradition." In *Journal of the American Academy of Religion* 66.1 (Spring 1998): 93–116.

Firth, Raymond. "Offering and Sacrifice: Problems of Organization." In *Journal of the Royal Anthropological Institute* 93 (1963): 12–24.

Faherty, Robert L. "Sacrifice." In *The New Encyclopædia Britannica*, 15th ed., vol. 26, 791–798. Chicago: Encyclopædia Britannica, 2002.

Foucault, Michel. "Nietzsche, Genealogy, History." Translated by Donald F. Bouchard and Sherry Simon. In *The Foucault Reader*, edited by Paul Rabinow, 76–100. New York: Random House, 1984.

Fradenburg, L. O. Aranye. *Sacrifice Your Love: Psychoanalysis, Historicism, Chaucer*. Minneapolis: University of Minnesota Press, 2002.

Frazer, James George. *The Golden Bough: A Study in Magic and Religion*. 3rd ed. New York: St. Martin's Press, 1990.

Freud, Sigmund. *Beyond the Pleasure Principle*. In *The Standard Edition of the Complete Psychological Works of Sigmund Freud*, translated and edited by James Strachey, in collaboration with Anna Freud, and assisted by Alix Strachey and Alan Tyson, vol. XVIII, 1–64. London: Hogarth Press and The Institute of Psycho-analysis, 1955.

———. "Mourning and Melancholia." In *The Standard Edition of the Complete Psychological Works of Sigmund Freud*, translated and edited by James Strachey, in collaboration with Anna Freud, and assisted by Alix Strachey and Alan Tyson, vol. XIV, 237–260. London: Hogarth Press and The Institute of Psycho-analysis, 1957.

———. *Totem and Taboo: Some Points of Agreement between the Mental Lives of Savages and Neurotics*. In *The Standard Edition of the Complete Psychological Works of Sigmund Freud*, translated and edited by James Strachey, in collaboration with Anna Freud, and assisted by Alix Strachey and Alan Tyson, vol. XIII, vii–162. London: Hogarth Press and The Institute of Psycho-analysis, 1955.

Froment-Meurice, Marc. "In (the) Place of Being, Antigone (The *Retrait* of the Polis)." In *That Is to Say: Heidegger's Poetics*, translated by Jan Plug, 121–148. Stanford, Calif.: Stanford University Press, 1998.

Gasché, Rodolphe. *The Tain of the Mirror: Derrida and the Philosophy of Reflection*. Cambridge, Mass.: Harvard University Press, 1986.

———. "Yes Absolutely." In *Inventions of Difference: On Jacques Derrida*, 199–226. Cambridge, Mass.: Harvard University Press, 1994.

Gemerchak, Christopher M. *The Sunday of the Negative: Reading Bataille Reading Hegel*. Albany: State University of New York Press, 2003.

Gibson, Thomas. *Sacrifice and Sharing in the Philippine Highlands: Religion and Society among the Buid of Mindoro*. London: Athlone Press, 1986.

Girard, René. *The Scapegoat*. Translated by Yvonne Freccero. Baltimore, Md.: Johns Hopkins University Press, 1986.

———. *Things Hidden since the Foundation of the World*. Translated by Stephen Bann and Michael Metteer. Stanford, Calif.: Stanford University Press, 1987.

———. *Violence and the Sacred*. Translated by Patrick Gregory. Baltimore, Md.: Johns Hopkins University Press, 1977.

Godbout, Jacques T., in collaboration with Alain Caillé. *The World of the Gift*. Translated by Donald Winkler. Montreal and Kingston: McGill-Queen's University Press, 1998.

Godelier, Maurice. *The Enigma of the Gift*. Translated by Nora Scott. Chicago: University of Chicago Press, 1999.

Bibliography

Golden, Stephanie. *Slaying the Mermaid: Women and the Culture of Sacrifice.* New York: Three Rivers Press, 1998.

Goldenweiser, A. A. "Totemism, An Analytical Study." In *The Journal of American Folklore* 23.88 (April–June 1910): 179–293.

Goux, Jean-Joseph. *Symbolic Economies: After Marx and Freud.* Translated by Jennifer Curtiss Gage. Ithaca, N.Y.: Cornell University Press, 1990.

Gray, George Buchanan. *Sacrifice in the Old Testament: Its Theory and Practice.* New York: Ktav Publishing House, 1971.

Gusdorf, Georges. *L'expérience humaine du sacrifice.* Paris: Presses Universitaires de France, 1948.

Hamacher, Werner. *Pleroma — Reading in Hegel.* Translated by Nicholas Walker and Simon Jarvis. Stanford, Calif.: Stanford University Press, 1998.

Hamerton-Kelly, Robert G., ed. *Violent Origins: Walter Burkert, René Girard, and Jonathan Z. Smith on Ritual Killing and Cultural Formation.* Stanford, Calif.: Stanford University Press, 1987.

Harner, Michael. "The Enigma of Aztec Sacrifice." In *Natural History* 86.4 (April 1977): 46–51.

Harris, Marvin. *Cannibals and Kings: The Origins of Cultures.* New York: Random House, 1977.

Heesterman, J. C. *The Broken World of Sacrifice: An Essay in Ancient Indian Ritual.* Chicago: University of Chicago Press, 1993.

Hegel, G. W. F. *Lectures on the Philosophy of Religion.* Edited by Peter C. Hodgson. Translated by R. F. Brown, P. C. Hodgson, and J. M. Stewart, with the assistance of J. P. Fitzer and H. S. Harris. Berkeley: University of California Press, 1984–1987.

———. *Phenomenology of Spirit.* Translated by A. V. Miller. Oxford: Oxford University Press, 1977.

———. *Science of Logic.* Translated by A. V. Miller. New York: Humanities Press, 1969.

Heidegger, Martin. *Being and Time.* Translated by John Macquarrie and Edward Robinson. New York: Harper & Row, 1962.

———. *Hölderlin's Hymn "The Ister."* Translated by William McNeill and Julia Davis. Bloomington: Indiana University Press, 1996.

———. *Hölderlins Hymnen "Germanien" und "Der Rhein."* In *Gesamtausgabe,* vol. 39. Frankfurt am Main: Vittorio Klostermann, 1980.

———. "The Onto-Theo-Logical Constitution of Metaphysics." In *Identity and Difference,* translated by Joan Stambaugh, 42–74. New York: Harper & Row, 1969.

———. "The Origin of the Work of Art." In *Poetry, Language, Thought,* translated by Albert Hofstadter, 15–87. New York: Harper & Row, 1971.

———. "Postscript to 'What Is Metaphysics?'" Translated by William McNeill. In *Pathmarks,* edited by William McNeill, 231–238. Cambridge: Cambridge University Press, 1998.

———. "The Thing." In *Poetry, Language, Thought,* translated by Albert Hofstadter, 163–186. New York: Harper & Row, 1971.

Henninger, Joseph. "Sacrifice." Translated by Matthew J. O'Connell. In *The Encyclopedia of Religion,* edited by Mircea Eliade, vol. 12, 544–557. New York: Macmillan, 1987.

Hollywood, Amy. *Sensible Ecstasy: Mysticism, Sexual Difference, and the Demands of History.* Chicago: University of Chicago Press, 2002.

Horkheimer, Max, and Theodor W. Adorno. *Dialectic of Enlightenment.* Translated by John Cumming. New York: Continuum, 1972.

Hubert, Henri, and Marcel Mauss. *Sacrifice: Its Nature and Function.* Translated by W. D. Halls. Chicago: University of Chicago Press, 1964.

Hyde, Lewis. *The Gift: Imagination and the Erotic Life of Property.* New York: Vintage Books, 1979.

Hyppolite, Jean. *Genesis and Structure of Hegel's* Phenomenology of Spirit. Translated by Samuel Cherniak and John Heckman. Evanston, Ill.: Northwestern University Press, 1974.

Irigaray, Luce. "Belief Itself." In *Sexes and Genealogies*, translated by Gillian C. Gill, 23–53. New York: Columbia University Press, 1993.

———. "The Eternal Irony of the Community." In *Speculum of the Other Woman*, translated by Gillian C. Gill, 214–226. Ithaca, N.Y.: Cornell University Press, 1985.

———. "Women, the Sacred, Money." In *Sexes and Genealogies*, translated by Gillian C. Gill, 73–88. New York: Columbia University Press, 1993.

James, E. O. *Sacrifice and Sacrament.* New York: Barnes & Noble, 1962.

Jay, Nancy. *Throughout Your Generations Forever: Sacrifice, Religion, and Paternity.* Chicago: University of Chicago Press, 1992.

Jensen, Adolf E. *Myth and Cult among Primitive Peoples.* Translated by Marianna Tax Choldin and Wolfgang Weissleder. Chicago: University of Chicago Press, 1963.

Jones, Robert Alun. "Robertson Smith, Durkheim, and Sacrifice: An Historical Context for *The Elementary Forms of the Religious Life.*" In *Journal of the History of the Behavioral Sciences* 17 (1981): 184–205.

Jung, C. G. "The Sacrifice." In *The Collected Works of C. G. Jung*, vol. 5: *Symbols of Transformation: An Analysis of the Prelude to a Case of Schizophrenia*, 2nd ed., translated by R. F. C. Hull, 394–444. Princeton, N.J.: Princeton University Press, 1956.

———. "Transformation Symbolism in the Mass." In *The Collected Works of C. G. Jung*, vol. 11: *Psychology and Religion: West and East*, 2nd ed., translated by R. F. C. Hull, 201–296. Princeton, N.J.: Princeton University Press, 1969.

Kafka, Franz. *Letters to Friends, Family, and Editors.* Translated by Richard Winston and Clara Winston. New York: Schocken Books, 1977.

Kant, Immanuel. *Critique of Judgement.* Translated by J. H. Bernard. New York: Hafner Press, 1951.

———. *Critique of Practical Reason.* Translated by Lewis White Beck. Indianapolis, Ind.: Bobbs-Merrill Company, 1956.

Kearney, Richard. "Myths and Scapegoats: The Case of René Girard." In *Theory, Culture & Society* 12 (1995): 1–14.

Keenan, Dennis King. *Death and Responsibility: The "Work" of Levinas.* Albany: State University of New York Press, 1999.

Kierkegaard, Søren. *Fear and Trembling: Dialectical Lyric.* In *Fear and Trembling and Repetition*, edited and translated by Howard V. Hong and Edna H. Hong, 1–123. Princeton, N.J.: Princeton University Press, 1983.

Kilpatrick, G. D. *The Eucharist in Bible and Liturgy.* Cambridge: Cambridge University Press, 1983.

Kosky, Jeffrey L. "The Disqualification of Intentionality: The Gift in Derrida, Levinas, and Michel Henry." In *Philosophy Today* Supplement (1997): 186–197.

Kristeva, Julia. *Powers of Horror: An Essay on Abjection.* Translated by Leon S. Roudiez. New York: Columbia University Press, 1982.

———. *Revolution in Poetic Language.* Translated by Margaret Waller. New York: Columbia University Press, 1984.

Kuper, Adam. *The Invention of Primitive Society: Transformations of an Illusion.* London: Routledge, 1988.

Lacan, Jacques. *Écrits: A Selection.* Translated by Alan Sheridan. New York: W. W. Norton & Company, 1977.

———. *The Four Fundamental Concepts of Psycho-analysis.* Edited by Jacques-Alain Miller. Translated by Alan Sheridan. New York: W. W. Norton & Company, 1981.

———. *The Seminar of Jacques Lacan, Book VII: The Ethics of Psychoanalysis, 1959–1960.* Edited by Jacques-Alain Miller. Translated by Dennis Porter. New York: W. W. Norton & Company, 1992.

Lacoue-Labarthe, Philippe. "Typography." Translated by Eduardo Cadava. In *Typography: Mimesis, Philosophy, Politics,* translated by Christopher Fynsk, 43–138. Stanford, Calif.: Stanford University Press, 1998.

Lang, Bernhard. *Sacred Games: A History of Christian Worship.* New Haven, Conn.: Yale University Press, 1997.

Lanternari, Vittorio. *La grande festa: Vita rituale e sistemi di produzione nelle società tradizionali,* 2nd ed. Bari: Dedalo libri, 1976.

Levenson, Jon D. *The Death and Resurrection of the Beloved Son: The Transformation of Child Sacrifice in Judaism and Christianity.* New Haven, Conn.: Yale University Press, 1993.

Levinas, Emmanuel. "Dying for . . ." In *Entre Nous: On Thinking-of-the-Other,* translated by Michael B. Smith and Barbara Harshav, 207–217. New York: Columbia University Press, 1998.

———. *Existence and Existents.* Translated by Alphonso Lingis. Dordrecht: Kluwer Academic Publishers, 1988.

———. "God and Philosophy." In *Of God Who Comes to Mind,* translated by Bettina Bergo, 55–78. Stanford, Calif.: Stanford University Press, 1998.

———. "Language and Proximity." In *Collected Philosophical Papers,* translated by Alphonso Lingis, 109–126. Dordrecht: Martinus Nijhoff, 1987.

———. "Meaning and Sense." In *Collected Philosophical Papers,* translated by Alphonso Lingis, 75–107. Dordrecht: Martinus Nijhoff, 1987.

———. "Messianic Texts." In *Difficult Freedom: Essays on Judaism,* translated by Seán Hand, 59–96. Baltimore, Md.: Johns Hopkins University Press, 1990.

———. *Otherwise than Being or Beyond Essence.* Translated by Alphonso Lingis. The Hague: Martinus Nijhoff, 1981.

———. "Philosophy and the Idea of Infinity." In *Collected Philosophical Papers,* translated by Alphonso Lingis, 47–59. Dordrecht: Martinus Nijhoff, 1987.

———. "Revelation in the Jewish Tradition." In *Beyond the Verse: Talmudic Readings and Lectures,* translated by Gary D. Mole, 129–150. Bloomington: Indiana University Press, 1994.

———. *Totality and Infinity: An Essay on Exteriority.* Translated by Alphonso Lingis. Pittsburgh, Pa.: Duquesne University Press, 1969.

———. "The Trace of the Other." Translated by Alphonso Lingis. In *Deconstruction in Context: Literature and Philosophy,* edited by Mark C. Taylor, 345–359. Chicago: University of Chicago Press, 1986.

Lévi-Strauss, Claude. *The Savage Mind.* Chicago: University of Chicago Press, 1966.

———. *Totemism.* Translated by Rodney Needham. Boston: Beacon Press, 1963.

Lienhardt, Godfrey. *Divinity and Experience: The Religion of the Dinka*. Oxford: Oxford University Press, 1961.

Lincoln, Bruce. *Death, War, and Sacrifice: Studies in Ideology and Practice*. Chicago: University of Chicago Press, 1991.

Luther, Martin. *A Treatise on the New Testament, That Is, the Holy Mass*. Translated by Jeremiah J. Schindel. Revised by E. Theodore Bachmann. In *Luther's Works*, edited by E. Theodore Bachmann, general editor Helmut T. Lehmann, vol. 35, 79–111. Philadelphia: Fortress Press, 1960.

Maccoby, Hyam. *The Sacred Executioner: Human Sacrifice and the Legacy of Guilt*. New York: Thames and Hudson, 1982.

Marin, Louis. "The Body of the Divinity Captured by Signs." In *Food for Thought*, translated by Mette Hjort, 3–25. Baltimore, Md.: Johns Hopkins University Press, 1989.

Marion, Jean-Luc. *God Without Being*. Translated by Thomas A. Carlson. Chicago: University of Chicago Press, 1991.

Marvin, Carolyn, and David W. Ingle. *Blood Sacrifice and the Nation: Totem Rituals and the American Flag*. Cambridge: Cambridge University Press, 1999.

Mauss, Marcel. *The Gift: The Form and Reason for Exchange in Archaic Societies*. Translated by W. D. Halls. New York: W. W. Norton & Company, 1990.

McKenna, Andrew J. *Violence and Difference: Girard, Derrida, and Deconstruction*. Urbana: University of Illinois Press, 1992.

McLennan, J. F. "The Worship of Animals and Plants." In *Fortnightly Review* 6–7 (1869–1870).

Merleau-Ponty, Maurice. "Hegel's Existentialism." In *Sense and Non-Sense*, translated by Hubert L. Dreyfus and Patricia Allen Dreyfus, 63–70. Evanston, Ill.: Northwestern University Press, 1964.

Middleton, John. *Lugbara Religion: Ritual and Authority among an East African People*. London: Oxford University Press, 1960.

Milbank, John. "Can a Gift Be Given? Prolegomena to a Future Trinitarian Metaphysic." In *Modern Theology* 11.1 (1995), 119–161.

———. "Stories of Sacrifice: From Wellhausen to Girard." In *Theory, Culture & Society* 12 (1995): 15–46.

Miller, Elaine P. "The Figure of (Self)-Sacrifice in Hegel's *Naturphilosophie*." In *Philosophy Today* Supplement (1997): 41–48.

Mizruchi, Susan L. *The Science of Sacrifice: American Literature and Modern Social Theory*. Princeton, N.J.: Princeton University Press, 1998.

Mleynek, Sherryll. "Abraham, Aristotle, and God: The Poetics of Sacrifice." In *Journal of the American Academy of Religion* 62.1 (Spring 1994): 107–121.

Nancy, Jean-Luc. "The Unsacrificable." Translated by Richard Livingston. In *Yale French Studies* 79 (1991): 20–38.

Nietzsche, Friedrich. *The Anti-Christ*. In *Twilight of the Idols and The Anti-Christ*, translated by R. J. Hollingdale, 113–187. Harmondsworth, Middlesex, England: Penguin Books, 1968.

———. *Beyond Good and Evil: Prelude to a Philosophy of the Future*. Translated by R. J. Hollingdale. Harmondsworth, Middlesex, England: Penguin Books, 1973.

———. *On the Genealogy of Morals: A Polemic*. Translated by Walter Kaufmann and R. J. Hollingdale. In *On the Genealogy of Morals and Ecce Homo*, 13–163. New York: Random House, 1967.

Bibliography

———. *Thus Spoke Zarathustra: A Book for All and None*. Translated by Walter Kaufmann. Harmondsworth, Middlesex, England: Penguin Books, 1978.

———. *Twilight of the Idols, or How to Philosophize with a Hammer*. In *Twilight of the Idols and The Anti-Christ*, translated by R. J. Hollingdale, 19–112. Harmondsworth, Middlesex, England: Penguin Books, 1968.

———. *The Will to Power*. Translated by Walter Kaufmann and R. J. Hollingdale. New York: Random House, 1967.

Nygren, Anders. *Agape and Eros*. Translated by Philip S. Watson. Philadelphia: Westminster Press, 1953.

Oliver, Kelly. "Fatherhood and the Promise of Ethics." In *Diacritics* 27.1 (Spring 1997): 45–57.

Pascal, Blaise. *Pensées*. Translated by A. J. Krailsheimer. Harmondsworth, Middlesex, England: Penguin Books, 1966.

Patočka, Jan. "Is Technological Civilization Decadent, and Why?" In *Heretical Essays in the Philosophy of History*, translated by Erazim Kohák, 95–118. Edited by James Dodd. Chicago: Open Court, 1996.

Patterson, Orlando. "Feast of Blood: 'Race,' Religion, and Human Sacrifice in the Postbellum South." In *Rituals of Blood: Consequences of Slavery in Two American Centuries*, 169–232. New York: Basic Civitas, 1998.

Peterman, G. W. *Paul's Gift From Philippi: Conventions of Gift Exchange and Christian Giving*. Cambridge: Cambridge University Press, 1997.

Plato. *Phaedo*. In *The Dialogues of Plato*, translated by Benjamin Jowett, edited by R. M. Hare and D. A. Russell, vol. 1, 101–175. London: Sphere Books, 1970.

Power, David N. *The Eucharistic Mystery: Revitalizing the Tradition*. New York: Crossroad, 1992.

Price, Robert M. *Deconstructing Jesus*. Amherst, N.Y.: Prometheus Books, 2000.

Reineke, Martha J. "Our Vital Necessity: Julia Kristeva's Theory of Sacrifice." In *Religion in French Feminist Thought: Critical Perspectives*, edited by Morny Joy, Kathleen O'Grady, and Judith L. Poxon, 101–116. London: Routledge, 2003.

———. *Sacrificed Lives: Kristeva on Women and Violence*. Bloomington: Indiana University Press, 1997.

Richardson, William J. "Lacan and the Enlightenment: Antigone's Choice." In *Research in Phenomenology* 24 (1994): 25–41.

Robbins, Jill. "Sacrifice." In *Critical Terms for Religious Studies*, edited by Mark C. Taylor, 285–297. Chicago: University of Chicago Press, 1998.

The Roman Missal: The Sacramentary. New York: Catholic Book Publishing, 1974.

Sahlins, Marshall. "Culture as Protein and Profit." In *New York Review of Books* 25.18 (November 23, 1978): 45–53.

Sallis, John. "Bread and Wine." In *Philosophy Today* (Spring 1997): 219–228.

———. "Sacrifice of Understanding." In *Echoes: After Heidegger*, 139–167. Bloomington: Indiana University Press, 1990.

———. "Tremorings—Withdrawals of the Sublime." In *Spacings—Of Reason and Imagination in Texts of Kant, Fichte, Hegel*, 82–131. Chicago: University of Chicago Press, 1987.

Saussure, Ferdinand de. *Course in General Linguistics*. Translated by Wade Baskin. Edited by Charles Bally and Albert Sechehaye, in collaboration with Albert Riedlinger. New York: McGraw-Hill, 1959.

Scarry, Elaine. *The Body in Pain: The Making and Unmaking of the World*. Oxford: Oxford University Press, 1985.

Schelling, F. W. J. von. *Ages of the World*. Translated by Judith Norman. In *The Abyss of Freedom/Ages of the World*, 105–182. Ann Arbor: University of Michigan Press, 1997.

———. *The Ages of the World*. Translated by Jason M. Wirth. Albany: State University of New York Press, 2000.

———. *Philosophical Investigations into the Essence of Human Freedom and Related Matters*. Translated by Priscilla Hayden-Roy. In *Philosophy of German Idealism*, edited by Ernst Behler, 217–284. New York: Continuum, 1987.

Schmidt, Dennis J. "Ruins and Roses: Hegel and Heidegger on Sacrifice, Mourning, and Memory." In *Endings: Questions of Memory in Hegel and Heidegger*, edited by Rebecca Comay and John McCumber, 97–113. Evanston, Ill.: Northwestern University Press, 1999.

———. "Why I Am So Happy." In *Research in Phenomenology* 24 (1994): 3–14.

Schmidt, Wilhelm. "Ethnologische Bemerkungen zu theologischen Opfertheorien." In *Jahrbuch des Missionshauses St. Gabriel* 1 (1922).

———. *The Origin and Growth of Religion: Facts and Theories*. Translated by H. J. Rose. London: Methuen & Co., 1931.

———. *Der Ursprung der Gottesidee: Eine Historisch-Kritische und Positive Studie*. Münster: Aschendorffsche Verlagsbuchhandlung, 1912–1955.

Schrift, Alan D. "Rethinking Exchange: Logics of the Gift in Cixous and Nietzsche." In *Philosophy Today* (Spring 1996): 197–205.

Schrift, Alan D., ed. *The Logic of the Gift: Toward an Ethic of Generosity*. London: Routledge, 1997.

Shell, Marc. *Art and Money*. Chicago: University of Chicago Press, 1995.

Shuger, Debora Kuller. *The Renaissance Bible: Scholarship, Sacrifice, and Subjectivity*. Berkeley: University of California Press, 1994.

Shulman, David. *The Hungry God: Hindu Tales of Filicide and Devotion*. Chicago: University of Chicago Press, 1993.

Simmel, Georg. *The Philosophy of Money*. Translated by Tom Bottomore and David Frisby. London: Routledge & Kegan Paul, 1978.

Smith, Brian K. "Capital Punishment and Human Sacrifice." In *Journal of the American Academy of Religion* 68.1 (March 2000): 3–25.

Smith, William Robertson. *Lectures on the Religion of the Semites: The Fundamental Institutions*. New York: Ktav Publishing House, 1969.

———. "Sacrifice." In *The Encyclopædia Britannica: A Dictionary of Arts, Sciences, and General Literature*, 9th ed., vol. XXI, 132–138. Edinburgh: Adam and Charles Black, 1886.

Spiegel, Shalom. *The Last Trial: On the Legends and Lore of the Command to Abraham to Offer Isaac as a Sacrifice: The Akedah*. Translated by Judah Goldin. Woodstock, Vt.: Jewish Lights Publishing, 1993.

Stevenson, Kenneth W. *Eucharist and Offering*. New York: Pueblo Publishing, 1986.

Strenski, Ivan. *Contesting Sacrifice: Religion, Nationalism, and Social Thought in France*. Chicago: University of Chicago Press, 2002.

———. *Theology and the First Theory of Sacrifice*. The Netherlands: Brill Academic Publishing, 2003.

Bibliography

Taylor, Mark C. "Christianity and the Capitalism of Spirit." In *About Religion: Economies of Faith in Virtual Culture*, 140–167. Chicago: University of Chicago Press, 1999.

Turner, Victor. "Sacrifice as Quintessential Process: Prophylaxis or Abandonment?" In *History of Religions* 16.3 (February 1977): 189–215.

Tylor, Edward Burnett. *Primitive Culture: Researches in the Development of Mythology, Philosophy, Religion, Language, Arts and Custom.* New York: Brentano's, 1924.

Urban, Hugh B. "The Path of Power: Impurity, Kingship, and Sacrifice in Assamese Tantra." In *Journal of the American Academy of Religion* 69.4 (December 2001): 777–816.

Valeri, Valerio. *Kingship and Sacrifice: Ritual and Society in Ancient Hawaii.* Translated from the author's unpublished French manuscript by Paula Wissing. Chicago: University of Chicago Press, 1985.

van der Leeuw, Gerardus. "Die *do-ut-des*-Formel in der Opfertheorie." In *Archiv für Religionwissenschaft* 20 (1920–1921): 241–253.

———. *Religion in Essence and Manifestation.* Translated by J. E. Turner. Princeton, N.J.: Princeton University Press, 1986.

Van Haute, Philippe. "Death and Sublimation in Lacan's Reading of *Antigone*." In *Levinas and Lacan: The Missed Encounter*, edited by Sarah Harasym, 102–120. Albany: State University of New York Press, 1998.

Vatican Council II: The Conciliar and Post Conciliar Documents, 1988 rev. ed. Edited by Austin Flannery. Northport, N.Y.: Costello Publishing, 1975.

Vernant, Jean-Pierre. *Mortals and Immortals: Collected Essays.* Princeton, N.J.: Princeton University Press, 1991.

Vernant, Jean-Pierre, and Pierre Vidal-Naquet. *Myth and Tragedy in Ancient Greece.* Translated by Janet Lloyd. New York: Zone Books, 1990.

Vorbichler, Anton. *Das Opfer auf den uns heute noch erreichbaren ältesten Stufen der Menschheitsgeschichte: Eine Begriffsstudie.* St.-Gabriel-Verlag: Mödling bei Wien, 1956.

Weber, Max. *The Protestant Ethic and the Spirit of Capitalism.* Translated by Talcott Parsons. Upper Saddle River, N.J.: Prentice Hall, 1958.

Weir, Allison. *Sacrificial Logics: Feminist Theory and the Critique of Identity.* London: Routledge, 1996.

Wellhausen, Julius. *Prolegomena to the History of Israel.* Translated by Black and Menzies. New York: Meridian Books, 1957.

Wiesel, Elie. "The Sacrifice of Isaac: A Survivor's Story." In *Messengers of God: Biblical Portraits and Legends*, translated by Marion Wiesel, 69–97. New York: Random House, 1976.

Wiggershaus, Rolf. *The Frankfurt School: Its History, Theories, and Political Significance.* Translated by Michael Robertson. Cambridge, Mass.: MIT Press, 1994.

Williams, Rowan. *Eucharistic Sacrifice—The Roots of a Metaphor.* Bramcote, Notts: Grove Books, 1982.

Wolff, Richard D., and Stephen A. Resnick. *Economics: Marxian versus Neoclassical.* Baltimore, Md.: Johns Hopkins University Press, 1987.

Wood, David. "Much Obliged." In *Philosophy Today* (Spring 1997): 135–140.

Wright, Kathleen. "Heidegger on Hegel's Antigone: The Memory of Gender and the Forgetfulness of the Ethical Difference." In *Endings: Questions of Memory in Hegel and Heidegger*, edited by Rebecca Comay and John McCumber, 160–173. Evanston, Ill.: Northwestern University Press, 1999.

Wyschogrod, Edith, Jean-Joseph Goux, and Eric Boynton, eds. *The Enigma of Gift and Sacrifice*. New York: Fordham University Press, 2002.

Yerkes, Royden Keith. *Sacrifice in Greek and Roman Religions and Early Judaism*. London: Adam and Charles Black, 1953.

Young, Frances M. *Sacrifice and the Death of Christ*. London: SCM Press, 1975.

———. *The Use of Sacrificial Ideas in Greek Christian Writers from the New Testament to John Chrysostom*. Cambridge: The Philadelphia Patristic Foundation, 1979.

Zito, Angela. *Of Body and Brush: Grand Sacrifice as Text/Performance in Eighteenth-Century China*. Chicago: University of Chicago Press, 1997.

Žižek, Slavoj. *The Abyss of Freedom*. In *The Abyss of Freedom/Ages of the World*, 1–104. Ann Arbor: University of Michigan Press, 1997.

———. *Enjoy Your Symptom! Jacques Lacan in Hollywood and out*. London: Routledge, 1992.

———. *For They Know Not What They Do: Enjoyment as a Political Factor*. London: Verso, 1991.

———. *The Fragile Absolute—or, Why Is the Christian Legacy Worth Fighting For?* London: Verso, 2000.

———. *The Indivisible Remainder: An Essay on Schelling and Related Matters*. London: Verso, 1996.

———. *The Metastases of Enjoyment: Six Essays on Women and Causality*. London: Verso, 1994.

———. *The Puppet and the Dwarf: The Perverse Core of Christianity*. Cambridge, Mass.: MIT Press, 2003.

———. *The Sublime Object of Ideology*. London: Verso, 1989.

———. *Tarrying with the Negative: Kant, Hegel, and the Critique of Ideology*. Durham, N.C.: Duke University Press, 1993.

———. *The Ticklish Subject: The Absent Centre of Political Ontology*. London: Verso, 1999.

INDEX

Abraham, 7, 59, 114, 123–124, 149–154, 185, 188
Abraham, Nicolas, 97, 185
Acéphale, 56, 57, 58
à-Dieu, 153–154, 185–188
Adorno, Theodor W., 21–22; *Dialectic of Enlightenment*, 21
agape, 7, 8, 114, 125–132, 182–184, 185, 188. *See also* love
Akedah, 59, 149–154
alienation, 7, 12, 26, 35, 89, 93, 94, 96, 100, 101, 113, 115, 116, 121, 123, 124, 132, 181, 184, 185
animism, 14
Anselm, 12; *Why God Became a Man*, 12
Antigone, 7, 114–123, 185, 188
Antigone, 116, 117, 118, 119
Aristotle, 116; *Poetics*, 116
art, 41, 42–43, 44, 118
ascetic ideal, 60, 64
asceticism, 10, 67, 68
Aufhebung, 21, 49–50, 51, 53, 54, 64, 138, 148, 164, 165
Aufklärung, 148
Augustine, 8, 174, 179–182, 187; *The City of God*, 180; "Sermon 272," 174, 187
Aquinas, Thomas, 29, 31; *Summa Theologiæ*, 31

bad conscience, 60, 69–70
Badiou, Alain, 126
Bataille, Georges, 4, 5, 6, 7, 42–43, 44, 45–58, 59, 134, 137, 165; "Hegel, Death, and Sacrifice," 5, 45, 48, 55; *Inner Experience*, 6, 59; *Theory of Religion*, 56, 58, 165
belief, 7, 8, 61–63, 70, 86, 89, 92–104, 157–158, 175, 186
Bergson, Henri, 158
bishop, 30, 31
Blanchot, Maurice, 3, 4, 5, 6, 46–48, 55–58, 64–66, 70, 71, 84, 114, 131, 143, 144, 149, 165, 166, 183; *The Infinite Conversation*, 6, 65; "Literature and the Right to Death," 3, 5, 46, 48; "The Negative

Community," 56; *The Space of Literature*, 46, 143; *The Unavowable Community*, 56, 165; *The Work of Fire*, 46; *The Writing of the Disaster*, 56, 144
Bloch, Maurice, 18, 19, 27; *Prey into Hunter*, 18, 27
body, 6, 7, 8, 11, 12, 15, 16, 19, 22, 23, 30, 34, 80–83, 87, 89–104, 114, 116, 121, 126, 130, 132, 138, 139, 155, 174, 178, 179–182, 184, 187
Burbidge, John, 164
Burkert, Walter, 26, 27; *Homo Necans*, 26

Cain, 124
Cassirer, Ernst, 21; *The Philosophy of Symbolic Forms*, 21
castration, 33, 35, 36, 67, 105
Christ, 7, 8, 12, 16, 17, 30, 31, 42, 61, 68, 114, 124–125, 130, 131, 138, 161, 163, 164, 165, 167, 168, 169, 178–185, 187. *See also* Jesus
Combs-Schilling, M. E., 23; *Sacred Performances*, 23
Comte, Auguste, 15, 16
Copjec, Joan, 105; *Read My Desire*, 105
Creon, 7, 114, 116–119
community, 5, 8, 15, 16, 25, 28, 38, 55–58, 62, 72, 94, 121, 149, 150, 161–169, 180, 188
creation from zero, 116, 131
crime, 92–93, 115–116
Cusa, Nicholas of, 11
Cyprian, Bishop of Carthage, 30; "Letter 63," 30

Daly, Robert J., 30; *Christian Sacrifice*, 30
Darwin, Charles, 13, 20, 175
de Heusch, Luc, 18, 22–23, 28; *Sacrifice in Africa*, 22
dead time, 78, 79, 82, 101. *See also* time
death, 1, 8, 10, 12, 13, 16, 20, 30, 41–44, 45–58, 66, 70, 72, 84, 95, 97, 100, 101, 114–123, 125–131, 137–153, 158, 162–173, 175, 179, 183, 185, 186, 187; being-towards-death, 7, 48, 56, 140–146; death

Index

death (*continued*)
of God, 8, 60, 101, 158, 164, 167, 169, 179; practicing (for) death, 7, 138–139, 141; the question of death, 5, 45, 58; symbolic death, 130, 131, 184
death drive, 34, 36, 41, 114, 116, 121, 122, 123, 130, 184
delusion, 86
demonic, 85, 138, 148, 149, 154, 182, 183, 185
Derrida, Jacques, 1, 4, 5, 7, 8, 13, 26, 49–55, 58, 61–63, 68, 89, 94, 95–98, 119–120, 124, 134–159, 160–173, 174, 175, 177, 178, 179, 182–183, 184, 185, 187; *Aporias*, 51, 52, 97, 119, 141, 142, 143, 146, 147, 151; "Before the Law," 170; "Désistance," 26; "Economimesis," 154; "Faith and Knowledge," 8, 158; "Force of Law," 94; "From Restricted to General Economy," 5, 7, 49, 134; *The Gift of Death*, 7, 13, 61, 68, 138, 146, 149, 177, 178, 179, 182, 183, 184; *Given Time*, 156; *Glas*, 7, 134, 154; *Margins of Philosophy*, 50; *Memoires for Paul de Man*, 97; "Mnemosyne," 97; "*Ousia* and *Grammē*," 50; *Positions*, 160; *The Post Card*, 95; *Writing and Difference*, 49
Descartes, René, 6, 74, 76–80, 81, 82, 83, 87, 153, 156; *Meditations on First Philosophy*, 6, 74, 76–80, 81, 82, 83, 87, 153, 156
Detienne, Marcel, 12, 13, 15, 18, 19, 22; *The Cuisine of Sacrifice among the Greeks*, 13; "Culinary Practices and the Spirit of Sacrifice," 13
dialectic, 5, 34, 41, 42, 44, 49, 51–52, 112, 113, 126, 127, 135, 136, 137, 165, 170
Didache, The, 30
Dike, 119
Dionysus, 19
(dis)incarnation, 81, 114, 122, 123, 130, 165, 166, 167, 169, 182, 183, 184, 185, 188. *See also* incarnation
doubt, 77–80, 82
Durkheim, Émile, 17, 19–20, 23, 26; *The Elementary Forms of Religious Life*, 19
dying to the Law, 130–131, 184

elemental, the, 80–81; the elemental substrate of life, 7, 98, 100, 103
Eliot, T. S., 9; *Four Quartets*, 9
enjoyment, 7, 35, 43, 44, 82, 93, 94, 102, 105, 114, 115, 122, 126, 127, 128, 130, 131. *See also* jouissance; surplus-enjoyment

Eteocles, 121
eternal recurrence, 65; eternal return, 3, 6, 59–73, 74
Eucharist, 8, 12, 16, 19, 30, 31, 90, 91, 93, 94, 99, 104, 174–188
Evans-Pritchard, E. E., 18, 22, 24, 28, 33; *Nuer Religion*, 22; *Theories of Primitive Religions*, 18
evil, 17, 67, 70, 128, 162, 163, 164, 167, 169, 175, 185
evil genius, 77, 78, 79, 80, 82
Exodus, 174
expenditure, 33, 39, 49, 50, 52, 53, 54, 58, 135, 136, 165, 168
externalization, 134, 161

fantasy, 41, 96, 98, 100, 101, 102, 104, 113, 170, 186
fetishism, 15, 16
Feuerbach, Ludwig, 26
fiction, 5, 46, 48, 52–54, 55, 137
Firth, Raymond, 24–25; *Offering and Sacrifice*, 24
forced choice, 7, 111, 113, 114, 115, 120, 121, 123, 124, 125, 132
forgiveness, 12, 70, 72
Fourth Lateran Council, 31
Frazer, James George, 16–17; *The Golden Bough*, 16
freedom, 14, 46–47, 69, 74, 76, 77, 80, 81, 108, 110, 112, 129, 138, 142, 144, 145, 150, 158
Frege, Gottlob, 40, 44
Freud, Sigmund, 5, 7, 20, 26, 34, 36, 55–58, 95–98, 126, 127, 175, 185; *Beyond the Pleasure Principle*, 95; *Totem and Taboo*, 20
Frobenius, Leo, 22
Froment-Meurice, Marc, 118; "In (the) Place of Being, Antigone (The *Retrait* of the Polis)," 118

Gasché, Rodolphe, 172; *Inventions of Difference*, 172; *The Tain of the Mirror*, 172; "Yes Absolutely," 172
Genesis, 149, 150, 153
Gibson, Thomas, 23; *Sacrifice and Sharing in the Philippine Highlands*, 23
gift, 13, 14, 15, 17, 19, 20, 21, 22, 39, 57, 91, 138, 139, 140, 141, 146, 147, 148, 149, 153, 156, 157, 166, 180, 181, 182, 183; giftlogic, 17, 19, 20
Girard, René, 5, 6, 15, 25–26, 27, 55–58, 89,

Index

DENNIS KING KEENAN is Professor of Philosophy at Fairfield University. He is author of *Death and Responsibility: The "Work" of Levinas* and editor of *Hegel and Contemporary Continental Philosophy.*